Florida A&M University, Tallahassee
Florida Atlantic University, Boca Raton
Florida Gulf Coast University, Ft. Myers
Florida International University, Miami
Florida State University, Tallahassee
University of Central Florida, Orlando
University of Florida, Gainesville
University of North Florida, Jacksonville
University of South Florida, Tampa
University of West Florida, Pensacola

The Making of
a Modern City

Philanthropy, Civic Culture, and the Baltimore YMCA

Jessica I. Elfenbein

University Press of Florida

Gainesville · Tallahassee · Tampa · Boca Raton

Pensacola · Orlando · Miami · Jacksonville · Ft. Myers

*To Kevin Manning,
a fearless leader,
I appreciate your
generous welcome to
this special place-
Stevenson is lucky
to have you!*

Jessica N

*ACE Fellow
2009-2010*

06 05 04 03 02 01   6 5 4 3 2 1

Library of Congress Cataloging-in-Publication Data
Elfenbein, Jessica I.
The making of a modern city: philanthropy, civic culture, and the Baltimore YMCA /
Jessica I. Elfenbein.
p. cm.
Includes bibliographical references and index.
ISBN 0-8130-2435-8 (cloth: alk. paper)
1. Young Men's Christian Association (Baltimore, Md.)—History. 2. Charities—
Maryland—Baltimore—History. I. Title.
BV1050.B2 E44 2001
267'.397526—dc21 2001027353

Frontispiece: The Old Central YMCA, Saratoga and Charles Streets, ca. 1901. It opened
in 1878 and had a gymnasium, library, classrooms, and retail space but no dormitory
rooms to let. It ceased YMCA operations in 1908. Since then it has been used as an office
building. It is now being converted into thirty-six moderately priced apartments in hopes
of attracting residents downtown. The turrets have long been removed. YMCA
Collection, University of Baltimore Archives.

The University Press of Florida is the scholarly publishing agency for the State University
System of Florida, comprising Florida A&M University, Florida Atlantic University,
Florida Gulf Coast University, Florida International University, Florida State University,
University of Central Florida, University of Florida, University of North Florida,
University of South Florida, and University of West Florida.

University Press of Florida
15 Northwest 15th Street
Gainesville, FL 32611–2079
http://www.upf.com

For Robert Feinstein

Contents

Illustrations

Acknowledgments

I've loved this project from the time I began doing dissertation research in the winter of 1993 to the completion of revisions to this book in the fall of 2000. My interest in the role of faith in the making of American culture, something I first encountered when I met D. L. Moody as a high school student, abides. My fascination with urban history and the challenges faced by city dwellers continues. My interest in the role of philanthropy in the city is keen. I have been lucky to have found kindred souls who share and support these interests. At the University of Delaware, where this project began, I had the wise counsel of Guy Alchon, my dissertation adviser. Ann Boylan and Carol Hoffecker were both generous in their support of me and this project, far exceeding what was required or, indeed, what I expected. Over fifteen years, Howard Gillette has been a thoughtful critic, supporter, and mentor, representing the kind of public-spirited historian I wish to be.

At Delaware I had a great dissertation group, whose motto, "Just Do It," belied keen intellectual interest not only in our own projects but in each other's work. To Gary Daynes and Neva Jean Specht, I am truly grateful. They gave companionship, camaraderie, and useful criticism at critical times. I am thankful, too, for the friendship and support of Kathy Steen and Jonathan Russ, other friends from the Delaware years.

Baltimore is a wonderful place to do urban history. Not only are there great resources, there is much important work to be done. My start in Baltimore history occurred in the mid–1980s during a stint in Mayor William Donald Schaefer's office doing public history programs. Knowing the city made coming back for dissertation work in the early 1990s easier and more fun.

I could not have done this project without the archives at the University of Baltimore. The collection there is a fascinating effort to document the work of nonprofit and civic organizations in nineteenth- and twentieth-century Baltimore, truly the making of a modern city. UB is lucky to have Tom Hollowak as its archivist. I am lucky to have him as my dear friend, confidant, and regular lunch date. At UB I have found not only the Baltimore YMCA's wonderful archives and a fabulous archivist but also my professional home. Very early in my tenure at UB, Sue Briggs and Neil Kleinman showed faith in me and my work. I am grateful to them, and to Jeffrey Sawyer and Cathy Albrecht, my chairs in the Division of Legal, Ethical, and Historical Studies, who have been willing to support a junior colleague in the pursuit of new initiatives. Judy Pratt has provided great technical assistance throughout the process of writing this book.

Through this project I have met other historians in and around Baltimore who have allowed me to build a professional community that is richly textured and rewarding. I especially appreciate the ongoing interest of Dean Krimmel, Elaine Eff, Jack Breihan, Joe Arnold, Jeff Korman, John Sondheim, and Chester Wickwire.

The YMCA of Central Maryland has been keenly interested in this project. First Harold Mezile and later Lee Jensen allowed me access to staff and records. I am glad that this study is being published in time for their sesquicentennial in 2003.

I was very lucky to have gotten generous support for this project. As a graduate student I received dissertation fellowships from the Aspen Institute's Nonprofit Sector Research Fund and from the Louisville Institute for the Study of Protestantism in American Culture. My dissertation won the 1997 award for Outstanding Doctoral Dissertation in Nonprofit and Voluntary Action Research from the Association for Research on Nonprofit Organizations and Voluntary Action (ARNOVA). The University of Baltimore gave me research grants with which I completed revisions.

Earlier versions of portions of this book have been published in *Essays in Economic and Business History* (1997), 191–207, and in Nina Mjagkij and Margaret Spratt, eds., *Men and Women Adrift: The YMCA and YWCA in the City* (New York: New York University Press, 1997). My thanks to these publishers for permission to reprint in this work.

My parents, Iris Elfenbein and Dick Elfenbein, my sister, Melissa Bockelmann, and my in-laws, Beatrice and Julius Feinstein, have all shown great interest in this project and my career. Friends outside the academy supported me in many ways. I am especially grateful to Clare Garfield and Karen Brown. Thanks!

On the home front, I have been blessed with three beautiful children, Nora, Susannah, and Micah Feinstein. I knew my work had shaped their lives when, about six years ago, a woman who had just had a long conversation with my oldest child asked me whether our family had a "special relationship with the YMCA." What prompted her question was four-

and-a-half-year-old Nora's comment that her sister Susannah was "so lucky because her birthday is June 6 and that's the same day the YMCA was founded!" It's true that the YMCA was founded on June 6, 1844, in England and that Susannah Feinstein was born June 6, 1992, in Wilmington, Delaware. All three of my children have unwittingly given a great deal to the writing of this book. Their father and my best friend, Robert Feinstein, made all of this possible. He is a wonderful editor and husband, and to him I dedicate this book.

A Flexible Vessel

The Baltimore YMCA and Community Change

The nearly seventy-year-long reign of the "New Deal Order" has clearly ended.[1] American governments on all levels face an intensifying skepticism toward public provision of social services, which, in combination with fiscal retrenchment, has led to their withdrawal from entire areas of social service. As a result, American society will more and more repair (willingly or not) to nominally private and voluntaristic organizations such as the Young Men's Christian Association (YMCA) to meet these needs.[2]

The YMCA's involvement in the making of urban culture and the fulfillment of community needs is by no means new. In the years from 1852 to 1932, in response to the trinity of faith, service, and civic obligation, the Baltimore YMCA's leaders helped to shape a modern city and its approach to community welfare. "Civically engaged," in Robert Putnam's terms, many of the YMCA's leaders also participated in other associational realms, including those of local governance and private industry.[3] The YMCA's definition of civic need, therefore, was not created in a vacuum.

From 1852 to 1932, YMCA leaders set out to address the domestic, educational, recreational, and vocational issues most critical to the well-being of their targeted audience—young, Christian men of, or aspiring to, the middle class. As members of Baltimore's commercial and political elites, the YMCA's leaders (white and, after the 1880s, black, too) thus defined the organization's mission not solely in religious terms but in terms reflecting the forces at work as modern America emerged.[4]

At no time did the YMCA operate in isolation from either the market or the state. Rather, much of the story of Baltimore's development has been one of partnerships forged by the YMCA with business, government, and the churches. Although the advent of the New Deal in the early 1930s expanded and formalized large-scale government involvement in the provision of social services generally, and through the YMCA in particular, the close fit between the state and the association was not new. Almost from the beginning, the YMCA worked in tandem with local government to address social concerns. From the 1850s to the 1930s, the YMCA repeatedly identified and worked to correct community-wide problems in such areas as worker education, housing, and poverty. As a result, the story of the Baltimore YMCA offers an opportunity to inquire further into the associational aspects of America's urban and political history. This particular association, moreover, is an interesting example of an institution at once creative and transitional, one that illuminates the personalities, ideas, and politics involved as the urban classes negotiated modernity.

Throughout its first eighty years, the YMCA was unwaveringly committed to a catholic and welcoming worldview, one dedicated to saving men from the moral ravages of the industrial world by leading them to Jesus. George Williams, a draper, along with eleven coworkers, founded the organization in London in 1844 in response to the demoralizing influence on young men of urban squalor and industrial work. Not only did the London group grow, but the idea of the association spread. Within seven years the YMCA had been established in sixteen other cities in England, Scotland, and Ireland. In the summer of 1851 a world's fair was held in London. Some of the Americans and Canadians attending the fair visited the rooms of the YMCA and returned ready to create such an organization in their home cities. In 1852, at the invitation of the Maryland Baptist Union, the Baltimore YMCA was organized.[5]

The Baltimore YMCA was, in many regards, typical of those created in large industrial American cities.[6] Over the course of 150 years, it has had only two "association firsts"—in 1859 the West Baltimore YMCA designed and erected the first building in the country exclusively for association use, and in the early 1980s, as the logical outcome of character building and ecumenical programming, the YMCA of Central Maryland was the first to remove Jesus from the mission statement.[7] Despite these "firsts," little of the Baltimore YMCA's varied programs was truly original. Instead, much of it consisted of initiatives transplanted (and perhaps adapted) to Baltimore from other associations across the country. In part, this cross-pollination resulted from the professionalization of YMCA work. In the mid-1880s, Springfield College was created for the express purpose of training men as professional YMCA secretaries, a development that surely contributed to the prevalence of shared association strategies. Graduates served as YMCA secretaries in communities throughout the country. To advance their careers, these men moved to new communities to assume more responsible positions. This, together with state and na-

1. Located at Pierce and Schroeder Streets and featuring a bowling alley and library, this building, erected in 1859 by the West Baltimore YMCA, was the first structure in the United States designed for the exclusive use of the YMCA. Later used by a series of churches, it was demolished in the 1960s to make way for the ill-fated expansion of Route 70. YMCA Collection, University of Baltimore Archives.

tional conferences for both professional and lay leaders, helped to spread ideas and concepts throughout the YMCA movement.

Despite shared information and expertise, local differences affected the YMCA's role as city builder. Perhaps the most unusual and important facet of Baltimore exceptionalism began when the YMCA became involved with Johns Hopkins University (JHU) at the time of its creation in 1876. Levering Hall, the campus YMCA at JHU, became a conduit through which passed much of the work of the university's Department of History, Political Economy, and Political Science. The partnership that resulted between Levering Hall, JHU, the Charity Organization Society (COS), and the Johns Hopkins Hospital allowed the YMCA to play a critical role in the making of modern philanthropy from 1880 to 1900, the impact of which was felt across the country for years to come.[8]

Perhaps because city government remained smaller and ineffective longer in Baltimore than in comparably sized cities, beginning in the 1850s the YMCA quickly became adept at setting a public agenda by responding to community needs through programs that would later be assumed by the state, by industry, or by another nonprofit created especially for that purpose.[9] For example, as early as 1866, feeling that newsboys in the city were at risk and also a potential danger to the community, James Drill, president of the YMCA, successfully lobbied the city council for an appropriation of $500 to start the News Boys' Home. Begun under the auspices of the YMCA, the home soon became an independent entity, while government involvement in the YMCA continued unabated. The information provided by the friendly visits made by members of Levering Hall, among others, provided city agencies with requisite data justifying the enactment of new legislation on tenement housing by 1907.[10] City officials, including Baltimore mayor James Preston, lauded the association's civic leadership and used it as a quasi-governmental agency in areas such as youth programming and education. Then, too, in the 1910s, in response to a growing immigrant population, the Baltimore YMCA offered a widespread and popular program, English for Foreigners, which in 1920 attracted nearly 10,000 students of Polish, Greek, Russian, and Serbian descent. When the city schools began offering a comprehensive Americanization program in 1922, the YMCA removed itself from the business.[11] Finally, when the burden of providing for sailors left unemployed by the Great Depression became too great, the federal government interceded by using the YMCA's Anchorage branch as a base of operations for the provision of services to seamen.

Similar partnerships between the YMCA and industry were also common. Not only did the YMCA provide direct services to employees through corporate welfare programs in the railroad and manufacturing industries, the association also provided housing and housing referrals to workers relocating for jobs in Baltimore. In addition, much of the YMCA's job training and educational programs was tailored to meet the needs of local industry. Repeatedly, YMCA leaders sought guidance from Baltimore's business leaders on how best the association could meet their needs.

The relationship of the Baltimore YMCA, its leaders and members, both to the state and to the market supports Theda Skocpol's assertion that such voluntary associations have historically "operated in close symbiosis" with the welfare state. The Baltimore YMCA, typical of this pattern, both pressured local government for the creation of public social programs and worked in partnership with the government to administer and expand programs after their establishment.[12]

With the exception of a few early, local, spontaneous voluntary associations, Skocpol contends that what she calls first-wave associationalism, or "Tocqueville romanticism," has been rare in American life. She criticizes those who juxtapose local voluntarism with the "dreaded" bureaucratic state and those, like Putnam, who assume that spontaneous social association, like bowling leagues, is primary while government and politics are derivative. She argues instead that American civic associations such as the YMCA were in fact representative of a second wave of voluntary group formation in the United States, which was encouraged by events such as the Civil War, World War I, and the New Deal. The experience of the Baltimore YMCA supports the contention that voluntary associations grew up not isolated from but in tandem with political events, processes, and institutions.[13]

Sociologists, political scientists, and other participants in the shaping of public policy have, until recently, had little incentive to pay attention to the nonprofit sector. Since the 1950s, however, historians, in their effort to reinterpret American culture, especially as it developed after the Civil War, have studied the associational state. Peter Dobkin Hall asserts that historians have gradually come to agree that "a fundamental reconstructing of public life began to take place in the 1870s and 1880s, which emerged as a national force with the Progressive movement at the turn of the century, and which . . . framed public life for the rest of the [twentieth] century."[14]

But for all of the insights into the current debate offered by Putnam, Skocpol, and associational historians, there is one question left unanswered—why do some organizations evolve and prosper while others decline or disappear outright? The Baltimore YMCA has been a uniquely flexible vessel, and during its first eighty years, it maintained a single mission of leading young men to Jesus through a variety of timely means. The YMCA employed eminently practical attractions such as vocational training and housing while also offering programs, such as sports and games, that were fun. All of the association's programs included a big dollop of training in character building, stewardship, citizenship, faith, and service. And they melded concerns that today are often divorced in our attempt to use the construct of public and private spheres to bring order to the world.

The most important key to the YMCA's success, however, was its willingness to maintain linkages with the public and private sectors. Even after the period covered by this study, the YMCA continued to address concerns we now typically associate with the public arena, including job training, summer camp programs for disadvantaged youth, and affordable transitional housing, as well as services for the private sector such as customized corporate wellness programs.[15] In forging and maintaining such connections between the public and private sectors, the YMCA has acted counter to the disengaging tendencies of modern American life.

For nearly a century, political rhetoric in the United States has shifted between an emphasis on cooperation and an emphasis on conflict between the public and private sectors, chiefly between private institutions and the instrumentalities of the state. Yet, as Lester Salamon astutely points out, some of the same language, the "rhetoric of conflict," was also used to describe the relationships between government and the third sector—private voluntary or nonprofit organizations. As Salamon has observed, such rhetoric has been useful in helping to "protect a sense of private initiative in the pursuit of public purposes and . . . the right and capacity of people to take the initiative to improve their own lives." On the other hand, the rhetoric has obscured "the growth of vitally important supportive relationships between the nonprofit organizations and the state."[16] It has caused serious misunderstandings of voluntarism and associationalism by scholars ranging from Marvin Olasky to Christopher Lasch, the latter of whom, embracing Tocqueville romanticism, claims, "Democracy works best when men and women do things for themselves, with the help of their friends and neighbors, instead of depending on the state."[17]

Dismissing the idea that capitalism may create intractable problems like poverty and underemployment, Olasky claims that only personal contact of the sort provided by the COS's Friendly Visitors can solve society's problems. Most disturbing is Olasky's claim that at some golden moment in the 1870s and 1880s, individuals took responsibility for making personal contact with the downtrodden, and the world was a better place.[18]

Although there has always been and will always be a need for face-to-face democracy, the YMCA's history suggests that even in the allegedly simpler times of the mid-nineteenth century, person-to-person compassion alone could not confront all of the social ills of a complex, capitalistic society. Advocating the need for a return to simple charity of that sort misunderstands or perhaps simply ignores the early yet sustained and reasonably successful care that bureaucratized organizations like the YMCA offered.

The case of the Baltimore YMCA suggests that while there has long been personal involvement in the provision of social services, there has also long been organized, bureaucratized intervention not only by nonprofit, voluntary organizations such as the YMCA, but also by government and business. The story of the Baltimore YMCA reveals that the association was a conduit through which both public and corporate funds were channeled to provide programs with relative efficiency and flexibility.

If this study does nothing more than suggest the permeability of analytical categories of "public," "private," and "third" sector, it has served a useful function. Successful associationalism has been, at least from the 1850s, the story of cooperative endeavor.[19] It is the story of the collaboration and interaction of three sectors—government, business, and nonprofit—in an ongoing quest for a viable civil society.

Despite a long and rich history and evident local pride, neither Baltimore nor its institutions have enjoyed the sort of intense historical study that Philadelphia and Boston have attracted. The congruence of an under-researched city such as Baltimore with its long-ignored but important YMCA thus offers a particularly attractive opportunity. Through eight thematic chapters, this study utilizes Baltimore's YMCA as both the subject and the vehicle of its analysis. By doing so it attempts an "urban biography"—an effort to reveal how religious sensibility, ethnicity, views of male obligation and impulse, and the idea of public ordering through private institutions gave shape not only to Baltimore but to some of the salient tendencies of the modern United States.

By making use of a thematic organizational structure rather than traditional narrative, this study offers a window on the intersecting layers of idea and activity that characterized Baltimore in the period from the 1850s to the 1930s. Individual chapters explore themes ranging from the YMCA's impact on the city's religious, racial, and educational landscape, to how the association helped bring modern philanthropy to Baltimore; the ways in which the YMCA worked with local industry to create loyal workers while enhancing the workplace, to a study of how YMCA members housed and cared for young men and boys.

1

"An Aggressive Christian Enterprise"

The YMCA and Baltimore's Faith Community, 1852–1882

In 1851, the Reverend John W. M. Williams became the pastor of the white First Baptist Church of Baltimore, a church whose membership consisted of 36 men and 160 women. The dearth of men at First Baptist was so serious that observers suggested that its name be changed to the "First *Female* Baptist Church of Baltimore" because, as Williams later remembered, the church was "without a deacon or a Sunday school superintendent, or a single male teacher, or a man who could lead in public prayer." Williams served the congregation for thirty-three years. He worked closely with the female majority, describing them as "wise, prudent, sensible, working women, who cheered the heart of their young pastor, and helped him in his work. Such women as Paul refers to 'who labor with us in the gospel.'" But, while Williams had faith in the women of his congregation, he was also concerned about the fate of young white men in the city. On 18 November 1852, he attended the organizational meeting of the YMCA of Baltimore.[1]

While the 80 percent female membership at Baltimore's First Baptist Church represented an extreme gender imbalance, women had constituted the majority of church members in white American Protestant congregations for a long time.[2] Scholars have attributed the rise of women in reform and voluntary associations, and the emergence of women in the public sphere, to this "feminization" of American Protestantism.[3] This chapter examines the effect of the feminized or emasculated church on the creation and growth of the Baltimore YMCA and the association's rise to institutional credibility and religious legitimacy from the time of its founding in 1852 until the arrival thirty years later of William H. Morriss, its first truly professional general secretary.

Baltimore has long been important to American Christianity. In addition to being the ecclesiastical center and earliest diocese of the Roman Catholic Church in America, Baltimore was the birthplace of American

Methodism. Moreover, the city had long been a center of Presbyterian and Episcopalian activity and an early stronghold of Quakers and Baptists. In 1859, there were 158 different church congregations in Baltimore, representing more than two dozen religious denominations. By the beginning of the twentieth century, Baltimore boasted nearly 600 church buildings.[4]

Despite the large number of congregations, some lay and clerical leaders were concerned about the paucity of male church members. In November 1852, a committee of five men of the Maryland Baptist Union appealed to the clergy of the city's white evangelical churches. Under the leadership of Franklin Wilson, a thirty-year-old Baptist minister whose chronic respiratory problems precluded his employment as a congregational pastor, the committee urged the clergy to announce the formation of the YMCA from their pulpits and to ask young male congregants to attend a preliminary meeting. The committee members knew that men like themselves had already created YMCAs in Boston, New York, Philadelphia, and Washington, D.C., in an effort "to combine the young men of *all the Evangelical Churches* for the moral, mental, and religious improvement of themselves, and of all whom they can influence." To satisfy those goals, the YMCAs established libraries and reading rooms and charged members with welcoming newly arrived young men to the city by directing them to reputable boardinghouses, churches, and the association itself. The YMCA's goal was to welcome the newcomer, to "in every way throw around him good influences, so that he may feel he is not a stranger, but that noble and Christian spirits care for his soul."[5]

News of the association's success elsewhere spurred the effort in Baltimore. In November 1852, more than 100 young laymen, representing nearly all of the city's white evangelical churches, attended the organizational meeting of the YMCA at the First Presbyterian Church.[6] Those who joined the enterprise recognized the critical need for a counteroffensive to the myriad sinful temptations that urban areas like Baltimore offered in the 1850s. The YMCA's organizers worried that neither the church nor the state was equipped to cope with the rapid increase in population in urban areas or the challenges posed by so many newly arrived young males. The YMCA's early leaders quickly identified the needs that the young men's arrival precipitated, including the desire for safe and decent housing, vocational training, job placement, and leisure-time activities. Under the auspices of the fledgling association, YMCA leaders mobilized to redress these concerns.

YMCA members focused on assuring the moral safety of young men adrift in the city, many of whom were naive farm boys. They urged the new arrivals to avoid the temptations of the theater, the saloon, the ballroom, the gaming table, and prostitutes whose "feet go down to death, and whose steps take hold on hell." The YMCA's organizers cautioned that these temptations paraded "their daily and nightly allurements in our midst, to drag into temporal and eternal ruin hundreds of young men." To attack "this deadly work," the self-proclaimed "lovers of God" who led the YMCA advocated using the "companionship and sympathy of the virtuous" as their ammunition.[7]

With an eye toward welcoming all those with even a modicum of interest in religious affairs, the Baltimore YMCA took into membership any moral, young, white Christian man. The Baltimore YMCA grew quickly. By 1853, the association reported more than 500 members.[8]

Although the YMCA's leaders saw that the churches exercised only the weakest attraction to young men, they hoped that organizing through congregations would give their nascent organization an air of respectability and open an important network of contacts with socially responsible men. The YMCA sought formalized links to all white evangelical churches as both an affirmation of its commitment to what Secretary Morriss later dubbed "nondenominational Christianity" and a recruiting tool.[9] In 1852, the YMCA first organized standing committees to act as liaisons between individual church congregations and the association. YMCA leaders soon realized that, despite their faith in the redemptive qualities of nondenominationalism, it was impossible to attract representatives from each congregation of every denomination. Only one-third of the city's eligible congregations organized YMCA standing committees. Advocates of YMCA work believed that this lack of church cooperation, combined with the competition of other voluntary organizations favored by young men, such as the Mercantile Library, the Mechanics Institute, and the Odd Fellows, would slow the YMCA's growth.[10]

Initially, the YMCA's leaders thought that the most effective way for them to accomplish their goals was to avoid encroachment upon what they broadly called "the proper work of the church."[11] At the beginning, this was not difficult because the YMCA's mission was to help young men adapt to the rapidly industrializing city, a job that appeared to be largely separate and distinct from church work. Its members sought out newly arrived men and brought them to both moral and religious influences by helping them find suitable boarding places and employment and by forming a circulating library. In these ways, and by leading young men to "some place of worship on the Sabbath" and using "every means in their power" to surround the newcomer with "Christian associates," YMCA members performed their Christian and organizational duty.[12]

The YMCA's emphasis on religiosity was abiding yet flexible. After early attempts at public prayer meetings attracted few takers, association leaders became more savvy in their efforts to attract their targeted audience. As early as 1856, the YMCA began holding religious services in the halls of all of the city's fire companies.[13] The decision to customize prayer meetings for a particular audience was a harbinger of the YMCA's pragmatic practice of bringing programs to the people, rather than waiting passively to be discovered by an appreciative public.

This infusion of Christianity into the YMCA's programs quickly muddied the distinction between the association's mission and church work. Moreover, the YMCA's nondenominationalism had the largely unintended and unanticipated effect of supplanting the appeal traditional Protestant churches had for some young men. Thus, the YMCA's more masculine and nondenominational religiosity quickly upset the religious and social hegemony of the urban churches and their clergy.[14] In 1858, for example, J. Dean Smith, then YMCA president, declared, "I speak from the depth of my inmost soul, when I say, that I owe to this means [the YMCA], under God, my happiest and most profitable religious hours, and my dearest Christian friends."[15]

The YMCA welcomed men with church affiliations as well as those who were entirely unchurched. Going beyond the bounds of denominationalism was intended to help both young native Baltimoreans and those who were "constantly coming hither from surround and distant parts," men who the YMCA's leadership feared would "without right associations and influences . . . make shipwrecks of themselves forever." To provide the young men adrift in Baltimore with proper guidance and companionship, the YMCA's leaders repeatedly asked the city's ministers for their cooperation.[16]

Despite these appeals, ministerial involvement was limited. With the notable exceptions of Williams, Wilson, and a handful of other clerics, the vast majority of the association's early leaders and members were laymen. In 1854, Baltimore's YMCA reported only nine clergymen among its 512 members. While three of the ministers were YMCA officers that year, all of them severed their ties with the association by 1858.[17] The early YMCA leaders, themselves strongly tied to denominational churches, sought to use the association to compensate for what they saw as the churches' shortcomings. If the YMCA's organization was an indictment of the churches' ability to reach young men, then the dearth of clergy in the ranks of the YMCA's leadership is therefore not surprising.

The YMCA's leaders, in their attempt to reach young men adrift, sought appropriate opportunities. In 1857, Baltimore, like many other American cities, experienced an economic panic followed by labor unrest and religious revivals. The depression was serious, causing many of the nation's stock markets and banks to fail and leading to the collapse of a number of fledgling railroads. Prices plummeted, and businesses and factories closed, leaving thousands of workers unemployed. Nationwide, a total of 6,000 firms went under. However, the northeastern states were most seriously affected by the economic shock.[18] The YMCA quickly mobilized both to attract new members and to forestall labor unrest. In response to the Panic of 1857, the YMCA, beginning in November 1857, increased its emphasis on religious programming with a stepped-up series of noontime prayer meetings.

In addition to the all-male meetings held in the YMCA's room on Fayette Street downtown, the association held as many as four public meetings each day in various city churches and dance halls. At China Hall in West Baltimore, which had been "so often the scene of the gay revel," the YMCA conducted daily worship services. Association leaders proclaimed that under their guidance China Hall was transformed from a place "which once echoed the sensual music, the obscene jester, the excited political harangue" into a site of moral activity. The prayer meetings held at the Maryland Institute were the YMCA's most popular, attracting between 2,000 and 4,000 people each day.[19] The prayer meetings excited religious fervor in the larger community and captured some of the time and attention of restless Baltimoreans. While it is difficult to prove that the YMCA staved off labor unrest, its work in the wake of the Panic of 1857 was strongly supported by the association's solidly middle-class leadership.[20]

Part of the YMCA's success in organizing prayer meetings resulted from a deliberate avoidance of conflict with church services. YMCA prayer meetings were never scheduled for Sunday morning. Although the leaders of the Baltimore YMCA promoted nondenominationalism, they did not expressly seek to undercut the role of denominations in the Christian community. Many YMCA members were largely unconcerned about denominational difference, believing instead in the primacy of a true living church, which focused on satisfying a commitment to God through service to young men. Baltimore YMCA president J. Dean Smith, for example, denounced denominations and sects as "temporary and carnal," insisting

2. The Union Festival, held by the Baltimore YMCA in 1859 and 1860, was very popular but failed to raise enough money for the construction of a new YMCA building. The University of Baltimore Educational Foundation.

that "the unity of the church is spiritual and eternal." Smith concluded that nondenominational unity was "the great foundation principle, upon which our associations stand; it is our creed, and the exemplification of, and the teaching, the power, and beauty, of this Christian oneness, is the great mission of these associations."[21]

While the association struggled to establish institutional legitimacy, it also sought a permanent place on the urban landscape. Since its inception, the Baltimore YMCA had occupied rented quarters in a variety of buildings in the downtown business district. In 1859, however, with the experience of the prayer meetings of 1857 still fresh, YMCA leaders organized a "Union Festival" to raise money to build a YMCA hall. The YMCA's Ladies' Auxiliary, with the support of women from various churches and denominations, made and sold a variety of goods, netting $6,500 in four days, which though substantial, was not adequate for acquiring land and constructing a YMCA building.[22]

A lack of funds was not the only obstacle to YMCA work in the 1850s. Increasing sectional tensions affected the association's success. The debate over slavery divided not only Maryland's population but also the membership of Baltimore's YMCA. The sectional crisis threatened the viability of the association as membership dropped precipitously. Although from its inception the YMCA itself was neutral and forbade political discussion in its rooms, the debate over slavery frequently affected association membership. When the Civil War began, many members left both the YMCA and the city of Baltimore.[23]

Although the YMCA did not dissolve entirely, it was moribund during the war years.[24] It is likely that during the Civil War the membership of the Baltimore YMCA followed the model of associations in Washington, New York, and other cities and materially assisted the work of the U.S. Christian Commission. With its leadership drawn from YMCAs around the country, the Christian Commission was a voluntary organization that acted as a clearinghouse for all religious work in the armed forces of the North and South. Local associations raised funds, and the government provided suitable accommodations. Although some prosperous local associations were able to maintain services for their urban constituents while supporting the Christian Commission, many smaller associations merged into local branches of the Christian Commission. The Baltimore YMCA, like those in Chicago, New York, St. Paul, St. Louis, and Buffalo, served as a regional clearinghouse for the multitude of activities that were channeled through the Christian Commission.

Ultimately, the Christian Commission was most successful at recruiting "agents" who went to the front to minister to the soldiers' religious needs. By war's end, 5,000 men and women had given an average of thirty-eight days each without compensation. In addition to one-on-one battlefield assistance, the Christian Commission distributed thousands of religious tracts and Bibles. The Christian Commission far exceeded its goal of providing spiritual help to soldiers. It garnered much support for the YMCA in the postwar years. This gave the Baltimore YMCA the strength and respectability to overcome quickly much of the loss of membership it suffered during the war.[25]

After the Civil War, the Baltimore YMCA was quickly reconstituted, beginning again in earnest in 1866. The following year the association admitted 347 new members, pushing membership to over 700. Those who joined after the war were largely new to YMCA work. Most postwar leaders were also new to the association. Of the more than two dozen officers and committee members in 1868, only a handful had been involved with the YMCA in 1859.[26]

In the postwar years, the Baltimore YMCA began to employ innovative and proto-Progressive approaches to urban problems, bringing to the city the beginnings of scientific philanthropy, sophisticated workplace training, and a social service agenda, all of which were religiously infused. Invigorated by new members and leaders and strengthened by wartime service, the work of the YMCA shifted dramatically. It evolved into a religious association that no longer operated within the confines of church-set agendas but came to minister not only to young men but to boys and girls, men and women, largely outside the churches' domain.

The YMCA's work with children extended to include mission schools. In 1867, city authorities permitted the YMCA the free use of the Broadway Market Hall in Fells Point on Sundays for a large mission school and prayer meeting. In addition, the YMCA operated another mission school and prayer meeting at a building it owned on Abbott Street, also in East Baltimore. Through these schools, the YMCA's leaders hoped to reach "many neglected children" who, they feared, were not otherwise receiving religious training. To attract the young scholars, the YMCA distributed religious tracts and other ephemera. Many children who attended the mission schools were Sunday school scholars elsewhere who were attracted by the giveaways. In 1869, the YMCA reported that "quite a number of children after attending their own schools, would leave early in order to attend ours."[27]

At the same time that the YMCA experimented with new programs intended to benefit groups beyond its targeted constituency of young men, it also tried to maintain its traditional stance of neutrality in partisan matters. Perhaps as a gesture to unity in the postwar years, the leadership of the YMCA helped scores of young southern men "without money or acquaintances in the city" obtain employment. The YMCA stepped up its emphasis on nondenominationalism and evangelism, "not to form a new Christian community, but as a recruiting corps, to fill up from the world the ranks of the great army of the Lord."[28]

The YMCA's members proved to be effective evangelists. Despite drawing many men to the association, the YMCA's literature and leadership continued to proclaim that a member's most important religious obligation was loyalty to a denominational church, with association activities filling only what leisure time remained after professional, personal, and religious commitments were satisfied.[29] While cultivating "handmaiden" rhetoric that promoted the image of the YMCA and its work as "needed auxiliaries of the Church," Baltimore YMCA leaders simultaneously proclaimed that their work, because of its nondenominational nature, represented the "truest Christianity . . . that which best demonstrates the mission and sacrifices of Jesus Christ in the daily behavior of his disciples."[30]

Sometimes young men chose the YMCA as their spiritual home. Although the YMCA's founders had not intended to subvert the power of the churches, for some association leaders and members the YMCA eclipsed the churches' importance in their religious lives. The growing prominence of the YMCA as the spiritual home for some members after the war hastened the growth of nondenominationalism. The members began to "rally under one battle flag, 'The Standard of the Cross!'"[31]

The association's leaders attempted to ameliorate the impact of the YMCA's expanded religious programming on relations with the city's clergy. They offered the city's white evangelical ministers a weekly meeting place, through which they hoped to find a place "in their affections which will the more readily secure us their personal sympathy and support." In 1868, association leaders regretfully reported "that there are but few of the ministers of our city who seem to take an interest in our operations, or who visit our rooms." Despite the clergy's apathy, YMCA leaders continued to invite the city's ministers to support the association's work, claiming "their presence and encouragement would help us very much, and give tone and character to the enterprise in which we are engaged."[32] YMCA members remained optimistic that through their efforts, changes in the churches would be effected. Not only did some YMCA members go on to careers as YMCA secretaries, some trained to be Protestant ministers themselves.[33]

The systematic expansion of the YMCA's policy of nondenominationalism irked some clergy. Although ministers cloaked their criticism of the YMCA's encroachment on their territory, tension in the postwar period was very real.[34] Some YMCA secretaries interpreted their jobs as formal ministry and wore ministerial collars. The YMCA's International Committee, the North American policy-making body, instructed secretaries to "avoid anything that smacks of the cloth," as they had not been ordained as spiritual leaders and as YMCA secretaries were not entitled to the "distinctive garb of the clergy."[35] More important, the clergy's antipathy toward the YMCA was caused by the expansion of the association's activities after the Civil War beyond the needs of young men adrift. Children's meetings, sick and poor visitations, mission schools, street preaching, and open-air gatherings were among the YMCA's new enterprises that may have caused some critics to be concerned that the association's outreach to children, women, and destitute men could threaten the loyalty of the churches' traditional stalwarts.[36]

The YMCA's open-air meetings began in the summer of 1869 with 153 speakers participating in twenty different weekly forums, each attracting between 100 and 1,000 people. These meetings were held at the Causeway on Eastern Avenue in East Baltimore, a locality similar in its crowding and dirt to New York's Five Points neighborhood. There, speakers inveighed against the evil influences of "low groggeries [and] dance houses." During cold weather, the YMCA held weekly services in a small building in the neighborhood. Open-air meetings became more popular each year. Some Protestant ministers supported the open-air meetings because sermons were limited to topics on which evangelical Christians agreed, and the policy was neither to commend nor condemn any creed.[37]

Although a few ministers, like those who participated in the open-air meetings, worked cooperatively with the YMCA, relations between the majority of clergy and the association remained cool. Association supporters repeatedly tried to reassure the clergy that the YMCA's work was not intended to replace their own. The church, YMCA leaders proclaimed, was eminently qualified for all religious work and therefore it would be "simply absurd to suppose that the Association can be more effective." YMCA leaders assured the clergy that "we do not interfere in any way with the legitimate work of the church, or attempt to take out of her hands that which is peculiarly her own." To prove that claim, the YMCA reported in 1871 that it tried only to reach the unchurched, its lay leaders taking the "simple truth" and bringing it to "those who avoid the sanctuary."[38]

No one better ministered to the unchurched than Dwight Lyman Moody, who as the first evangelist invited under the YMCA's auspices held a series of revivals in Baltimore for seven months during the winter and spring of 1878–79.[39] In anticipation of Moody's visit, the Baltimore YMCA hastened the completion of its Central Building. Baltimore leaders invited Moody because they wanted to experience his evangelical ministry and because they knew that during his revivals, Moody supported the work of the local YMCA by lobbying or fund-raising on its behalf. In exchange, YMCA members supported Moody's work. In Baltimore, for example, Moody persuaded John Work Garrett, president of the B&O Railroad, to support the establishment of a railroad YMCA in the city.[40]

Moody's visit to Baltimore stirred up religious zeal and strengthened the association's role as a serious and legitimate participant in the city's religious life. At Moody's request and in hopes of winning some clerical support, the YMCA hosted a plenary meeting with representatives from ten Protestant denominations. Moody's visit also coincided with the YMCA's annual convention in Baltimore where, against his will, he was elected national president of the YMCA.[41]

Moody completed his stay in Baltimore in June 1879 and returned to his home in Massachusetts. Hoping to continue Moody's revival activities and his goal of extending the work of the "Church in Baltimore," YMCA leaders hired the evangelist E. W. Bliss as his replacement. In a letter to ministers across the city, the YMCA's leaders asserted that they expected Bliss to work without ministerial support, hoping "this great Christian enterprise may be carried on without interfering with the regular work of the Ministry in your own congregation."[42]

Although the YMCA remained committed to basic courtesy in its dealings with the city's clergy, by 1880 the association had proven itself a viable, independent force in the city's religious life. Ministerial approbation, while desirable, was no longer necessary to legitimate the YMCA's religious programming. Moody's visit proved the association's independence and institutional legitimacy as a faith organization. There was now no question about the YMCA's ability to stand unsupported by the ministerial community.

In 1881, the Baltimore YMCA publicly recognized that it had long been considered "an organization directly antagonistic to the church; working for its own ends, and laboring in a field properly coming under church government."[43] But that would all change, the YMCA promised, as the association refocused its attention to ministering exclusively to the needs of boys and young men. Hiring William Morriss as general secretary in 1882 helped the YMCA redouble and clarify its institutional commitment to bring young men to Jesus. Under Morriss's leadership, the YMCA excluded women and children.

Morriss sought to reach a more diverse group of young men, including railroad workers, college students, Germans, and African Americans. Morriss, a Quaker, was himself a proselytizing evangelist who saw the YMCA's fluctuating membership as a boon to his ministry. Early in his forty-one-year career with the Baltimore YMCA, Morriss realized that rarely did the YMCA's religious work alone reach young men, yet he believed that using athletics, education, and housing as incentives increased the possibility that a young man would gain exposure to the YMCA's religious mission and be led to Jesus. "That this is not done effectively or completely does not lessen the fact that it is our recognized aim," he concluded.[44]

In the thirty years following its founding in 1852, the Baltimore YMCA's leaders and members affirmed their need for religion that was masculine, accessible, and nondenominational. At its inception, the Baltimore YMCA had a tightly focused mission—to reach the flood of young men entering the city. These were men whom the established churches were largely failing to attract. Yet some leading members of the city's Protestant clergy supported the formation of the YMCA, concerned that "the lovers of sin," with their array of "daily and nightly allurements," were winning the battle for the souls of young men. In turn, the YMCA in its first years sought legitimation from the churches. The standing committees, in particular, were means not only of attracting new YMCA members but of attempting to work with and *through* the churches. This focused definition of mission and the companion efforts at nondenominationalism bred a comforting, assuring rhetoric that cast the YMCA as an "auxiliary" to the churches.

By the end of its first decade, however, the YMCA's rhetoric had already begun to clash with the realities of its programmatic efforts. The YMCA responded to the Panic of 1857 and the resulting economic dislocations by taking the lead in organizing religious programming for an audience far broader than just young men. If it was using techniques that the established churches had not employed, the YMCA was now reaching not only the unchurched but also women and children—audiences whom the churches had themselves often successfully cultivated.

While the coming of the Civil War led to a contraction in the YMCA's activities, after the war the YMCA emerged with renewed confidence and embarked upon a wide-ranging effort to provide services to children and adults, men and women. The rhetoric of the YMCA during this period, however, remained committed to the notion of a limited mission, devoted to serving the needs of young men, and to the very politic, deferential language of serving as the church's "auxiliary." Although early rhetoric described the YMCA's goal as supplementing the church—serving as its handmaiden—the association quickly replaced or superseded the role of denominational Protestant churches for some young men. By 1882, when William Morriss filled the position of general secretary, the Baltimore YMCA was emerging as an independent and legitimate institutional presence within the city's religious infrastructure. The YMCA plied a kind of Christianity that took its ministry well beyond the framework of the mainstream Protestant churches.

2

"The Next Best Thing to the Family Christian Home"

The YMCA, Housing, and Moral Stewardship, 1858–1890

In their mission to bring men to Jesus, leaders of the Baltimore YMCA made no fine distinctions between the public and private spheres. They ministered to young men not only in the rapidly changing public arenas of work and education but also in the private sphere dominated by spirituality and domesticity. While making available business skills and contacts they believed were necessary for making boys and young men into responsible citizens, YMCA leaders also provided tools of domesticity designed to make them good husbands. Housing and moral stewardship programs first emerged as priorities for the YMCA from 1858 through 1890.

In venturing into this realm, the YMCA's leaders found themselves confronted by the mythic components (real or ideal) of a proper Christian home. Their challenge was to construct housing and moral stewardship programs that would provide a Christian home consonant with domestic pieties for young men in the modern American city. In making a literal and figurative home, the YMCA found itself operating in the midst of a world with its own powerful language, mores, folkways, and traditions.

During the early nineteenth century, according to historian Elizabeth Blackmar, the language of housing rested on polarized categories in which a proper home life was one where, by definition, there was a "mature" male provider and a "virtuous" female caretaker.[1] But the traditional language and the sanctity of traditional housing arrangements were then besieged by the rise of the industrial city. With its agglomeration of large numbers of unmarried, unattached men and women, the city forced people into both new and long-marginal forms of housing, particularly boardinghouses and lodging houses.

Although boardinghouses were largely unknown in many smaller American cities until the mid-nineteenth century, they appeared early in New York. Blackmar argues that the youth, transience, and freedom from family ties and long-term commitments of young men, many of whom chose to live in boardinghouses, represented to genteel citizens "a condition of social immaturity that rejected the principles of family duty and selective obligation. . . . Viewed from a distance, the sharing of domestic space seemed to break down any one household's powers to define and order its relations with other households." She contends that economic uncertainty was another factor influencing the development of boardinghouses. "In an unstable economy, the selling of surplus housing space, and indeed the creation of that surplus through decisions about density and use, provided households with an additional source of cash." There were 50 boardinghouses in New York in 1790 and 150 in 1800.[2]

While there had been some boardinghouses earlier, in Baltimore it was the critical housing shortages of the postbellum period that convinced many respectable white families "of their duty to use at least one vacant room to surround some young man with home comforts and such influences as should help to stay the fearful tide of temptation." YMCA leaders were drawn to housing by their belief that "the downward career of many a young man has been traced to the soul-destroying influences which surround him in many boarding houses."[3]

Faced with a rapidly industrializing city, the Baltimore YMCA's involvement in housing began with efforts to match young men to safe, decent, and affordable boardinghouses. Convinced that making matches between newly arrived young men and respectable quarters could improve the quality of life in the city, YMCA leaders first sought out and then sanctioned "desirable places . . . where young men can find the comforts of a home."[4]

The kind of arrangement typified by the family boardinghouse, although not ideal, was viewed more favorably by the YMCA's leaders than were lodging houses.[5] A housing type that gained popularity in the late eighteenth century, the lodging house eliminated, according to historian Mark Peel, "many of the protective socializing rituals of full board. . . . Lodgers rented only a room, not boarding privileges. They ate their meals in cheap restaurants and socialized in nearby cafes and bars, spending much of their time away from home."[6] The men who lived in the increasingly popular lodging houses were "the great middle class of clerks, salesmen, skilled mechanics, and miscellaneous industrial workers." Most of them were unmarried and "without other abiding-place in the city."[7]

Not only was the lodging house different from the boardinghouse, it was also distinguishable from apartments and tenements. While the latter were "fitted for housekeeping," the lodging house was "cut up into separate rooms to be rented to single men and women or to childless married couples of limited means" who were willing to "undergo the inconveniences of life in one room and meals at a corner cafe."[8]

YMCA leaders were concerned that without thoughtful guidance, young workingmen might be ruined sexually and financially by an impersonal, immoral city. As early as 1858, the YMCA's Housing Aid Committee conspicuously posted lists of city boardinghouses known to be "kept by persons of a decided Christian character." In the 1860s, they kept a list of affordable, "good eligible boarding houses where Christian companionship could most likely be fostered," which was important "as companionship tends either to elevate or enervate." Over time the YMCA's boardinghouse list evolved into a register overseen by the Committee on Employment and Boarding, which listed the owner's name and religious denomination, along with the location, capacity, and rates of the house. Inclusion in the register required being "well recommended by some responsible party." The register was used not only by newly arrived young men but also by local people.[9]

Despite the concerns of urban elites like the YMCA's leaders, the popularity of boardinghouses and lodging houses grew quickly. By the end of the nineteenth century, they were quite common. Although some boardinghouses were morally unsavory, many others, including those sanctioned by the YMCA, were modeled on an idealized American family, where "shared meals and supervised interaction within the dining room and the parlor maintained the ethos of the family home."[10] Augusta Tucker's novel *Miss Susie Slagle's* offers a vision of respectable boardinghouse life in Baltimore in the late nineteenth and early twentieth centuries.[11] In 1885, upon her parents' deaths, thirty-five-year-old Miss Susie became a boardinghouse keeper. By 1912 (the year in which the story is set), the sixty-something Miss Susie was "plump, white-haired and had an hourglass figure," as well as "all the arrested physical charm of a voluptuous virgin coupled with the emotional unsteadiness of a woman who has never had a beau." She was extremely concerned about the well-being of her young charges: "she had known the American medical student for years with a profundity which would have amazed his mother and annoyed his sweetheart." Miss Susie's four-story boardinghouse on Biddle Street served two generations of male medical students at Johns Hopkins Hospital. Room assignments were based on medical school seniority. The bedrooms were small and "contained ordinary cheap machine-made bureaus, tables and chairs." The only ornamental features of the bedrooms were the black iron beds, which through years of use had been trans-

3. Sports teams were long a feature of YMCA life. This 1898 photograph of Central's track and field team highlights the camaraderie between the young men and Thomas Cornelius, their physical director. YMCA Collection, University of Baltimore Archives.

formed: "The black paint only etched the contours of arms, legs, muscles, tibia and the instruments which had come into use in the last quarter century." Miss Susie, a very good cook, served food family style. Meals began with the grace of Miss Susie's childhood: "Lord, bless this food to our use and ourselves to Thy service. For Christ's sake. Amen." The food was so plentiful and rich that "the Dean won't allow any student with heart troubles, a tendency toward gout, asthmatic symptoms or fallen arches to board at Miss Susie's. Mean sure death if he did. Gastric suicide in six months." A practicing Protestant, Miss Susie had two house rules. She prohibited smoking in bed. Her other rule concerned propriety. As one of her senior boarders announced, "It is a stag house at all times, even when Miss Susie goes to church conventions!"[12]

Boardinghouses sanctioned by the YMCA were of two types. Some, like Miss Susie's, were run by professional proprietors, but the majority were family homes in which one or two men were taken as boarders. Both types offered family-style meals. But even the best of them did not provide leisure-time activities, a shortcoming that spurred leaders to make the YMCA a place of recreation for young men. To stave off the temptation posed by bars and dance halls, the YMCA organized and shaped wholesome leisure-time activities: "In the heart of this great city, there is a home with doors ever open, where the stranger may find a welcome; those who have leisure hours a pleasant and profitable resort; those who are tired a refuge from temptation; and those who are in trouble, friends to sympathize and help."[13] The YMCA's rooms, "an antidote for club-houses and saloons," offered entertainment as well as the opportunity for quiet reading and study.[14]

The opening of the first Central YMCA Building in 1878 at Charles and Saratoga Streets, followed by William H. Morriss's arrival as general secretary soon after, stimulated the YMCA to redouble its Christian homemaking efforts. The association's goal was:

> *work by young men, for young men, to bring them to Christ.* It is our aim to make this building a Christian home, attractive, amusing, cheerful and instructive for young men. . . . We aim as an association to get hold of young men before they have wasted their strength in riotous living, to save their strength and increase it. We have the facilities for doing this, mentally, morally, physically, socially and spiritually. Every young man has within him the social element; this will be developed, sooner or later, for good or for evil. Young men will and must have amusement. We aim to give them pleasant companions, surrounded by Christian influence, healthy recreation, and innocent amusements.[15]

By giving vocational training and advice, along with religious, secular, and physical instruction in cheerful surroundings with "elevating companionship," the YMCA, even before it offered any housing, saw itself as a proxy for the Christian family home.[16]

While the YMCA was sanctioning boardinghouses and providing leisure-time spaces for men housed privately, its leaders also briefly experimented with their corporate capacity to provide housing for the homeless. As early as 1866, James M. Drill, then YMCA president, went to the Baltimore City Council asking for an appropriation to start a home for "hundreds of boys, newsboys and bootblacks [who] had no homes and no home comforts." With the $500 he received, the YMCA's homemaking became literal through its creation of the News Boys' Home in the upper rooms of a blacksmith shop on Holliday Street near city hall. The YMCA installed bunks "steamship style" and "fixed nice reading rooms with

4. So proud was the YMCA of its Central Building that its images adorned much of the association's printed material, including the *Weekly Bulletin*, a newsletter for members, in 1877. YMCA Collection, University of Baltimore Archives.

games." The News Boys' Home was created to help orphan boys locate gainful employment.[17] Within two years this enterprise captured the imagination of public benevolence and commanded the "liberal sympathy and support of Christians and lovers of the poor throughout our community." So successful was the News Boys' Home that it was soon incorporated as a separate institution. Building on the YMCA's foundation, the independent Boys' Home helped poor youth earn a livelihood while, according to an association chronicler, "slowly but surely laying the foundations of character, which will cause them to become, instead of lost and ruined wrecks, honest and upright members of society; better than all else, Christian men."[18]

Following the Panic of 1873, the YMCA made a second foray into housing for the destitute with its Friendly Inn on West Lombard Street, two blocks from the inner harbor, where "the hungry are fed and the homeless sheltered." The Friendly Inn offered food, shelter, and help obtaining employment to homeless patrons, many of whom had been responsible community members. The YMCA committee that operated the Friendly Inn claimed that there was "no better channel" for "Christian and other people who wish to practice charity in aiding needy and deserving men." To do so, association members sold meal and lodging tickets for distribution to homeless men who redeemed them at the Friendly Inn.[19]

The Friendly Inn had seventy single beds, which were filled "nearly every night," and a soup kitchen in the basement that fed hundreds of men weekly. After the labor unrest of 1877, the YMCA reported that "many who enter the door of this humble but well arranged establishment once lived in wealth and comfort and occupied high positions."[20] Featuring mandatory religious services, the spiritual work of the Friendly Inn resembled that of traditional city missions. The Friendly Inn closed permanently in 1881 when, upon the eve of Morriss's arrival as general secretary, the association redirected its energy toward young businessmen and away from tramps and the working poor.[21]

The News Boys' Home and the Friendly Inn were exceptions. Generally, YMCA leaders strove to serve young men at risk while keeping the truly destitute and homeless away from the association.[22] YMCA leaders believed that for young middle-class bachelors, it was a matter of preventing contact with the danger posed by saloons and prostitutes. Hardcore homeless men were steered to the city's established charitable agencies.[23] In 1895, for example, the association's Executive Committee considered ways to keep "all questionable characters and tramps" from the reading room and discussed men who habitually made the reading room "a loafing room," and who, they believed, hindered their ability to reach a "class of young men who may . . . enjoy the fellowship and benefits of uniting with our Association."[24]

Concomitant with the YMCA's focus on safe and decent housing for young men adrift was the association's concern with defining appropriate male sexuality, and the desirable comportment of husbands and fathers. One of the earliest efforts in this area began in 1886 when the Baltimore association (as part of a national YMCA initiative) became the local agent for a sexual purity program known as the White Cross.[25] This was an egalitarian view of sexuality that required of men the same sexual conduct expected of women. Whereas the male portion of the program was called the White Cross League or White Cross Society and operated out of YMCAs, the White Shield, the women's program, was administered by the Women's Christian Temperance Union (WCTU).

Frances Willard, a leader of the WCTU, coined the phrase "the white life for two." Although Willard never spelled out exactly what the "white life" entailed, historian Barbara Epstein suggests that Willard was concerned not only with virginity before marriage but with minimal sex within marriage as well. Willard was interested in enabling women to have some control of their sexual and reproductive lives. The "white life" attempted to reverse standard male-oriented ideas about sexuality and give women some power in sexual relationships. It assumed that good women had only minimal sexual drives. Before the national YMCA took on the administration of the White Cross, it was briefly run under the aegis of the WCTU's Department of Social Purity, which required men to promise to "treat all women with respect . . . to maintain the law of purity as equally binding upon men and women . . . to use all possible means to fulfill the command, 'Keep thyself pure.'"[26] The goal of the White Cross was "a single moral standard for men and women, and it asks the Church in all its branches to maintain the single standard and by practice as well as by precept assure the world that what is sin in the woman is sin in the man."[27]

Through leadership of the White Cross, the YMCA's leaders faced head-on the double standard inherent in sexual relationships of the late nineteenth century. According to an 1887 YMCA report, "the double standard prevails today, the [sexually active single] woman being hopelessly condemned while the man goes free. On this point a great battle is yet to be fought, and the White Cross now calls upon Christians far and wide to meet the issue."[28] Recognizing no distinction between the public and private spheres, YMCA leaders believed it was incumbent on the association to take on the work of the White Cross because there were few other venues for the teaching of sexual virtue. Who better to teach young men "purity of private life" or the dangers of "self-pollution"?

> The minister cannot teach these things from the pulpit, for it would be indelicate, as he has to talk to both sexes. The school-teacher is not asked to, as it is no part of mental training, . . . And so it is left to whom to teach in this important field? Why to the parent. And how often does he or she do it? . . . Is it not the truth that the vast majority of fathers right here in our Christian land utterly evade their duty in this matter?[29]

By its nature, argued the YMCA, the work of pushing personal purity was "quiet and unobtrusive." In support of the goals of the White Cross, members of the Baltimore YMCA purchased and distributed thousands of tracts on ideal sexual behavior for young men, the titles of which included *True Manliness*, *O, Stop Him*, and *Early Manhood—Some of Its Dangers*.[30] The YMCA also held public White Cross League meetings (which often featured physicians speaking on issues related to personal hygiene) and sent its members to visit churches to enlist ministers' support. In 1886, White Cross membership in Baltimore was 121. Two years later, membership was 352, in 1889 it was 474, and it reached its peak of 632 in 1890.[31] Apparently the speakers and the tracts were very persuasive. In 1895, the

White Cross Society held a National Purity Congress in Baltimore at which even self-professed disbelieving young male reporters were "sufficiently moved to join the White Cross League."[32]

Topics addressed by the White Cross through its tracts and lectures dealt not only with the prohibition against premarital sex but also with the dangers of masturbation. For example, the 1888 YMCA tract *Personal Purity* (for men only) editorialized on the widespread practice of masturbation in schools: "So bad has the habit become that in one of the largest schools in the United States, which is under State control, the authorities will not allow any boy to have side-pockets in his pants." The White Cross League opposed masturbation both on grounds of immorality and because of the erroneous (but widespread) belief that a single ejaculation was the equivalent of "forty ounces of that . . . life-blood."[33]

The YMCA's embrace of the White Cross movement is another example of male interest in homemaking in its largest sense—men as partners in the making of Christian homes. And, although not intentional, according to historian David J. Pivar, the White Cross Society proved to be "a tremendous boost to the woman's movement. Through its appeal to young men it educated both young men and women to the new ideal man-woman relationship." According to Pivar, the White Cross Society, like the women's movement, "further spiritualized sexuality. The society tacitly agreed that women's moral standards were higher than men's." Ultimately, the goal of the White Cross and White Shield groups, in Pivar's view, "implied the sanctification of womanhood."[34]

A nuanced reading of the role of the White Cross Society and, in fact, the range of YMCA housing and moral stewardship programs suggest that association leaders believed that for individual wholeness, the artificial distinctions of the private and public sphere were irrelevant. It was, therefore, as appropriate for the YMCA to train a young man in telegraphy as it was to provide him with information on the dangers of masturbation. Again, there was no cognitive dissonance in pursuing the personal and the professional simultaneously, and, in the view of YMCA leaders, such efforts were to be increased.

Although homosexuality was not a topic explicitly mentioned in any of the YMCA's moral stewardship programs, there is no question that it existed within the YMCA. In his 1937 novel *A Scarlet Pansy*, Robert Scully begins his fictionalized account of a gay man's sexual coming-of-age in the 1890s by describing his seduction at the hands of a YMCA secretary at the Central YMCA in Baltimore. (Such a seduction could not have taken place in the YMCA's dorms in the 1890s, however, because it was not until 1908 that the new Central featured housing.)[35]

In much the way that the YMCA's leaders developed an alternative to the "feminized" church, so they fashioned a new rhetoric for, and a new model of, male domesticity. The YMCA thus unwittingly created an alternative to the dominant gender-based nineteenth-century language of housing, mores, and manners—which blurred (or, more accurately, melded) the neat divisions of the prevailing rhetoric. Leaders made the YMCA into "the next best thing to the family Christian home."[36] Association volunteers and staff offered young men training and guidance for both the marketplace and the home by respecting no separation of public and private domains.

3

Not Bowling Alone

Faith, Science, and the Moral Imagination
of YMCA Leaders, 1880–1920

Between the 1880s and the 1920s, the Baltimore YMCA emerged as a multifaceted organization serving a range of community needs. Volunteer leaders such as James Carey Thomas, Joshua Levering, and Francis Albertson (F. A.) White, along with William H. Morriss, general secretary of the Baltimore YMCA from 1882 until 1923, pioneered in the use of modern methods in that era's war on poverty. They encouraged the growth of a meritocracy by establishing a far-reaching web of educational programs catering to able, aspiring students. They served *in loco parentis* to nurture and house young men and boys in facilities throughout the city. They reached out to male workers in a variety of industrial settings in an attempt to humanize work, and they began formal service to German-Americans and African Americans.

That so much occurred at and through the Baltimore YMCA in the years from 1880 to 1920 surely reflects the times. These decades encompassed the arrival of urban American modernity. The modern industrial corporation, vast immigrations and migrations, and the rise of the modern city all were indications of the acceleration of historical time that historians have termed the "incorporation of America."[1] In the face of these larger changes, new civic leaders emerged. Impelled by faith, fascinated by the spectacle of the burgeoning city, and believing in the promise of scientific and industrial progress, YMCA leaders used their moral imagination to turn the association ever more explicitly into an instrument of progress. The YMCA's broad mission of bringing men to Jesus, coupled with its elastic and adaptable program, allowed leaders to envision it as a change agent. By doing so, they helped to make the Baltimore YMCA vital to the Social Gospel.[2]

The Social Gospel grew within American Protestantism between the 1880s and the start of the Great Depression in 1929. Fundamentally, it attempted a Christian response to the changing realities and problems of an increasingly industrialized and urbanized nation. The Social Gospel's advocates tried to adapt the Protestant tradition of an earlier rural America to the changing demands of a newly industrial, organized, and multiethnic society. Such Applied Christianity posed the question, "What would Jesus do?" usually in such a way as to leave little doubt that had Christ bothered to visit, he would have urged reform.

In 1882, Morriss became the Baltimore YMCA's general secretary. Born in England in 1851, Morriss came to the United States as a young man. He served as assistant to the general secretary of the Washington, D.C., YMCA before taking on the top job for the Poughkeepsie, New York, YMCA in 1875, a position he held until he was called to Baltimore.[3] Morriss hesitated before accepting the Baltimore job:

> Unless I felt the call of duty urging me to this apparently greater field for usefulness, nothing could induce me to leave my present home. ... It is only in the consciousness that God calls me to work for Him that I dare think of going out into this unknown field and my earnest prayer is that if we are brought together it may be apparent that his hand is in every act and word of the Association.[4]

When Morriss arrived, membership at the Baltimore YMCA totaled 701, and the association occupied one building. When he retired forty-one years later, paid members exceeded 7,000, and the association owned three buildings, rented two others, ran 35 club centers, employed 42 officers, and engaged 442 volunteer managers.[5] Under Morriss's leadership, the Baltimore YMCA created special branches and programs for industrial employees, affirming and formalizing earlier more tenuous links between the YMCA and Baltimore's workers.

In 1901, reporter Ernest H. Abbott observed religious life in America for a series of articles in *Outlook* magazine. To get information from the leadership of the Roman Catholic Church and, incidentally, to meet with the president of the Johns Hopkins University (JHU), Abbott began his trip in Baltimore. He remained longer than planned because Morriss allowed him an unexpected introduction to the city's workingmen and labor leaders, a fact that surprised Abbott. In his experience most YMCA secretaries were "out of touch (though not out of sympathy) with the workingman." Abbott described Morriss as having "evident good breeding, strong personality, businesslike ways, broad sympathies, alert mind—the kind of true gentleman we Americans are proud to think only a democracy can produce."[6]

Under Morriss's leadership, religion suffused the Baltimore YMCA even as program offerings expanded. A Quaker involved with the Homewood Meeting and most citywide religious activities, Morriss was an evangelist. He called his product "nondenominational Christianity" and reported that it had "favorable access practically everywhere—shops, office buildings, clubs, industrial plants, railroads, and homes."[7] Morriss saw the YMCA's fluctuating membership as a boon to his ministry. "In a church there is practically the same congregation year after year; here we have from 40 to 50 percent change every year. We are in contact with new groups of men and boys every year."[8] Like the lay leaders with whom he worked, Morriss understood the YMCA's mission in religious terms. While he realized that the spiritual work by itself rarely attracted young men, he was convinced that "every department of the Association is religious." He believed that it was the YMCA's purpose to have every participant "exposed to the distinctly Christian message. That this is not done effectively or completely does not lessen the fact that is our recognized aim, and the classes on the gymnasium floor, the educational classes, dormitory and other groups of men who come for specific purposes are visited and made aware of the compelling and controlling motive of the Association."[9]

In addition to his work with the YMCA, Morriss identified with many civic enterprises, especially those related to the welfare of boys and men. An avid bicyclist, Morriss sought to improve parks, playgrounds, and athletic competitions. He worked with the Boy Scouts and the News Boys' Home. He was one of the founders of the YMCA College in Springfield, Massachusetts, in 1885.[10] Along with YMCA leaders James Carey Thomas and Eugene Levering, he lobbied for the construction of public baths in Baltimore.[11]

Morriss's wife, Mary Elizabeth Haviland Morriss, was active in women's club work and civic activities in Baltimore. She, like the wives of the YMCA's volunteer leaders, acted as both a manager of the YMCA's Ladies' Auxiliary and a director of the YWCA. Her husband, meanwhile, was involved with the YWCA, for years serving on its male advisory board.[12]

The Morrisses had two sons and a daughter, Margaret Shove Morriss ("Peggy Push"), who graduated from Goucher College in 1904 and completed a Ph.D. in history at Bryn Mawr College. Like her parents, she was involved with the YWCA. During World War I, while her father selected YMCA secretaries for service in France, Peggy Morriss left her teaching job at Mount Holyoke College to serve as a recreational director with the

5. James Carey Thomas, M.D., a longtime leader of the Baltimore YMCA, served as its president from 1877 to 1881 and as vice president from 1882 to 1896. A Quaker, Thomas was a civic leader who served as a trustee for the Johns Hopkins University and Hospital. At his death, a room was furnished and named in his honor at the Central YMCA Building. YMCA Collection, University of Baltimore Archives.

YWCA's War Work Council in France. In 1923, the year of her father's retirement, she became the dean of Pembroke, the women's college at Brown University, a position she held until she retired in 1950.[13] At his retirement, William Morriss worked from the Providence, Rhode Island, association conducting a service for disabled YMCA secretaries, and he was involved in many of the campus activities at Pembroke. He died on Thanksgiving Day 1939 at the age of eighty-eight.[14]

The interlocking interests of native-born white Baltimoreans James Carey Thomas, Joshua Levering, and F. A. White, each of whom served as YMCA president during Morriss's Baltimore tenure, encompassed not only that association but also the YWCA and many other civic, business, and religious groups. Their benevolent activities, combined with those of their families, offer a window into the moral imagination of Baltimore's elite—the ways they volunteered their time, talents, and resources to improve the community—in these years. Examining the community involvements of these men and their wives, parents, children, and siblings allows insight into patterns of voluntarism among urban leaders.

James Carey Thomas's involvement in the YMCA began in 1866 when he founded the YMCA's News Boys' Home. He was an officer of the YMCA for almost twenty years, serving as president from 1877 to 1881 and vice president from 1882 to 1896. A physician, he focused his voluntary activities largely on men and boys. In addition to the YMCA, he was involved with the State Manual Labor School, the Society for the Prevention of Vice, and the Sunday Afternoon Mission School for the boys of South Baltimore, which he organized himself. Thomas's interest in modernity and science was manifest through his leadership of JHU where he served as trustee. Thomas supported JHU and its campus YMCA, Levering Hall, and was also the best friend of JHU's president, Daniel Gilman. When Thomas died on 8 November 1897, Gilman was so distraught he "didn't know where to turn."[15]

Thomas's wife, Mary Whitall, a Philadelphia native, moved to Baltimore when they married in 1854. Gurneyite Quakers, the Thomases shared a commitment to civic leadership, the Society of Friends, and their many children. Martha Carey (M. Carey) Thomas, the oldest (and best known) child, was, like Peggy Morriss, a staunch feminist. She studied at Cornell, received a Ph.D. from the University of Zurich, became president of Bryn Mawr College, and set a new standard in education for women.[16] Another daughter, Helen, married Simon Flexner, Abraham Flexner's brother, who served on the JHU Medical School faculty and was a member of Levering Hall before becoming the longtime director of the Rockefeller Institute for Medical Research.[17]

When the evangelist Dwight Lyman Moody came to Baltimore in the winter of 1878–79, James Thomas was YMCA president and head of the local committee that sponsored his stay. Mary Thomas was the organizer and principal speaker at Moody's women's meetings, having "the pleasure as she preached of seeing women rise like rockets all over the floor shouting that they were saved." As a result of her experience with Moody, Mrs. Thomas felt at one with God, writing in 1885 that "God is so vivid to me that it is such an entire oneness I cannot seem to know any difference."[18]

Mary Thomas led many of Baltimore's women's organizations. She was a founder and president of both the Women's Christian Temperance Union (WCTU) and the YMCA's Ladies' Auxiliary. She, like several of her daughters and daughters-in-law, was also active in the YWCA.[19] Mary Thomas also regularly attended sessions of the Magistrate's Court before which women were tried, where she "sustained and supported the defendant by her presence and bore silent witness before the judge that he was responsible to the feminine half of the community even though it possessed no political power. . . . Dressed in the simple, nunlike costume she habitually wore, she sat day after day on a courtroom bench and followed

6. Joshua Levering served the Baltimore YMCA as vice president from 1879 to 1884 and as president from 1885 to 1896. A Baptist Sabbatarian, Levering was a prosperous tea and coffee importer. His twin, Eugene Levering, gave Levering Hall, the campus YMCA, to Johns Hopkins University. YMCA Collection, University of Baltimore Archives.

the proceedings."[20] At her death, a resolution from the YWCA proclaimed, "She has shown us what it is like to be Christ."[21]

Joshua Levering, like his twin Eugene, Jr., was a Baptist stalwart and partner in a prosperous tea and coffee importing business. In addition to his work on the International Committee of the YMCA, Joshua Levering led the Baltimore YMCA for twenty years alongside Morriss, as vice president from 1879 to 1884, and as president from 1885 to 1896. He also worked with the YWCA, serving as a member and then as chairman of its male advisory board.[22]

A Sabbatarian, Joshua Levering was the longtime president of both the Lord's Day Alliance, which fought against the liberalization of Baltimore's Sunday laws, and the House of Refuge for Boys. A Prohibitionist, he was that party's nominee for state comptroller in 1891, governor in 1895, and president in 1896.[23] A director of both the National Bank of Baltimore and Provident Savings Bank, Joshua Levering died in 1935 at the age of ninety.

Like his brother, Eugene Levering was a Sunday school teacher and an organizer of new Baptist churches throughout Baltimore. Believing in voluntary action through civic involvement, he served as an officer of the

Association for the Improvement of the Condition of the Poor, the Society for the Suppression of Vice, the Baltimore Charity Organization Society, and the Home for Incurables. He was also president of the Baltimore Board of Trade and an organizer of the Merchants and Manufacturers Committee. In 1893, he purchased a large building on Fayette Street in downtown Baltimore, which he converted into a nationally celebrated workingmen's lodging house.[24] A trustee of both JHU and George Washington University, Eugene Levering was president of the National Bank of Commerce, an organizer of the Baltimore Trust and Guarantee Company, and a director of the insurance company United States Fidelity & Guaranty.[25]

Although he lost an 1886 bid for Congress on the Prohibition ticket, Eugene Levering enjoyed years of appointive public service ranging from his tenure as a commissioner and later chairman of the Public Bath Commission, to serving at the behest of several mayors on committees charged with tasks as varied as investigating the condition of the poor and assessing the effect of the great Baltimore fire of 1904.[26]

Eugene Levering never held office in the YMCA, but his beneficence in building Levering Hall, the campus YMCA at JHU, shaped the association's role in Baltimore's organization of modern "scientific" philanthropy, the Charity Organization Society movement.[27] At his death in 1928, the *Baltimore Sun* reported:

> Neither Eugene Levering nor any of his family belonged to the spectacular class of the mercantile and banking world. . . . They were quiet folk, but strong. They achieved much without noise. But they were not Laodiceans. They were people of decided, of unalterable convictions in regard to what they considered moral fundamentals. . . . Eugene Levering . . . was true in every fiber of mind and soul. Nor can there be any doubt as to his civic status. He was in the front of good citizens, always intensely interested in the public welfare, always ready to help anything that made for the public good.[28]

The Levering women committed to the YMCA and YWCA, too.[29]

Francis A. White, the third president of the YMCA during Morriss's tenure, came from a civically and YMCA-engaged background.[30] The son of Jane E. Janney, a niece of Johns Hopkins, and Francis White, F. A. White was born in Baltimore in 1860 and educated at Haverford College. He began his business life as a clerk in a wholesale provision house. He married Sarah P. Ellicott, who, like his mother and father, also served on the YWCA's board.

Francis A. White joined the committee work of the YMCA in 1888. He became vice president in 1898 and president in 1901. Under White's administration, the new Central YMCA Building at Franklin and Cathedral Streets was funded and built in 1908.[31] Once his presidential tenure ended, he stayed on as director and trustee. He alone among the association's two dozen officers listed his profession as "Capitalist."[32]

Like that of the Morrisses, the Thomases, the Leverings, and his own relations, White's civic involvement went beyond the YMCA. A Republican, White was also a member of the advisory committee of the Women's Hospital and a director of the Provident Savings Bank and the Friendly Inn.[33]

The work of Morriss and the YMCA's lay leaders paralleled the development of a new era in philanthropy that, like the YMCA itself, began in England. The new philanthropy, based on the collection and analysis of allegedly "scientific" evidence, started in 1869 with the establishment of the London Charity Organization Society. The charity movement came to the United States in the late 1870s and formally to Baltimore early in the 1880s. Better administration of private charitable activities achieved by husbanding the community's private charitable resources so that money would be available to give adequate assistance to all worthy cases while fraudulent claims were weeded out was its goal. To ascertain a person's level of need, well-documented investigations were done first by volunteer friendly visitors and later by paid agents. Although the charity organization philosophy was premised on a series of preconceived moral judgments and presuppositions about the poor, in time the extensive data gathered by these groups revealed to their leaders and the general public that poverty had little to do with character flaws. It resulted instead from involuntary unemployment, industrial accidents, and low wages, among other effects of widespread industrialization.[34]

This summary assessment of the accomplishments and civic involvements of the YMCA's leaders in the years spanning 1880 to 1920 underscores how families such as the Morrisses, Thomases, Leverings, and Whites, like others in the charity organization world, came to look upon the attainment of social justice as a more important field of endeavor than the administration of private benevolence. It begins to explore, too, how the YMCA came to be an organization capable of embracing "Progressive" goals, ones that promoted unabashedly "modern" ideas such as scientific philanthropy, meritocracy, corporate welfare, and moral homemaking for both the white Anglo Christian mainstream and marginalized ethnic and racial minorities. The YMCA's leaders, this review shows, drew on the twin wellsprings of a faith-driven sense of mission and a willing engagement with the new industrial order.

In the minds of the YMCA's leaders, these forces were not antagonistic or even mutually exclusive. For them, the YMCA was an institutional expression of their own optimistic melding of faith and modernity, their own sense of Christian mission applied to the new industrial order. The alliance of this missionary sensibility and a willingness to engage new and emerging urban conditions were the hallmarks of the Baltimore YMCA's creative contribution to the making of a twentieth-century city.

4

The YMCA and the Coming
of Modern Philanthropy, 1880–1900

Modern philanthropy came early to Baltimore. Nationally, it was the end of the 1890s before the leaders of most charity organization societies, settlement houses, and public welfare institutions as well as professors and students of political economy came to believe that pauperism was both a cause and effect of social ills. Yet by the mid-1880s, the philanthropic scene in Baltimore already had the markings and signal characteristics of the modern social welfare services infrastructure. Likewise, where nationally a new view of poverty that defined the problem in terms of insufficiency and insecurity rather than exclusively as a matter of dependency gained currency at the turn of the century, Baltimore's modern philanthropy was shaped by a remarkably close and innovative collaboration forged by the YMCA, the Johns Hopkins University (JHU), the Johns Hopkins Hospital (JHH), and Baltimore's Charity Organization Society (COS), which had identified and promoted this view of poverty at least a decade earlier.[1] By examining the roles of the participating organizations and their leaders, this chapter focuses on the development of a symbiotic, pioneering partnership. It explores, too, the abundance of new ideas about the problem of poverty and attempts at its solution that this collaboration engendered, and the new methods of scientific philanthropy and modern social science these partners employed in Baltimore in the years from 1880 to 1900.

The YMCA's contribution to this alliance ranged from the spiritual to the technical, from the theoretical to bricks and mortar. As we have already seen, the YMCA's leaders melded a faith-driven sense of mission to a willing engagement with the new industrial order. This applied Christianity was reflected in a range of YMCA programs that strove to permit middle-class–aspiring boys and young men to gain the tools—ethical and educational, spiritual and economic—to make the most of this new industrial world. The hallmarks of this programming were education and prevention.

After William H. Morriss's arrival as general secretary in 1882, the Baltimore YMCA worked aggressively to focus its resources almost exclusively on boys and young men aspiring to the middle class. The association's "aim and effort," its "sole intent and purpose," was to "make intelligent Christian citizens" of young men. The decision to restrict programming to this constituency meant that opportunities abounded for other groups to adopt and adapt the prevention- and education-based self-help principles, concepts, and techniques of the YMCA in addressing the needs of women and girls, the elderly, and the destitute. The most obvious example of this adaptation in Baltimore was the creation of the YWCA in 1883.[2]

Although the YMCA plainly disavowed work with the poor ("we are not a society for the relief of the destitute . . . and [have] no fund for such a purpose"), its leaders acknowledged the widespread interest members had in poor relief, "as individuals [they] have shown themselves willing to succor the distressed."[3]

Among the YMCA's members most committed to the eradication of poverty were the student and faculty members of Levering Hall, the campus branch of the YMCA at JHU, founded in 1883 and endowed by Eugene Levering in 1889. Explaining the object of his gifts, which included not only $20,000 for building Levering Hall but additional funds for a lecture series, Levering wrote that his purpose was to "aid in promoting religious influences in the JHU, upon the principles of Christian union and of unsectarian fellowship."[4] As the only on-campus entity catering to the religious needs and spiritual impulses of the JHU community, Levering Hall emerged as the nerve center for the new philanthropy's assault on poverty. Levering Hall's members, students no doubt of Tolstoy and Toynbee, not only served as foot soldiers in the war but were central to the creation of an effective alliance that collectively rethought and modernized philanthropy in Baltimore.

To this alliance the Baltimore YMCA also brought its leaders' extensive contacts with the clergy, business executives, politicians, and others who had a stake in the city's civic success. JHU, as a rather radical start-up entity, and the COS, as a new enterprise, lacked the credibility and resources that the YMCA had already developed. Just as significantly, the YMCA's leaders had begun to employ their collective moral imagination for the articulation of a vision of an attainable and desirable civil society, which stressed prevention and education-focused social services. The

7. Levering Hall, the campus YMCA at Johns Hopkins University, was endowed by Eugene Levering in 1889. Its activities shaped the YMCA's role in bringing modern philanthropy to Baltimore. The building pictured, the second Levering Hall, is on the Homewood campus of JHU. YMCA Collection, University of Baltimore Archives.

moral imaginings of the YMCA leaders were open to and supportive of collaborative efforts to tackle the problems and redress Baltimore's needs. Collaborative enterprise was consistent with the YMCA leaders' sense of mission—their commitment to being an aggressive Christian enterprise unshackled by denominational limitations.

This collaboration began, of course, only after JHU and JHH had been conceived. In 1867, six years before his death, the Quaker merchant Johns Hopkins began overhauling the city's educational, medical, and philanthropic landscape. Hopkins, a man who believed that two things were sure to endure, "[a] university, for there will always be youth; [and] a hospital, for there will always be suffering," founded JHU and JHH.[5] He chose twelve trustees to form a corporation for the university. Of these men, nine—including Francis White (F. A. White's father) and James Carey Thomas—were also named by Hopkins to be trustees of the hospital. Hopkins made the boards interlocking to underscore his hope that they would work closely together. It was his "wish and purpose" that the hospital would "ultimately form a part of the medical school," which would, in turn, be part of the university. The idea of linking the hospital and the university through a school of medicine would prove immensely important to JHU and JHH's success and to their strong influence on American education and the coming of modern philanthropy to Baltimore.[6]

Although Johns Hopkins gave scant indication of the kind of educational institution he envisioned, he divided his $7 million estate between the university and the hospital. Hopkins's gift of $3.5 million to JHU was the largest single bequest that, to that time, had ever been made to an American institution of higher learning. He devoted only two paragraphs of his will to JHU. Yet notwithstanding the founder's vague plan, the trustees moved quickly to create a new American university. The board met only once while Hopkins was alive, but after his death they mobilized and sought expert advice from the presidents of Cornell, Harvard, and the University of Michigan about the ideal modern American university. What developed was consensus that Daniel Coit Gilman, a Connecticut native, Yale graduate, president of the University of California, and educational visionary, should be JHU's president. The trustees succeeded in hiring Gilman, who believed that the time was ripe for a nationally prominent university different from any then in operation.[7]

Gilman started at JHU in May 1875. He spent the following year formulating plans and visiting European universities. Gilman wanted to establish JHU as the first all-graduate American university by promoting to advanced students "scholarship of the first order" modeled after the German university. But, feeling that Baltimore's youth had particular claims upon Hopkins's legacy and thus should not be compelled to go away from home to be trained to enter JHU, the trustees and Gilman agreed to offer a bachelor's degree to undergraduates in a curriculum that generally required three years for completion.[8]

Gilman was committed to a university that cherished freedom of thought and speech and that was free of sectarian and political biases. He sought productive scholars and scientists. The faculty he planned to assemble would be "so catholic in spirit; so learned as to what has been discovered and so keen to explore new fields of research; so skillful as teachers; so cooperative as builders; and so comprehensive in the specialties to which they are devoted,—that pupils will flock to their instruction, first from Maryland and the states near to it,—but soon also from the remotest parts of the land."[9]

JHU opened in 1876. Under Gilman's leadership, it helped define Baltimore's early transition from old-fashioned almsgiving to modern philanthropy. The creation of JHU, and especially its Department of History, Political Economy, and Political Science, accelerated the development of modern philanthropy by underscoring the importance of the application of scientific methods to the identification and remediation of social ills, and by providing, through the university's press and professional journals, the means for disseminating data.[10] Believing that the successful diffusion of research was critical to the common good, Gilman was himself personally committed to publication.[11]

Even before the opening of JHU, the organized provision of social services in Baltimore had begun. After the Civil War, public poor relief around the country was in bad repute. Public indifference toward the helpless resulted, according to Robert Bremner, from society's emphasis on self-help, "the religion of the respectable in the vigorous young republic." The aim of public relief was the prevention of starvation and death as economically as possible, yet the ideal of economical administration was often defeated because relief was managed by politicians who tended, according to Bremner, to be "kindhearted, inefficient, or corrupt—or all three." Even while there was maladministration of public poor relief, private charity flourished. Many of the well-to-do who made contributions to charity naively believed that if the poor could develop good character they would soon become self-supporting. Endemic causes of poverty were not then considered. In response to widespread dissatisfaction about the way charity was handled, the charity organization movement, which had begun in London in 1869, was embraced and quickly replicated in many American cities. It pioneered an allegedly scientific philanthropy that, in an effort to separate worthy from unworthy poor, looked into the personal circumstances of those applying for aid. These societies sought to coordinate the work of numerous and sometimes competing extant philanthropic organizations. They hoped to avoid duplication, root out impostors, and encourage the investigation of appeals. Thus, scientific philanthropy began as a revolt against the old-fashioned spendthrift almsgiving.[12]

Coordinated relief started in Baltimore in 1870 with the Association for the Improvement of the Condition of the Poor (AICP), which, despite a constitution to the contrary, quickly became almost entirely an almsgiving society. Wanting a more scientific approach to giving, critics of the AICP in 1881 organized the COS. Daniel Gilman, president of JHU, was the force behind its organization.[13]

Gilman and the other founders wanted the Baltimore COS to act as a central bureau to organize charity. They hoped that the COS would educate and improve those who "had not." They anathematized indiscriminate almsgiving. While the COS did not plan to distribute alms, it wished to see all deserving people receive proper and adequate care. COS leaders believed that by eliminating duplication, fraud, and waste, community resources would increase. The COS also wished "to raise the needy above the need of relief," "to encourage thrift, self-dependence and industry; . . . to teach the poor the laws of health and economy; to show them where there are facilities for the improvement of themselves and their children; to carry to them the best social influences."[14] The COS proposed to differentiate its programs from those of the AICP by studying the causes of pauperism and by collecting social statistics on poverty. Implicit in this proposal was the hope of making philanthropy a practical social science, based on "scientific" principles that provided a body of pertinent data from which useful conclusions might be drawn. Applicants registered at a central office. The COS investigated each applicant's need.

Whereas traditional charity aimed to give relief to the destitute, feed the hungry, shelter the homeless, and heal the sick, the developing modern philanthropy hoped to address and prevent the root causes of destitution, hunger, homelessness, and sickness. In their work and in their missions, the YMCA and similar groups offered an important transition between traditional charity's emphasis on the relief of suffering and modern philanthropy's focus on the elimination of its root causes. The YMCA and other transitional organizations such as the COS embraced a view that held distress to be preventable, especially through the inculcation of thrift and useful skills. Many of the programs developed by the YMCA, COS, and other reform groups during this period featured education and prevention as critical components of a new and increasingly complex conception of philanthropy. Their programs moved away from the simple act of filling a physical need. Instead, they attempted to supersede such an act and obviate its necessity by providing training and employment for the poor. Another hallmark of the YMCA and similar groups was their focus on those at risk rather than truly destitute people.[15]

In the early 1880s, while the YMCA pioneered effective self-help programs, which ranged from systematic efforts to secure employment for out-of-work men, to vocational instruction designed to enhance workers' job skills, to caretaking programs that prepared young men for stable home lives, the COS was slow getting started. The public and scholars alike were largely indifferent to its goals. The work of the COS centered on the Provident Wood Yard and Friendly Inn where unemployed and transient men could earn an immediate economic benefit—ranging from a pittance or a day's board and lodging—by chopping a required number of wooden blocks.[16] Based on the principle of "work rather than relief," the COS hoped to drive away professional beggars. This work test was long used by the COS to separate the "worthy" from the "unworthy" poor. To enable concerned citizens to participate, this Friendly Inn (like the YMCA's Friendly Inn before it) sold tickets to "responsible individuals" who in turn gave them to needy men for redemption for room or board, a practice that, ironically, obviated the recipients' need to work as the price of assuring donors that their money was being responsibly spent.[17]

In 1885, the Baltimore COS began to evolve into a vital force in the field of social welfare. That year John Glenn, a blind, prosperous real estate dealer, joined the organization. He became chairman of its executive committee in 1886.[18] Glenn helped the COS to move away from the administration of the Friendly Inn and to focus instead on rationalizing the provision of social services by various groups within the city. Glenn insisted on business efficiency and economy in the practice of charity. He wished to "remove much of the sentiment from the administration of charity" and to make it instead an efficient business transaction. Glenn "looked with abhorrence" and "considered as sheer waste" random almsgiving. For him, a donation ought to be accompanied by an "effort to promote industry, temperance, economy, and self denial on the part of the recipients."[19]

COS work thus came to emphasize the prevention of distress rather than its relief. In 1892, for example, the COS championed industrial education (and self-reliance for women) by strongly supporting the introduction of sewing into the curriculum of public schools. During the depression of 1893–94, the COS organized charitable agencies and businesses into the Citizens' Central Relief Committee, which, in the era before the public provision of social services, coordinated most relief activities and based them on work rather than on direct relief.[20] The COS's success that winter expanded its authority and influence. Also, relations between the COS and AICP improved. For nearly twenty years the two groups "were working in the main through different district centers with separate registration and application bureaus," each with its own system of record keeping and annual meetings. Even before formal federation in 1902, the two groups held meetings of agents together, jointly registered families, created joint districts, and hired a shared secretary. The COS sought out material sources of relief, and the AICP helped when these could not be secured and in the treatment of emergent and temporary needs.[21] In 1905, three years after federating, the two groups changed their name to the Federated Charities of Baltimore.

Along with Daniel Gilman, John Glenn was instrumental in linking the considerable resources of the YMCA, the COS, and Hopkins together as partners in the implementation and design of modern philanthropy in Baltimore. Under Glenn's leadership, the COS built up a staff of 236 volunteer visitors by 1890, and 310 by 1893.[22] Many of these visitors were JHU students who expressed their concern about social welfare through the activities of Levering Hall.

Because JHU had no school of theology, "as the University is truly nonsectarian in its aims and purposes," Levering Hall became both the focus of religious life on campus and the nerve center for social welfare work. In 1889, the *New York Christian Advocate*, a Methodist newspaper, reported that Levering Hall and the YMCA it housed would please those who thought of the JHU as "a hotbed of rationalism" because in it were found "so many earnest, active Christian men whose influence is not diminishing, but, on the contrary, is continually increasing."[23]

It is perhaps surprising that some of the most modern scientific thinkers had a profound commitment to Applied Christianity, especially as it was practiced through Levering Hall, a campus YMCA. Ira Remsen, professor of chemistry, had no question but that as knowledge about the physical universe increased, ideas of the Creator would also become "larger, broader, grander," which would, in turn, lead humanity to "worship with a truer adoration, and a feeling of more perfect reverence." Psychology professor G. Stanley Hall believed that psychological insights would "effect a complete atonement between modern culture and religious sentiments and verities." Gilman himself believed that science pointed "more and more steadily to the plans of a great designer."[24]

Membership in Levering Hall was large and varied, exceeding 250 in 1892. Early on, the group became "so popular and so truly catholic in its spirit, that Jews have been permitted to join as well as those who were brought up on the Westminster Catechism."[25] Among the advantages of Levering Hall membership was "Christian Work," which afforded students "splendid opportunities" to "use this city as a laboratory for economic study," as the discipline of political economy required. Association leaders encouraged members, particularly those from outside Baltimore, to participate in the city's social work. During the winter of 1887, for example, students assisted in the work of the COS, the South Baltimore

Working-men's Club, the North East Baltimore Adult Mission, and unde-nominational Christian missions throughout the city.[26]

In 1888, John R. Commons, a JHU graduate student in political economy, who later became a scholar in labor history and economics, participated in the Levering Hall experiment. His professor, Richard T. Ely, had him visit the city's building and loan associations and also encouraged him to join the COS as a friendly visitor. The COS assigned Commons a Civil War veteran who was "down with tuberculosis in the third story of a rattle-shack tenement. . . . He had never been able to get a pension." So Commons spent a year gaining insight into practical politics while "getting a pension for him." From his experience with the COS not only did Commons gain raw data, which he translated into reports for the university's joint history and economics seminar and an article for one of Professor Herbert Baxter Adams's journals, he also became "a minister of the Gospel" through his activities as both a social worker and a graduate student in economics.[27]

JHU's *Student Handbook*, produced by Levering Hall members, re-ported that students like Commons who were attracted by the study of charity administration could find abundant opportunities in Baltimore. In 1890, for example, Dr. David I. Green, a Hopkins alumnus and COS worker, gave weekly tours of Baltimore's philanthropic and service institu-tions to university men interested in social welfare work.[28] Baltimore, ac-cording to Levering Hall chroniclers, offered "institutions of every sort, liberally supported by municipal aid or private benevolence." Levering Hall members compiled the *Directory of Baltimore Charities*, which was published by the COS. So impressive were Levering Hall's programs that the national YMCA held it up as a model for other college associations.[29]

In addition to the support it received from faculty members such as Bernard Steiner, Ely, Adams, M. D. Learned, and Ira Remsen, Levering Hall attracted friends from the larger community.[30] Sustaining member-ships were held by Joshua and Eugene Levering and their mother, Ann Levering, James Carey Thomas, Francis White, Francis T. King, and Miles White, Jr., among others.

Although faculty members and student volunteers helped to guide the activities of Levering Hall, in 1892 JHU's trustees made an appropria-tion for the appointment of a part-time general secretary for the campus YMCA. Charles S. Estes, a graduate student in history who received his Ph.D. from JHU in 1895, served as general secretary for four years. He was replaced in 1896 by Clyde B. Furst, a graduate student in English, who would later serve as secretary of the Carnegie Foundation for the Advancement of Teaching.[31]

Lawrence House, Baltimore's first settlement house, became a key component of Levering Hall's social science practicum. Founded in 1893 by Edward A. Lawrence, Jr., a Congregational minister who attracted crowds of JHU students to his services, and Frank D. Thomson, a graduate student in history and economics at JHU, Lawrence House began in Winans' Tenements in the heart of the tenement district in southwest Baltimore.[32] It included a Boys' Club, a Boys' School, and a Girls' Sewing School for neighborhood children. The JHU *Student Handbook* reported that Lawrence Settlement House was a "good field for practical studies and observations of social problems" and "the only place in Baltimore with such admirable opportunities for social science work." Lawrence House commended itself to university men interested in sociological studies, "since the region is the only purely tenement district in the city, and there is ample opportunity to work along a variety of lines." No religious exercises were held in connection with Lawrence House, and "all earnest men and women are welcomed as helpers." Volunteers came from several churches, the Social Science Club of the Woman's College (now Goucher College), and JHU's Levering Hall. The Reverend Lawrence, in a talk to members of Levering Hall, "likened the work in Christian lines in the city to a well-spread table of good things." He described opportunities in regular church work, Sunday school, missions, the COS, and his settlement house, which he invited JHU students to make into a "veritable University Settlement."[33]

Lawrence died unexpectedly soon after the settlement house opened. After his death, the Lawrence Memorial Association, with Bernard C. Steiner, longtime faculty officer of Levering Hall as its president, kept the settlement work going.[34]

Early on, JHU students in the Department of History, Political Economy, and Political Science worked through Levering Hall to use Baltimore as a laboratory to show the relations of the past to the present. Herbert B. Adams and Richard T. Ely, both German-trained scholars and faculty members of Levering Hall, coordinated this effort.[35] Adams, a historian who had received his Ph.D. from the University of Heidelberg in 1876, was an original member of the JHU faculty. He organized the Johns Hopkins Historical and Political Science Association and began publishing Johns Hopkins University Studies in Historical and Political Science. Under his guidance, students, many of whom became great scholars, founded the American Historical Association at JHU in 1884. Ely, a Chris-

tian socialist and leading intellectual in the national Progressive movement, taught political economy at JHU from 1881 until 1892, when he left
to head the University of Wisconsin's Department of Political Economy.
Dorothy Ross described Ely as the "most radical spokesman" for Christian socialism. Ely made contact with Christian reformers and wrote
widely for the popular and religious press.[36] Ely and Adams, along with
JHU students of "historico-politics" who shared their mentors' reformist
impulses, depicted laissez-faire policies as not simply wasteful and cruel
but also inappropriate for an industrializing yet democratic nation. Ely
played a pivotal role in setting the early reform agenda of the American
Economic Association.[37]

As a result of the efforts of professors such as Ely and Adams, John
Glenn reported that JHU was the first university in the country where
social welfare work was "almost a part of the curriculum."[38] The active
engagement of Hopkins students with the work of the COS pleased Glenn
greatly, as he had a desire that educated young men should become ac-
quainted with the "experience of wise and thoughtful philanthropists" so
that when they became community leaders—ministers, lawyers, doctors,
teachers, editors, or writers—they themselves might each contribute to the
"up-lifting of the down-cast."[39] Glenn persuaded JHU students interested
in social welfare to supplement their academic studies with practical work
on the COS District Board. Daniel Gilman assisted Glenn by opening the
university's building to the COS for its meetings and by bringing Amos G.
Warner, a student in the Department of History, Political Economy, and
Political Science, to the secretaryship of the COS. Gilman arranged for
sociological courses on charities to be given at JHU to develop and spread
the ideals of "scientific charity." By joining forces with the COS and those
at JHU most concerned with social welfare work, the leaders of the Baltimore YMCA enabled Levering Hall to become the conduit for the practical application of theoretical models of social welfare work and the creation of critical links between the university and the city.[40]

John Glenn's highly successful efforts to bring national attention to
Baltimore's philanthropic work strengthened the impetus for the inclusion
of social welfare work in JHU's formal curriculum and extracurricular
activities. In 1887, under the auspices of the COS, Glenn first organized a
local conference on charities in Baltimore where three of the five sessions
were held at the Central YMCA. A fourth session focusing on the relation
of hospital work to organized charity was held at the still uncompleted
JHH. All told, more than 175 men and women attended, including leaders
of Baltimore's religious, social service, health, and educational institu-

tions. Baltimore mayor James Hodges spoke. James Carey Thomas was there in his capacity as president of the Thomas Wilson Fuel Saving Society. His wife, Mary Whitall Thomas, represented the Maryland Women's Christian Temperance Union. Miles White, Jr., Francis A. White's brother, and secretary of the Miles White Beneficial Society, participated. Nearly two dozen JHU students attended. From JHU's faculty, the conference attracted Richard T. Ely, Daniel Gilman, G. Stanley Hall, Joseph Jastrow, and Ira Remsen. The conference also drew participants from outside Baltimore including Lyman Abbott, editor of the *Christian Union*; Charles L. Brace, secretary of the Children's Aid Society of New York; Charles D. Kellogg, general secretary of the New York COS; and F. B. Sanborn, secretary of the American Social Science Association, among others.[41]

Glenn was also able to persuade the National Conference of Charities to hold its meeting in Baltimore in 1890.[42] "There never was a more representative body collected from our citizens," Glenn reported. The meeting was a success due in large part to the efforts of Herbert B. Adams, who persuaded the Associated Press to disseminate news of the meeting, the result of which was that reports were "spread more widely than ever before." Although Gilman was in Europe and missed the conference, Glenn related, "the conference itself would have been an extreme gratification to you and you would have had . . . the pleasure of hearing the part taken by yourself and your university in the consideration of these social problems not only fully recognized but recommended to others as an example."[43]

Gilman and Glenn's abiding interest in modern philanthropy and scientific management were more than reflections of the prevailing, and increasingly corporatized, culture of late-nineteenth-century America. They very specifically reflected developments in Baltimore's cultural scene, which in the period from 1880 to 1900 was charged not only with the scientific and political economy inquiries of JHU but also with the modern medical and public health innovations that flowed from JHH.[44]

Whereas the university trustees were unfettered by a founder's vision for their institution, the hospital trustees were both blessed and burdened by Johns Hopkins's explicit instructions about the hospital's size, location, and general character. Before his death, Hopkins designated a site in East Baltimore that was ample enough to allow for a physical plant accommodating 400 patients. The hospital grounds were to be planted with trees and flowers and surrounded by iron railings. Hopkins's plans included a nurses' training center and an orphanage for needy black children.[45]

The hospital opened in 1889, and the medical school opened four years later. Admission standards were the highest of any medical school in the country. All students were required to hold a bachelor's degree.[46] The medical school curriculum was four years long and linked opportunities and resources at the university and the hospital.[47]

The medical school attracted some students who were preparing for work as medical missionaries. Before and even after a special YMCA of the Medical Department was created late in the 1890s, these and other male medical students and medical faculty often joined Levering Hall. Women medical students had the option of joining the YWCA of the Medical Department, which offered limited services—Bible classes, travel assistance, and housing referrals.[48]

John Glenn continued supporting social welfare work through links between Hopkins, the YMCA, and the COS until his death in 1896. At a special COS meeting held at Levering Hall at which his contributions were celebrated, Daniel Gilman eulogized Glenn as a scientific investigator and thinker on the causes of poverty, the very epitome of the ideal facilitator of scientific philanthropy. "Like a wise researcher, he went to the original sources of information, the stories of the poor. He inquired, like a good physician, into the causes of distress, and he watched, with the most careful attention, the results that followed from the remedies proposed."[49]

Gilman, too, was a complex man. He took personally the imperative he defined for a modern university to have as its central feature "original research." During his quarter century at JHU he promoted the concept of "profitable investigation" as it was practiced by Glenn and by JHU faculty and students. This was scholarly research that was routinely translated into service to the city, the state, and the federal government in areas as diverse as sanitary reforms, water purification, taxation, public education, and charitable and philanthropic activities. Applying scholarly research to civic undertakings was a hallmark of both Gilman and JHU under his leadership. In addition to defining JHU's mission and founding the COS, Gilman served on the city's Charter Reform Commission and on the school board, where, according to H. L. Mencken, he quickly became "the real boss of the whole school system."[50]

The legacy left by the generation of philanthropy workers who worked with Gilman and Glenn testifies to their impact. Many of the students they mentored through Levering Hall contacts took their JHU training and went on to important social science jobs around the country through which they shaped modern philanthropy. For example, E.R.L. Gould came to JHU in 1881 for graduate studies in economics. After receiving his Ph.D., he taught at JHU and at the University of Chicago. He then had a distinguished career in applied economics and municipal reform that featured leadership positions in New York City's charter revision, the Federal Bureau of Statistics of Labor, and finally the model tenements movement in New York City. According to his biographer, "it is not difficult to trace in Gould's awakened consciousness of pending municipal and social problems, while at Baltimore, the beginnings that led to his subsequent career as a municipal administrator and a social reformer."[51]

Abraham Flexner was another JHU student whose life was touched by Gilman and Glenn. A Jew from Louisville, Kentucky, Flexner came to JHU in 1884 as an undergraduate. He majored in classics and graduated in 1886. After teaching and founding his own elementary school in Louisville, Flexner had a long and distinguished career doing research and setting policy for the Carnegie Foundation, Rockefeller's General Education Board, and the Institute for Advanced Study at Princeton. He credited his time at JHU as the turning point in his life. The impact of his college training was lasting. "Those who know something of my work long after Gilman's day . . . will recognize Gilman's influence in all I have done or tried to do."[52]

Amos G. Warner was yet another JHU–Levering Hall alumnus who applied his training to the study of modern philanthropy. During his graduate studies in economics at JHU, Warner served as secretary of the Baltimore COS. He left that position in 1889, a year after receiving his Ph.D., to chair the Economics Department at the University of Nebraska. In 1891, President Benjamin Harrison called Warner to become the first superintendent of charities for the District of Columbia, a post he held for two years. He left to become professor of economics and social science at Stanford University. In 1894, he published his book, *American Charities*, which he dedicated to John Glenn. Warner's book was a classic in the development of modern philanthropy. In it he attempted to be systematic and empirical in reaching conclusions about the needy. According to Walter I. Trattner, Warner's book showed that "in most cases misfortune was more important than misconduct in causing dependency."[53] Although Warner died young, his life's work was motivated by a commitment to social justice. According to his biographer, it was the "influence of social righteousness [that] ever reflected from his pure heart and lofty mind."[54]

Another former JHU student, Jeffrey Brackett, headed Baltimore's Commission on City Charities. The impulse to reform municipal charitable policy came after the election of 1895 when Mayor Alceaus Hooper appointed "a board of trustees of the Poor who believed in the principles of the COS," three of whom, including the president of the board, were COS managers. Brackett, a COS agent, surveyed the entire field of municipal charities and saw his recommendations for their improvement incorporated into the city's 1898 charter. Like other Levering Hall–affiliated JHU faculty and alumni, Brackett gained national prominence through his pathbreaking work in the fields of scientific social welfare and modern philanthropy.[55]

Although John R. Commons never completed the graduate training he began at JHU, he became a scholar in the field of labor history and economics. In addition to teaching at the University of Wisconsin, Commons worked closely with Robert M. La Follette, Sr., helping to draft the Wisconsin Civil Service Law and the Public Utilities Law. He was also involved with reform initiatives related to industrial relations, unemployment, and the minimum wage.[56]

JHU faculty and administrators, too, left their mark on the nascent fields of social welfare studies and modern philanthropy. Daniel Gilman himself left JHU in 1900 to become the first president of the Carnegie Institution in Washington, D.C. Simon Flexner, a Jewish Levering Hall faculty member (Abraham's brother and James Carey Thomas's son-in-law), taught at the medical school for ten years before becoming the first director of the Rockefeller Institute for Medical Research.

The combination of the YMCA, COS, JHU, and JHH made for a heady mix in Baltimore that affected more than those with a Hopkins affiliation. For example, Mary Richmond's pioneering efforts in modern social work began in Baltimore during this exhilarating period. Hired by Gilman and Glenn to be assistant treasurer of the COS in 1888, she became general secretary in 1891 and worked directly with many Levering Hall volunteers. Richmond pioneered the casework system in social work and wrote her first book in 1889 based on her experiences with friendly visits in Baltimore. From 1900 to 1909, Richmond served as secretary for the Philadelphia COS. She then went on to a long career with the Russell Sage Foundation, where she was joined by John M. Glenn, John Glenn's nephew, and another former Baltimore COS leader.[57]

In conclusion, two aspects of the collaboration among the YMCA, Hopkins, and the COS warrant further comment. First, there is, to some contemporary readers, the rather curious parentage of modern philanthropy, with one parent, the Hopkins entities, seemingly firmly entrenched in a rigorously scientific, rationalistic world, and the other parent—the YMCA and COS—approaching the problem of poverty with a spiritually suffused rhetoric and an Applied Christian perspective. Second, there is simply the YMCA's surprising willingness to enter into this partnership.

Many accounts of the rise of modern America present a picture of a nation whose cultural life was nearly bifurcated. On one side of the divide was arrayed the public realm, an arena dominated by the forces of science, law, technological innovation, and the amoral imperatives of a capitalistic economic system—and on the other, the private sphere, where spiritual concerns and religious feelings predominated.

This chapter has shed light on a collaboration that did not respect any division between the two spheres. If anything, the partnership forged among the YMCA, Hopkins, and the COS seemed to draw much of its power precisely from its ability to tap the resources of both the private and public realms. Far from inducing cognitive dissonance, the words and works of the participants reveal a sense that in efforts like this collaboration many involved felt that they made their world whole.

As to the YMCA's willingness to enter into this partnership, it is worth recalling the "handmaiden" rhetoric of the YMCA-church relationship and the association's ostensible efforts to work collaboratively with the mainstream Protestant denominations. The YMCA's willingness to enter into a partnership with Hopkins and the COS at a time when the latter were untested local institutions reveals another facet of the association's commitment to serving community needs. In remaining true to their focus on boys and young men who were aspiring to become middle class, YMCA leaders such as Morriss, Thomas, Levering, and White early on recognized that partnering afforded an opportunity to extend the association's mission and influence, without compromising its resources.

The cumulative effect of the work of individuals including John Glenn, Daniel Gilman, and Mary Richmond, and of institutions like the YMCA, COS, and Hopkins, created modern philanthropic work in Baltimore and helped to define a national standard. The YMCA played a central role in this transformation by repeatedly employing educational and preventive measures and carefully devoting critical resources to address emerging community needs. The Baltimore YMCA, along with the COS, and companion organizations such as the YWCA were critical transitional organizations that early on bridged the divide between the reformist instincts of the nineteenth century and the Progressive-minded modern philanthropy of the twentieth century. In addition, because of the partnership between the YMCA, COS, and Hopkins not only did modern philanthropy come early to Baltimore; tales of its journey were told nationwide through JHU's press and journals, and through the students, faculty, and staff who took their Levering Hall social science training and applied it in communities across the country. The concentration of so many thinkers and doers in the fields of social welfare and scientific philanthropy in the Baltimore of this period is remarkable.

5

"A Place of Resort and Help for Their Young Men"

Baltimore's Black YMCA, 1885–1925

Despite an abiding interest in poverty and scientific philanthropy, in matters of race relations the white YMCA was largely absent. Black community leaders challenged the YMCA, eventually creating an important community institution known as the Druid Hill Avenue YMCA. Long a mainstay in West Baltimore, the city's oldest and perhaps most significant African-American neighborhood, the Druid Hill YMCA was known simply as the "Colored YMCA" in its pre-1900, pre–Druid Hill Avenue days.[1] Ironically, the story of the Druid Hill YMCA's establishment and growth (when it has been told at all) has been whitewashed. It has been told in the tradition of celebratory history: A group of upstanding black men came together to do good in and for their community. Despite great odds and limited resources, they succeeded. Their legacy continues today.[2] Although this version of the Druid Hill Avenue YMCA's history is not *untrue*, it raises questions far more provocative than those it answers. Why, for example, would men persevere in their efforts to be accepted by a club that didn't want them? Where did the white YMCA stand on matters of race? How close was the white YMCA's rhetoric to reality? Once created, what was the relationship between the black YMCA and the community? What role did the black press play in this institution's expansion? How important were issues of class?

To understand this story better, it is helpful to review briefly both the history of the Baltimore YMCA and the national YMCA's handling of the race issue. In November 1852, the white Maryland Baptist Union issued the call that led to the establishment of a YMCA in Baltimore, among the first in the United States. From the beginning, the white YMCA used pantheistic and catholic rhetoric to describe its simple goal of leading men to Jesus by offering an attractive alternative to the myriad temptations industrial cities posed to young men "adrift."[3] From its inception, Baltimore's YMCA was exclusively white. Yet by the mid-nineteenth century, the city's

African-American community was sizable, long established, and predominantly free.[4]

The exclusion of African Americans from the YMCA was not unique to Baltimore. Before the Civil War, most YMCAs simply evaded the issue of race, and in Baltimore, as in most associations nationally, partisan political talk was forbidden. During Reconstruction, the YMCA nationally began to encourage a Jim Crow policy by allowing African Americans to organize their own branches and "join the Christian brotherhood on 'separate-but-equal' terms." The black elite welcomed the YMCA's tripartite mission to develop the body, mind, and spirit and embraced the association's character building programs, viewing them as a means for racial advancement.[5]

In 1876, the International YMCA (the national policy group to which local YMCAs belonged) appointed its first secretary to promote association work among African Americans in the South. From 1876 to 1891, two white men served successively as the YMCA's international secretary for "colored work."[6] In 1890, William A. Hunton, a Canadian, was appointed to the position, becoming the highest-ranking black YMCA official in the United States. Hunton assisted African Americans as they established YMCAs in cities. Under his leadership, Baltimore's Colored YMCA became a reality. The branch prospered under Jesse E. Moorland, who in 1898 was hired as Hunton's assistant. Hunton then turned his attention to college work, and Moorland took charge of helping urban YMCAs with fund-raising and membership drives. Upon Hunton's death in 1916, Moorland became the senior African-American international secretary.[7]

The roots and antecedents of Baltimore's black YMCA go back to 1869 when Bishop Alexander Wayman of the Bethel AME Church invited fellow clergy to join him in the formation of a Pastors' Union to "discuss all problems affecting Negroes, including drunkenness and idleness and the possibility of establishing a Colored YMCA," an idea that did not then materialize.[8] In 1885, a precursor to Baltimore's Colored YMCA began at the Old Union Baptist Church, located at Guilford Avenue near Lexington Street. The group's work was limited to discussions of religious issues. Members held meetings at their homes. In 1888, this group began calling itself the "Colored YMCA."[9]

The next year, the white Central YMCA (whose records mentioned race for the first time in 1883 when its leaders denied rental of their hall to "colored people") appointed a committee, which, after considering "the question of a Branch of our association for Colored Men," recommended an indefinite postponement.[10] More fruitful efforts began in March 1891

8. In 1869, Bishop Alexander Wayman of the Bethel AME Church invited fellow clergy to join him in considering the formation of a Colored YMCA. Although it didn't materialize, Wayman's name was long invoked in connection with the Druid Hill Avenue YMCA. The University of Baltimore Educational Foundation.

when representatives of two black groups visited Secretary William H. Morriss hoping to enlist his support for the creation of a black YMCA branch. The time was ripe. Not only was Hunton newly appointed as secretary for colored work, but the deterioration of race relations and the tightening of the color line nationally affected the YMCA, which, at its national convention in 1891, "officially acknowledged the long-established de facto segregation of African Americans." That year, too, delegates to the national convention recognized "Colored Associations" as legitimate facets of YMCA work.[11] Both local African-American groups and the YMCA's International Committee lobbied the Baltimore association. Acceding to their requests, as well as to those of his own Executive Committee, Morriss attended a convention of "Colored Associations" at Richmond, Virginia.[12] His attendance notwithstanding, no immediate action resulted.

Despite the lack of support from the local white YMCA leaders, some young men persevered in their efforts to create a black association in Baltimore. In 1892, an interdenominational group of church-going young black men who desired to be "under the direction . . . of the YMCA of Maryland" worked with an advisory committee of black clergy to lobby for the YMCA's blessing. They also sought a meeting place "centrally located in the city where young men who are victims of evil association may be gathered and led into Christian society." It was, the clergy reported, difficult to "save our young men from the many agents of vice which are actively at work in this city." Although the churches and Sunday schools were "doing good work," additional help was needed. The black clergy's rhetoric mirrored language white clergy used in the 1850s and again in the 1870s and 1880s to convince their congregants and other concerned citizens of the need for a YMCA for white young men. The language is eerily familiar.[13]

The dearth of organizations serving young black people in Baltimore in the late nineteenth century bears out the clergy's concerns. In 1892, Levering Hall researchers for Baltimore's COS identified only the House of Reformation and the Industrial Home for Colored Girls as providing services to "colored minors."[14] These organizations were inappropriate for the constituency defined by the young men hoping to organize a YMCA, their clergy, or Hunton, the international secretary for "colored work," who came to Baltimore in the summer of 1892, remarkably at Central YMCA's invitation, to "look over the field," confer, and advise. Hunton asked YMCA president Joshua Levering for support, estimating that it would cost about $1,400 to operate the Colored YMCA for the first year. Of this, he thought that $500 could be raised "from the colored people, from all sources, membership fees, baths, entertainment, etc." Hunton wished for "means for physical cleanliness . . . reading room, library and night school, and the other uplifting influences of a 'Christian home away from home.'"[15]

The white YMCA's response was tepid at best: "We cannot see our way clear . . . to appropriate from our already overtaxed treasury the sum that seems to be necessary to put this Association in good working order." Based on consultations with friends "who are especially interested in the work among colored young men," a special fund was proposed, but here too the Central YMCA hedged, reporting "of this we cannot be at all sure."[16]

Despite the Central YMCA's reticence and their leaders' conclusion that "it was thought best by them and by us not to organize as a branch but as an independent Association, under their own direct management," the black community organized a YMCA during 1892. They rented a twelve-room house at 416 W. Biddle Street, where, Central believed, "they will be able to supply a much needed place of resort and help for their young men."[17] Their work was commended by Hunton, under whose supervision the branch placed itself.

The 1890s was a decade of good intentions but limited action for Baltimore's Colored YMCA.[18] By 1896, the house on Biddle Street was sold and the branch was homeless. Central's response was long on high-minded lip service but short on meaningful financial support: "What a splendid thing it would be . . . if at this crisis, a building could be bought and equipped in first class style for the Association."[19] Central's leaders limited their financial support to forgiving a twelve dollar debt owed by the Colored branch, a gesture encouraged by Morriss, who believed the black group's financial security to be so tenuous that without loan forgiveness the branch "may disband and a few of its official members assume its present obligations."[20]

The Colored YMCA instead maintained "steady work on a modest scale" at a smaller structure at 436 West Biddle Street.[21] But those efforts were not enough to address the needs of the black community as perceived both by black clergy, who were "anxious for the establishment of a well equipped" Colored YMCA, and by Central's white leaders, who reported that Baltimore's black population of about 85,000 included 15,000 young men whose need for a YMCA was "very evident to any thoughtful citizen."[22]

In the quarter century preceding World War I, young men from rural areas and graduates of black colleges went in great numbers to urban areas, attracted by the lure of jobs and better housing in the growing cities, and, oftentimes, also propelled by a desire to escape the racism and discrimination of their birthplaces. While the experience of the migrants who moved north between 1890 and 1915 has been largely eclipsed by the attention focused on the Great Migration, the harsh realities of their situation and the need to protect them from the city's evils was a primary goal of YMCA supporters not only in Baltimore but in other major cities, too. For example, in 1899, the Reverend Dr. Charles T. Walker, the nationally known pastor of New York City's Mount Olivet Baptist Church, led the creation of a black YMCA to serve as a home for southern migrants in Manhattan. Walker raised money from his own congregants and the black community at large for a year's lease on a building on West 53rd Street, "the Main Street for respectable folk of Negro Tenderloin." Walker then successfully appealed to the white New York YMCA for membership for the branch. When the black population began to move to Harlem early in the twentieth century, a branch was created there. In 1919, the 53rd Street branch relocated to Harlem, where in the 1920s it became "the biggest Y in America."[23]

In Baltimore, despite the apparent serious limitations of the local work, many applauded the contributions made by African-American YMCAs nationally. A Dr. Talmage, whose weekly sermon appeared in the *Afro-American* newspaper, reported in 1898 that the country's YMCAs were doing "a glorious work. They have fine reading rooms, and all the influences are of the best kind, and are now adding gymnasiums and bowling alleys, where, without evil surroundings, our young men may get physical as well as spiritual improvement." This was important because, in Talmage's estimation, the community was "dwindling away to a narrow-chested, weak-armed, feeble-voiced race. When God calls us to a work he wants physical as well as spiritual athletes."[24]

Many observers (both black and white) understood the efforts of the YMCA as an important antidote to larger destructive societal trends. "Everything that the forces of evil can do to ruin these young men is being done and the recent outbreaks of lawlessness and rowdyism is sufficient evidence of the power of the influences thus exerted," reported the Central YMCA's white leadership in 1899. Central's leaders proclaimed that what was needed to "place the [colored] branch on a firm basis" was "help from the white people."[25] That recognition notwithstanding, little tangible assistance followed.

In a June 1898 editorial, Baltimore's *Afro-American* critiqued the racial policies of the local YMCA as representative of the racism racking institutions nationwide: "Our present Christian civilization and the institutions of the country are pervaded with an 'invisible' word, which is . . . productive of such results as are humiliating as well as exasperating to a large percentage of the people who make up this republic." At that time, many predominantly black institutions and organizations were labeled "colored," while those white groups actively supporting Jim Crow policies did not identify their racial limitations by beginning their name with "white":

Over the portals of the great majority of Christian churches are words although invisible, [which say] "for white people only." Ostensibly our white fellow citizens have not the courage to resurrect and reestablish the antebellum sign, "No Negroes and no dogs allowed in here," but in a striking hypocrisy indicative of supreme cowardice they are content to wound and outrage the feelings of their colored brethren by sailing under false colors. There ought to be some law, and it should be rigidly enforced, whereby every so-called public establishment, whether ecclesiastical or otherwise, whose business is conducted for white people alone, should state plainly this declaration in its charter and be placed in its forefront. To openly declare that an institution is for the public, and then deny a portion of that public its privilege on account of color is not only systematic lying but an outrage.

To prove that African Americans, "the most catholic minded of the people who make up the American public," were also "guilty of innocent, but systematic lying," the writer used the case of Baltimore's YMCA. The Central association, "although it would appear, on its face, as if it were for 'men' regardless of color," was restricted to whites only. The building on Biddle Street, the editorialist continued, "publicly and unwisely proclaims an untruth when it prefixes to its title 'colored'" when in fact it would "take men of all races." Therefore, only the Biddle Street branch could "justly, honestly, and honorably bear the title "Y.M.C.A.""[26]

Despite both the rhetoric and philosophy of inclusion, it appears that the Druid Hill YMCA's constituency was nearly all black. Given the exclusionary policies of so many other organizations and the growing need of the African-American community in Baltimore, the black community embraced the association's efforts to provide services. On the eve of the twentieth century, the Colored YMCA's programs were expanded and professionalized. By February 1899, W. Edward Williams, a college graduate and the Colored YMCA's first paid secretary (whose hiring was "made possible by the generosity of the Central Association," which attempted but failed to raise $600 to cover his annual salary), was "in the field . . . actively engaged in pushing on the work." At the same time, W. H. Murray, a Baltimore public school vice principal, was elected president.[27] Williams and Murray were concerned about the thousands of young black men in Baltimore who were "looking, perhaps unconsciously for . . . help" from the risks the city posed: "the saloon, the club, and other places of evil," which opened attractive doors to them. With the exception of the church, Williams believed there was "no place of moral resort, of physical and mental and spiritual helpfulness to our young men" in the city. The result was they went astray and became "in large number rowdies."[28]

With that reality in mind, Williams helped craft the Colored branch's mission:

> to band together young men whose lives and action will tell against rowdyism, impurity and vice in any form, and who will endeavor to bring other young men in touch with the YMCA. To make men workers, by securing work for them. To help them to be and keep pure, by giving them pure examples and bring them in touch with pure men. To help them towards intelligence, by supplying them means to profitably spend and improve the spare hours. To lead them to God; by living Godly lives ourselves and thus preach to them of the power and love of God.[29]

Williams succeeded in attracting members and funds. During his first year as secretary, paid membership increased from 13 to 166 and contributions from the black community reached $500. Many of the new members worked for hotels or private families. They used the facilities most heavily from September through May. During the summer, many members were "away in the country and at the seashore with the families of their employers and at the hotels."[30] Under Williams's leadership the branch purchased a building at the southeast corner of Hoffman Street and Druid Hill Avenue for $2,000, giving the branch its lasting moniker—the Druid Hill Avenue YMCA.[31]

Despite his successes, Williams left after two years "to accept the charge of a church in the city," Grace Presbyterian, because unlike William Morriss he didn't believe the YMCA offered him the opportunity to do "the spiritual work" for which he was "better fitted." He leaned "too much toward the ministry or at least the Evangelistic work to be satisfied with the details of a local Secretary's work."[32] P. A. Goines, an experienced association worker and secretary in the YMCA's Army Department, replaced Williams.[33]

Chronic money problems plagued the black YMCA, whose leaders repeatedly urged all "white and colored friends" to give to save "from careless and sinful lives the thousands of young colored men of Baltimore." In reality, self-help from within the black community accomplished much of what was achieved before 1915. In the first years, the largesse of Central included no cash but "some of our old papers and magazines." In 1894, Central denied a request for financial aid, saying "it was impossible to assist." The following year, a request from Hunton generated $50 for the black association. The annual appropriation from Central to the Colored YMCA was the smallest made to any branch in Baltimore, averaging $100 or less. In 1900, the Druid Hill YMCA published a report highlighting the branch's financial, spiritual, intellectual, and physical accomplishments entitled "What the Colored [YMCA] Has Done for Itself . . . Without Aid from the White People."[34]

Financial shortcomings were manifest in the building at Druid Hill Avenue and Hoffman Street, which had a small gym, reading room, and office.[35] Chronic underfunding caused chronic physical plant and equipment deficiencies. It took five years to raise funds sufficient to install baths; this was especially damning given the shortage of both indoor plumbing and public baths in Baltimore.[36]

The flawed facilities remained an issue even as the branch moved to another building five blocks north at 1619 Druid Hill Avenue in 1908 or 1909. Located in the Fourteenth Ward, where the black population would increase 67 percent between 1910 and 1920, the new building was just north of the Seventeenth Ward, which, with a black population of 16,736 in 1920, would become the "center of the colored population."[37] Both the Fourteenth Ward and the southern part of the Seventeenth Ward had increasingly serious housing and social problems. The small houses on alley streets were becoming overcrowded, with many housing two or three families, adversely affecting the health, social, and civic life beyond just the immediate area. Tuberculosis and venereal disease were especially serious threats, as was the shortage of safe recreational options.[38]

Like the earlier facilities, this one quickly proved wanting. Central reported that "in spite of limitations of an inadequate building . . . a fine work has been done for colored young men and boys. It speaks volumes for what might be done if facilities were provided in any way commensurate with those for white young men and boys."[39] Despite its shortcomings, the branch featured many of the same services offered by Central and other white branches, such as education, employment, and boardinghouse referrals.[40] Just as Central ministered to young men of or aspiring to the middle class, the black branch was sometimes criticized for catering to the "'kid glove' class rather than helping those who really need help."[41] To ambitious young men, the branch offered a Bible class, a literary society, and an employment bureau to "secure work for members and other worthy men out of employment." Finding "Christian young men of good character" for positions such as "porters, waiters, coachmen, footmen, [and] bell-boys" was the bureau's goal. A Junior Department was also created. Classes in English, first aid, and physiology began in 1899. Arithmetic, shorthand, and political science were soon added.[42]

Educational offerings advanced careers. For example, George H. Arthur and W. H. Beckett studied religion as well as secular topics at the Druid Hill YMCA. They then earned highly coveted International YMCA certificates for their stellar Bible study examinations in 1903. Arthur, a five-year Druid Hill employee who worked first as a janitor and later as a typewriter and stenographer, left the YMCA to work for Chicago's police department: "all of his training for the position was had in our association." Beckett left Baltimore for the YMCA Training School at Springfield, Massachusetts (which Morriss had helped found), to study to become a secretary in the Colored Department.[43]

Personal enrichment was a focus of some of Druid Hill's programs. In 1899, Mary Richmond, general secretary of the Baltimore Charity Organization Society, spoke on the "True Method of Giving Charity." Her speech was described as "the great event of the month." A lecture, "How to Lessen the Criminal among Our People," attracted more than 300 people in 1905.[44]

The Druid Hill YMCA presented cultural programs, including Samuel Taylor Coleridge's adaptation of Henry Wadsworth Longfellow's *Hiawatha* with a fifty-two-piece orchestra in 1903 and again in 1904. The branch's leaders were "convinced that the uplifting influences upon our own people of such music . . . is well worth the task of its management, especially when 'rag-time' music has even found its way in many of the Sunday Schools, to say nothing of the homes of the people." White members of Central's board of directors bought tickets, and a party of five whites occupied a box at the concert, which was held at a black theater.[45]

The colored work in Baltimore was tightly linked to other black YMCA initiatives around the country. In December 1899, for example, Baltimore hosted the Eleventh Annual Conference of Colored YMCAs from Virginia, West Virginia, Maryland, and Washington, D.C. Nearly 600 men attended.[46]

Like other black YMCAs nationally, Baltimore was profoundly affected when in December 1910, Julius Rosenwald, the president of Sears Roebuck, offered $25,000 to every community in the country that raised $75,000 toward the erection of a black YMCA over five years. He would give $25,000 after $50,000 raised locally was expended for land and building. In Baltimore, the white community raised $50,000, and the black community agreed to raise $25,000. After $15,000 of that $25,000 was paid, work on the new building would begin.[47]

Jesse E. Moorland directed the November 1912 campaign to raise the $25,000 contribution from the black community for the new building planned for a 60-by-100-foot lot on Druid Hill Avenue on the same block where the branch was already operating. Moorland was then a fifteen-year YMCA worker and an "earnest Christian intensely interested in the uplift of young men, and full of optimism," who had already led similar fund-raising drives in Chicago, Philadelphia, Atlanta, and Washington, D.C., among other cities.[48] In Baltimore, 100 men volunteered in ten districts to solicit subscriptions from 6,000 prospects over the ten days of the campaign. Their motto was "What others have done, we can do." Each volunteer got "a certificate empowering him with the authority to solicit funds." Anyone soliciting without a valid certificate was to be "handled according to law."[49]

The size and scope of the 1912 fund-raising effort was unprecedented. Although the black community had given at "rallies for church purposes," never before had "large sums, such as fifty, one hundred and two hundred" dollars, been asked. Halfway through the campaign, less than a third of the $25,000 had been pledged. The "ridiculously small" contributions several "well to do men" made surprised and dismayed the campaign's organizers and the editors of Baltimore's *Afro-American*, who believed that "many of our citizens do not realize what it really means to enter into a campaign of this kind."[50] Moorland urged every man "to give in keeping with his means." Those who earned their livelihood from the patronage of the black community were key. "The race made his success possible and he should be willing to give generously. . . . Those who owe their success to the race owe the race a duty and should discharge the same by being morally and financially in all movements that tend toward race betterment."[51]

The *Afro-American*'s editorial staff encouraged the community to participate fully while it chided black leaders to give generously: "These men owe it to themselves as well as to the people they serve to return something to those who have made it possible for them to be where they are." Those who were "giving five dollars where they ought to give fifty, and giving ten where they ought to give one hundred" were declared "a disgrace to the race." Some of the donations were "ridiculously small so much so that the individuals giving them ought to be heartily ashamed of themselves for even offering them." In contrast, those earning "a pittance" gave "more than the men who are making thousands." In response, the *Afro-American*'s writer proposed publishing a list of donors and the amounts pledged "so that the people of the city will know in the future just upon whom they can depend."[52]

So big was the campaign that "all of the newspapers, especially the race papers" covered it. At its deadline, the campaign appeared to have succeeded, and even the *Baltimore Sun* praised the black community for securing more than $31,000 in pledges. The *Afro-American* commented: "The colored people of Baltimore are to be congratulated for the splendid effort they made in raising $31,000 for a new building for the Y[MCA]. ... $25,000 was the amount called for, but as Bishop Wayman used to say 'Colored folks in Baltimore always overdo the thing.' It was a glorious victory ... both for the association and for Baltimore." The largest single donor was James W. Hughes, who subscribed $300 and was president of the association in July 1918 when the first public tours were given. Hughes proclaimed, "I am glad I gave my money. This building is needed and will be a God send to our people."[53]

The 1912 kudos proved premature. By 1915, only a third of the $31,000 pledged was in hand.[54] The balance proved elusive, causing both the building's delay and the need for additional fund-raising. The *Afro-American* was again heavily involved, urging readers to "Make your Xmas and New Year's gift to the YMCA an investment that you will never regret. . . . Your gift . . . will help some boy and bless some man."[55] In December 1917 when the building's ground breaking was held, nearly $9,000 was still needed to reach the $25,000 goal.[56] Nine months later, the Druid Hill YMCA held an "Over-the-Top" campaign designed to collect $8,000 from the 1,375 people whose 1912 pledges remained unpaid. The YMCA's plan to publish "in the public press, a full and complete list of all the names of individuals who have paid no portion of the amount pledged by them" was softened when Druid Hill's leaders declared that "if each one . . . pays one dollar on their pledge, . . . we will have no need to publish any names."[57]

World War I complicated fund-raising efforts because the black community was inundated with funding requests. Concurrent with appeals for the new building came requests to support black troops through military YMCAs.[58] As the new building was under construction, the Druid Hill branch itself supported war work by providing social and recreational activities for black army and navy men "who may have a few hours in Baltimore." The association's temporary recreation center at 1533 Druid Hill Avenue was used as "a real home" for soldiers on furlough in Balti-

9. The Druid Hill Avenue YMCA Building, located at 1619 Druid Hill Avenue, opened in 1919, the result of a challenge grant from Julius Rosenwald and of the generosity of local citizens, black and white. It was immediately popular, attracting an average of more than a thousand visitors per day.

more. According to the *Afro-American*, "the Sammies know the value of the YMCA."[59]

Even as the Druid Hill YMCA served military men in town, events were held to generate interest and support for the new building. In February 1918, the *Afro-American* supported a membership campaign with a goal of 1,000 new members. "A city with probably the largest colored population of any city in the Union, with the many men and boys who need just what the Association will be shortly so well equipped to furnish, ought to take first rank at least in matter of membership."[60] The day before the campaign's scheduled end, 242 more members were needed.[61] Secretary S. S. Booker made a final appeal to the congregation at Ames ME Church, where the men were "wild with enthusiasm" and more than 30 joined within ten minutes. Those men then fanned out in different directions, "each one determined to go the limit in order to win. The interest was at fever heat and everybody was talking about the campaign. No conversation was complete without the question—'Are you a member of the Y?'" The men were successful. In the final day, 328 new members were secured, bringing the total to 1,108.[62]

Despite the success of the membership campaign, when Druid Hill's cornerstone was laid in April 1918 (six months after the second fundraiser began) nearly $9,000 in pledges remained unpaid. New sources were tapped. Black clergy passed the collection plate and sold souvenir bricks for a dollar. On YMCA Day, "every minister" in the black community was asked to speak of the YMCA's work and make an offering to the building fund. Pharmacists allowed their drugstores to be used as a distribution system for free tickets for a "monster patriotic mass meeting" at Ford's Theater on the YMCA's behalf.[63]

The *Afro-American* was unwaveringly committed to the YMCA. As pledges went unmet, the newspaper reported that the completion of the new building depended on black citizens paying their pledges. Failure was not an option: "The need for such a plant is too urgent, the time for it is most opportune and the generous gifts of our good white friends mean too much." Said Booker, "This IS a 100 per cent proposition and I am confident that the citizens of Baltimore will put it thru with flying colors. Five other cities are doing the same thing this year and WE MUST DO IT, that's all."[64]

By the summer of 1918, the financial situation was critical. The building was being erected on a "pay as you go plan" and "when the money gives out the work will stop." The campaign's 240 volunteers canvassed "home and church, minister and layman, shop and industrial plant" in order to attract notice from those whose pledges remained unpaid and from groups ranging from "churches, social service clubs, business and professional clubs, to chauffeurs, waiters, janitors, porters, butlers, bellmen and workingmen of Baltimore for a united pull in the common cause." Unlike the 1912 campaign, there was "no amount too small."[65]

The 1918 campaign started well. After ten days, more than $2,500 in cash had been received and the volunteers were "full of ginger and confident of getting $8,000 . . . and thus sav[ing] the honor and integrity of the colored citizens of Baltimore." Teams were organized at Sparrows Point and "at all of the big firms of the city where a large number of colored men work." By October 1918, the campaign lagged. Only $3,000 of the required $8,000 had been raised, and there was cash enough for only two weeks of construction.[66]

To alleviate the cash shortage, short-term savings were realized by leaving the swimming pool unfinished, thus seriously compromising the YMCA's service to a recreation-hungry community. Despite that, the building's opening was celebrated. In his dedicatory address, Moorland sketched the history of the colored work in Baltimore, told of the new building campaign in 1912, and lauded Booker for his "indefatigable work in collecting the necessary pledges among the colored people." Booker in turn described his struggle to collect $25,000 in pledges made by the black community over his four-year tenure in Baltimore. He ended with an appeal to raise the $1,300 necessary to complete the fund-raising![67] The *Afro-American* itself "had the honor and the privilege of giving the last hundred dollars," which allowed the association to "go over the top and emerge with every brick in the . . . structure paid for."[68] The building's opening festivities lasted for more than a week and featured events such as Chauffeurs Night, Church Night, Organization Night, Boys Night, and a Patriotic Mass Meeting. Throughout the week, the building was "thronged with visitors."[69]

Furnished, the building cost approximately $110,000, of which $25,000 came from the African-American community, $50,000 from "White friends," and $25,000 from Rosenwald. At the opening, the Druid Hill YMCA had a mortgage of $12,000 but was current with all bills. Of all the black YMCA buildings then erected (including those in Washington, D.C., Philadelphia, Chicago, Indianapolis, Kansas City, and Cincinnati), Baltimore's was reportedly the only one in which the black community's quota had been fully paid at the time of the building's dedication.[70] The vagaries of fund-raising and other budgetary problems helped the Druid Hill board decide that they would "be gratified to come under the control of the Baltimore Association" (thereby becoming a formal branch of the Baltimore YMCA).[71]

The Central YMCA reported that the "thoroughly modern structure" designed and built by George R. Morris was "not only architecturally beautiful [and] semi-fireproof," it was also "thoroughly substantial and adapted to modern Association work." In addition to "commodious reception rooms" and "a fine gymnasium with running track," the building featured the unfinished swimming pool, separate Boys' and Men's Departments, an auditorium and classrooms on the second floor, and fifty-two "simply but substantially furnished" dormitory rooms with a capacity of seventy-one boarders on the third and fourth floors.[72]

The building served both local residents and those new to the city. The dormitory provided an important base for newly arrived men. The 1920 federal census offers a snapshot of the Druid Hill YMCA's dormitory residents. All forty-two residents were literate and spoke English. Most were young (more than half were between seventeen and twenty-six years of age), single, born in the region (nearly 75 percent were born in Maryland and Virginia), and employed. Many of the lodgers held service jobs with hotels or private families. The census taker identified one-third of the residents as black and two-thirds as mulatto.[73]

Soon after the building's opening, the Central YMCA's leaders proclaimed that their investment at Druid Hill was "one of the best the Association . . . ever made." The building was "the central influence in the life of the colored population in this section of the city." Blacks and whites both saw the branch as an important center for the black community, "the centre of the interdenominational religious life of the colored community" and "the center of the social and religious work among colored people."[74]

The new building was immediately popular. Its opening coincided with a population explosion in Baltimore. Between 1920 and 1924, the city's total population increased by more than 50,000, to 785,242, of which there were 36,452 black boys and men between ten and forty-nine years of age.[75] In 1920, the Druid Hill YMCA's membership was 1,605. Daily attendance was 950. There were 101 students enrolled in educational classes and 312 in Bible studies. The dormitories were occupied by 1,875 different men. The branch matched 45 men with churches and provided opportunities for 210 others to serve on a plethora of association committees.[76]

The YMCA's work was supported by "the leading colored people of the city," who would "increase their support when needed." The membership of the Druid Hill branch was then made up of "ministers, teachers, lawyers, doctors, dentists, pharmacists, chauffeurs, contractors, painters, waiters, porters, insurance men and laborers." The branch served as a community center by providing rooms for groups such as the Medical Association, Teachers' Association, Male Ushers' Club, and benevolent organizations.[77]

As the building's beauty and utility were celebrated, what was not apparent was that besides the unfinished swimming pool, other corners had been cut in the construction and finishing of the building.[78] By 1924, the YMCA's own surveyors were struck by the poor conditions, observing "either the amount of the fund to be spent was fixed without regard to the standards of Association service or else it was assumed that the standards of equipment could be disregarded in a building for colored men and boys." The building was "exceedingly disappointing" and could not compare "for a moment" with the Central Building, ten years its senior. The gym was too short for standard games. The combination of intensive use (1,000 people used the building daily) and the poor quality of materials caused the locker rooms and showers to be in deplorable condition. The dormitories were the only part of the physical operation that met standards, but they were criticized for providing mostly doubles. The lot itself was too small, and the building was only half the size necessary to meet demand.[79]

Although there were clearly commonalities in the program of the Druid Hill YMCA and the association's white operations, there was also clear separation. Leaders such as Morriss, James Carey Thomas, Joshua Levering, and F. A. White attempted to negotiate a modernity that was characterized by a profoundly racist society in which the Jim Crow edict of separate but equal long stood unchallenged by them and their peers. Whereas the white YMCA proved to be a pathbreaking organization in areas including adult and continuing education, vocational training, and even housing, in the area of race relations, Baltimore YMCA leaders both black and white long tolerated the status quo of racial segregation.

6

"A Program of Helpful Cooperation"

The Railroad and Industrial Work of the YMCA, 1879–1933

In 1901, a former president of the Baltimore Federation of Labor reported "religion is in a bad way in Baltimore . . . the churches do not welcome the workingmen, and the workingmen do not care for the churches." He suggested that ministers give lectures on industrial questions on Sundays. But from his experience he believed that would never happen because the churches were under the control of the employing classes: "You hear sermons about everything else, but you don't hear any sermons about the workingman." The labor leader also favored the YMCA's youth work as a Christianizing influence for workers and their families. A lapsed Catholic himself, he encouraged his two sons to join the YMCA. His insights were reported by Ernest H. Abbott, a reporter for *Outlook* magazine who was introduced to him and other city labor leaders through William H. Morriss, the Baltimore YMCA's longtime general secretary.[1]

Under Morriss's leadership, the YMCA developed what it termed "industrial work," creating special branches and programs for industrial employees and affirming and formalizing earlier, more tenuous, links between the YMCA and Baltimore's workers. Morriss, along with leaders such as James Carey Thomas, Joshua Levering, and F. A. White, sought to enhance the religious, social, athletic, and educational experiences of workers.

In its industrial work, as elsewhere in its operations, the Baltimore YMCA demonstrated a capacity to respond to the changing circumstances and needs of its constituency—namely young men having or aspiring to middle-class values and rank. The YMCA's programs for industrial employees, especially its efforts to reach the workers of expanding industries such as railroads and modern manufacturers, provide an excellent example of its broad and flexible mission.

For many railroad men, affiliation with the YMCA was important as a career boost even before industrial work formally began. For example, a superintendent of the Texas Pacific Railroad claimed that his affiliation with the association enabled his rise in the railroad's corporate culture: "My belonging to the YMCA made the officials have confidence in me. I was promoted to assistant to the President, and now I am superintendent of the valley branch, and a little good business advice caused it all. The advice gave me the first boost, and the YMCA drew me up and held me there."[2]

Anecdotal evidence notwithstanding, reaching a broad-based cross section of workers in the harsh new industrial world of post–Civil War America was a daunting challenge for the YMCA. Industries experienced wave after wave of consolidations, mergers, and bankruptcies. Labor-management relations were rocky. The national economy gyrated dramatically with periods of rapid growth and steep decline. Most notable in the latter group were the depressions of 1873 and 1893. Wage cuts and layoffs precipitated the great railroad strikes of 1877 and 1886, the Homestead strike of 1892, and the Pullman strike of 1894.

These "earthquakes," according to historian Henry F. May, caused Protestant leaders to change their thinking.[3] Increasingly, ministers and other religious leaders became aware of a "necessity for new Christian social doctrine." Because of the labor unrest of the late nineteenth century, religious commentators, "despairing at the increase of social conflict, concluded that the only solution lay in spiritual regeneration." Although the chasm between Protestant clergy and the industrial workers to whom they hoped to minister was not new, the great social crises of the late nineteenth century "forced clerical observers to admit the existence of problems ignored, or waved aside, by the pat theorists of earlier times."[4]

Against this background of stressful changes and enmity, the Baltimore YMCA's efforts to reach the rapidly expanding ranks of industrial workers came early and were revealingly stubborn. The association's success required modifying or abandoning programs, changing facility sites, and maintaining an unusual and delicate coalition of labor and management. The industrial work of the YMCA was an important harbinger of both the Social Gospel—Applied Christianity—and corporate welfare work that, though pioneering in the 1870s, became commonplace in the twentieth century.[5]

The industrial work of the Baltimore YMCA was remarkable both for bringing to workers a kind of Christianity they found accessible and for satisfying the historically contentious needs of workers and management through what Stuart Brandes calls "welfare capitalism": "service provided for the comfort or improvement of employees which was neither a necessity of the industry nor required by law."[6] Welfare capitalism programs, Lisa M. Fine argues, spawned a new definition of workplace manliness, which was expressed not through "his participation in an alternative working class culture but in his compliance with middle class emblems of decorum." The result was that "cooperation with the team" became the hallmark of the new workingman.[7]

To varying degrees, the YMCA's industrial work became an important vehicle for the delivery of corporate welfare programs to industries across Baltimore. The railroads enthusiastically embraced the YMCA. Merchant marines and local manufacturers also formed partnerships with the YMCA for the provision of religious, recreational, educational, and housing programs for workers.

The Baltimore YMCA's involvement in industrial work began as a result of the 1870s labor unrest. The fallout from the depression of 1873 was especially cruel to railroad workers. For workers on the Baltimore and Ohio Railroad (B&O), there were terrible changes. Overtime payments ceased. Daily wages were dramatically reduced. Firemen and brakemen saw their pay slashed or lost their jobs. Work-related injuries became more common. In July 1877, B&O president John Work Garrett added insult to injury by simultaneously increasing shareholders' dividends 10 percent while cutting workers' wages 10 percent more. Garrett's move sparked labor strife throughout the line. For the brakemen and firemen who remained employed, falling wages, compounded by half-time employment, resulted in salaries that were about one-quarter of what they had been four years earlier. Although elsewhere in the country the strikes of July 1877 were violent from the outset, in Baltimore the striking firemen were first reported to be quiet, orderly, sober, and successful in stopping all B&O freight in the city.[8]

Despite popular support for railroad workers, the strike's peaceful beginning in Baltimore, and enmity against local strikebreakers and state militiamen brought in to quell strikers in Martinsburg, West Virginia, the railroad, after all, was keenly important to the economic life of the region. Garrett and Maryland's governor John Carroll wanted the strike ended. Fearing violence in Baltimore, Carroll brought the Maryland National Guard into the city, a move that itself triggered violence. Nine civilians were killed, and more than twenty were seriously injured. In response, 2,000 federal troops and 500 marines were called in to quell Baltimore's agitators by a show of force designed to discourage further worker insurrection. Within a week the strike weakened and then ended. Workers returned to 10 percent wage cuts and layoffs. Yet despite the railroad's apparent victory in Baltimore, the protest spread to other places and other railroad lines.[9]

The Baltimore uprising forced public awareness of the grievances of the railroad workers and the intransigence of Garrett's railroad. An aroused public pleaded for reforms of the industry and for government supervision. In response, the railroad reacted favorably to the YMCA's overtures to aid the railroad workers.[10] The concern of association leaders about the plight of railroad workers was sincere. They offered what they believed was "the better way" to solve the railroad problem while benefiting both employee and employer. From the start, YMCA railroad branches offered Bible study and prayer meetings, a safe haven for railroad workers, and a forum through which public awareness of railroad workers was raised, with special attention focused on issues related to occupational safety. According to Clarence Hicks, an industrial relations expert who gained experience as a YMCA railroad secretary, "the Railroad "Y" pioneered in creating a program of helpful cooperation based upon unity of interest between employer and employees."[11]

In addition to contentious labor issues, railroad employment featured unusual work conditions. Employees running the trains spent a great deal of time away from home. Railroad men, like many transient workers, chose between "utter loneliness on the one hand and warmth and cheer in the realm of moral danger on the other." Railroad centers were notoriously blighted with saloons, "flophouses," and gambling dens. Often these were the only places where trainmen on the road could find food and lodging. Intoxicated or exhausted workers were an unattractive prospect in an industry where expensive goods and many lives depended on close control of large and powerful high-speed engines. In an effort to create a third path—an alternative to those dismal choices—the YMCA created railroad branches. By 1878, after meeting with representatives from various railroads, the Baltimore YMCA was working with railroad men, finding "Christian men in all ranks and departments of the railroad service [who] assist us in endeavoring to win over those who are living in sin and exposed to danger." Rail companies forged an alliance with the YMCA for a joint-venture welfare organization for workers isolated by their work from home and family, and as a way to address the public's perception of the railroad industry's deficencies.[12]

The B&O Railroad branch was the first in Baltimore to offer significant programming run by paid professionals. In the spring of 1879, D. L. Moody and E. D. Ingersoll, both businessmen-turned-evangelists, called upon Garrett on behalf of the Baltimore YMCA. Ingersoll, the first permanent traveling railroad secretary of the YMCA's International Committee, had the job of convincing management that railroad branches represented "not a philanthropy, but simply good business for the railroad company."[13] He and Moody lobbied Garrett to introduce railroad YMCAs along the B&O's rail lines. Moody assured Garrett of his personal knowledge of "the good results accomplished in . . . the railway department of the work of the Association."[14]

At Moody's suggestion, a full-time secretary, Edward E. Sheldon, was hired to serve the B&O Railroad's Baltimore employees, a job he held for twenty-two years. Sheldon was "one of the little band of pioneer YMCA secretaries . . . [and] about the first employed officer on any of the railroads in this country." He was charged with making the rooms "more attractive to railroad men socially and intellectually than any saloon"; organizing and leading Christian railroad men in visitation and care of the sick and injured; working to make "better men" through personal and religious reform; and arranging evening classes in subjects such as penmanship and mathematics that would make railroad workers "more valuable servants of the company." YMCA leaders were gratified that Sheldon's work, "carried on exclusively in the interests of railroad men," was paid for by the railroad.[15]

Part of management's willingness to embrace the YMCA resulted from the bloody strikes that began along the B&O in 1877 and eventually tied up all five American trunk lines and major rail centers. In the wake of these disruptions, railroad executives tried to improve their workers' general conditions. Management's underlying theory was that "well-housed, well-fed, properly educated Christians do not strike."[16] Nationally, many railroad operators supported the YMCA's entry into railroad work. Between 1872 and 1883, annual contributions of railroad companies to railroad YMCAs grew from $3,000 to more than $50,000. The number of railroad YMCAs increased quickly from 39 in 1879 to 230 in 1911.[17]

Railroad branches pleased railroad executives like Garrett, who reported that the YMCA's efforts were "fruitful of good results." The "numerous visits made and other attentions shown to employees, where sick or injured, have been much appreciated."[18] Railroad executives endorsed and encouraged the movement, which they "considered of the highest importance in developing spiritual, moral, mental, and physical improvement." As business enterprises with financial, not altruistic, ends, railroad corporations made donations only "when there is reasonable assurance that funds so appropriated will bring commensurate returns." The investment in the YMCA demonstrated that there was "both a direct and an indirect return to corporations contributing to benevolent institutions."[19]

W. R. Davenport, a builder of railroad cars, explained the willingness of many managers and owners to make corporate contributions to the railroad branches: "Railroad managers are beginning to see that Christian men save their companies largely in cost of repairs and in many ways, and that money spent in YMCA work among their men is the best paying investment they can make."[20] The nondenominational, yet religious, nature of the YMCA's Applied Christianity appealed to management. According to Davenport, "One of the prominent features in the success of the movement rests on the fact that it is free from sectarian complications, the religious work being of such a broad, general character that it can be participated in without entrenching upon denominational affiliations— being based upon the simple principles of morality that are accepted and recognized by all Christian people."[21]

The railroad YMCA, in Abbott's estimation, was "the only considerable organization . . . which is at all venturing to put the religious life of workingmen into institutional form." Its success, Abbott felt, should "suggest to the Church at large some possible measures."[22] From their beginnings, the railroad branches held formal religious services, some in the yards and depot and others at the Central YMCA. Even "in the face of ridicule and opposition," daily attendance at noonday prayer services for B&O workers at Locust Point averaged 40 in 1881. Twenty years later, the average attendance at the B&O's Sunday meetings was 154, with 5 men professing conversion weekly.[23]

The railroad YMCA was successful because, by design, it responded to the needs of its members. Trainmen's desire for one regular stopping-place at the end of their route determined the comfortable character of the railroad YMCA, which, aiming to be a second home for railroad workers, needed to be "free from unnecessary restrictions based on other people's notions of what is expedient for him to do or not to do." The railroad YMCA offered timetables, housing, and check cashing services, resulting in the members "mentally associat[ing] the Christian spirit with what in the minds of workingmen . . . [was] their strongest ethical motive—interest in the physical comfort and welfare of the individual, the personal desire on the part of one man that another should be contented and happy." The religious success of the railroad YMCA was that it "'put the Gospel' into the railroad worker's vernacular."[24]

The largesse of the railroad executives could easily have compromised the autonomy of the railroad YMCA. As early as 1879, when railroad branches gained the support of industrialists like Garrett, Cornelius Vanderbilt, and John Wanamaker, YMCA and railroad leaders discussed whether railroad branches should be independent organizations (like Levering Hall and the Druid Hill Avenue YMCA would come to be) or part of the corporate YMCA.[25] Ultimately the railroad branches came under the umbrella of their local association and proved useful in dispelling the YMCA's reputation as "a superior club" that dispensed "luxuries to the so called 'white collar' class" but that both lacked appeal and gave little attention to those workers most in need of its help. The outreach of the railroad branches and their practical ministry to railroad workers "won the attention and sympathy of many skeptics."[26]

The triangular relationship between management, the YMCA, and workers was especially critical in times of labor strife.[27] As John F. Moore, an early student of the YMCA's railroad work, noted, some corporations believed that the railroad branch would support them: "We have made you. Our funds have largely erected and equipped your buildings. Our monthly contributions enable you to meet your operations budgets. The hour has struck when we need a specific service you are qualified to render. Will you fail us now?" Meanwhile, some workers assumed the railroad branch's total loyalty: "We constitute your field. You were born and have been nurtured to serve us. We work on your committees. We constitute your membership. . . . you have been shouting from the housetops that you were the friend of railroad men. Now we are in trouble. Temporarily we are out of work, but we still regard ourselves as railroad employees. We need your sympathetic understanding. Will you fail us now?" Mediating between the desires of management and labor were some "leading railroad operators and outstanding railroad brotherhood leaders" who counseled that railroad branches "be saved from embarrassment by unreasonable demands made by either party so that when peace came the Movement might be in a position effectively to continue its ministry of good will to all." The key to the success of the YMCA's industrial work was that the joint venture of employer, employees, and the YMCA functioned independent of the larger, contentious relationship of labor and management.[28]

Although they contributed to railroad branches for many years, railroad executives often preferred using the YMCA's facilities to their own because employees bore part of the expense. The railroad corporation and employee members split the cost of the railroad YMCAs' building, programs, and personnel. In 1890, railroad corporations paid about 60 percent of the branches' operating budgets, with employees providing 40 percent. Twenty years later, the ratios had reversed. The railroad corporations' contributions to the railroad YMCA occasionally engendered criticism from what Abbott called the "more bitter" labor leaders against the YMCA but did not prevent amazing, if erratic, growth.[29]

Until the late 1880s, the railroad YMCA work in Baltimore used ad hoc facilities at the railroad yards, stations, and the Central branch. In 1887, the B&O Railroad YMCA purchased its own building at Stricker and Lombard Streets in West Baltimore, across Union Square from H. L. Mencken's house, with subscriptions of $5,000 (of which $3,000 came from trustees of Garrett's estate). The building, intended for the exclusive use of railroad men, featured a hall for 200, a parlor, reading and reception rooms, and a janitor's apartment.[30]

Unexpectedly, the B&O branch attracted neighborhood people, too. In 1889, Secretary Sheldon alerted the YMCA's Executive Committee that many of the men enjoying privileges of the branch were not railroad men. The paid membership peaked at only 280, with about equal numbers of people from the neighborhood and trainmen.[31] The lack of a gymnasium and bathing facilities, untimely B&O layoffs from the nearby Mount Clare shops, and, most important, a railroad policy that made the branch's privileges free to all railroad men caused the dearth of paid members. Memberships were available, but "the man who paid nothing for them would frequently be found using them, while the man whose money had supplied them had to do without."[32]

In 1894, the YMCA vacated the building at Stricker and Lombard Streets where, during six years, 219 public meetings and 599 meetings for young men were held, 69 conversions occurred, two churches grew, and 6 ministers and several professional YMCA workers were spawned. Also 325 students attended 552 class sessions, despite "great difficulties on account of lack of room and a poor constituency."[33] The neighborhood people acquired a new West Baltimore YMCA branch several blocks away.[34] The railroad branch continued its operations at Camden Yards and at the B&O's shops at Riverside in South Baltimore where many of the 800 employees were already interested in YMCA work, a small branch having opened there in 1891. The company-owned buildings at Riverside, however, were too small, and men were "actually turned away from the Sunday services for lack of room."[35]

In 1900, a "splendid new building" was erected adjacent to the tracks, where paid members had exclusive use of recreational and athletic facilities, while the baths, lockers, and washroom, furnished by the railroad, remained free. Paid membership grew from fewer than 100 in 1902 to 260 in 1904. With increased membership revenues and additional support from the railroad, the Riverside branch was remodeled to include a basement bowling alley, trackside portico, and sign that "smile[d] its welcome." A reading room, game room, and office were furnished with new books and pool tables "of the grown-up kind." A night secretary was hired to supply towels and soap to men coming in late. These improvements were intended to make the Riverside YMCA "the most attractive place in South Baltimore for the men."[36]

This branch was so successful that in 1908 the B&O Railroad erected an even larger and more substantial YMCA building at 1800 Webster Street, adjacent to the tracks at Riverside. The two-story brick colonial building was 36 feet wide and 100 feet long and cost $35,000. In the basement were bowling alleys, toilets, and a locker room. The first floor held a reception hall, reading room, and game room. Upstairs were an assembly room, a ladies' retiring room, classroom, four bedrooms, buffet kitchen, and two bathrooms. The attic contained a large dormitory.[37]

In addition to the B&O YMCA, the Philadelphia-based Pennsylvania Railroad (Pennsy) had an important presence and, by 1890, a railroad branch of its own in Baltimore. The making of the Pennsy branch began in 1888 when about 800 people attended a religious meeting for railroad men held at Immanuel Baptist Church near Pennsylvania Station. Edward Sheldon, Jennie Smith (the railroad superintendent of the WCTU), and several ministers spoke. A large number of Northern Central Railroad (NCRR) employees attended, hoping that the organization of a railroad branch near the Pennsylvania shops and depot would result.[38]

NCRR executives chose the YMCA after carefully examining the programs of several organizations attempting to meet the needs of railroad workers. They then advised the Baltimore YMCA of their desire to form a Pennsy Railroad branch to offer "a convenient place for social resort" to their 2,000 city employees. The Pennsy branch opened on 1 July 1890. The majority of its funds, including the secretary's $60 monthly salary, were appropriations from the railroad company. The consortium of railroads involved "contributed sufficient funds to keep the new venture from financial embarrassment without taking from it the necessity for hearty cooperation on the part of the members of the Branch." The number of dues-paying members in the Pennsy branch grew rapidly, going from 70 in 1890 to 403 in 1897, second only to Central.[39]

10. This imposing B&O Railroad YMCA branch, located at 1800 Webster Street, adjacent to the tracks in South Baltimore, was built in 1908 and is pictured here in 1920. Although the building was demolished, neighborhood residents recall going there for showers, bowling, and Thanksgiving dinners. YMCA Collection, University of Baltimore Archives.

The Pennsy branch's first home was at 118 W. North Avenue, several blocks from both the Mount Royal and Pennsylvania Stations. Despite the distance between the branch and many employees' homes, at the height of membership in 1897, 403, nearly 17 percent of all Baltimore Pennsy men, were members of the railroad branch, the highest percentage of any Pennsy YMCA outside Philadelphia. In 1900, Pennsy membership fell to 348.[40] To shore up membership, YMCA leaders encouraged more active participation from wives, sisters, and daughters, believing it was in the family's best interest "that an attractive place be provided for the male portion of the family, where he can spend his spare time surrounded by good influences."[41]

A more immediate tactic for increasing membership was relocating the branch to a building at 9–11 E. Lanvale Street, directly across from Pennsylvania Station. In 1900, membership exceeded 200. In 1915, the Pennsy's 400 members were invited to use the old Central Building at Charles and Saratoga Streets for athletics. In 1919, the branch was evicted from its rented quarters and moved to a room at Pennsylvania Station that had been used by the Red Cross. After World War I, there was first a dramatic increase in new members, then, just as suddenly, a membership contraction. Membership fluctuations complicated the branch's attempts to buy a building near the station. As late as 1923, the Pennsy branch was still "on the lookout for a site for a new building," because its parent corporation, unlike the B&O, never provided a company-owned home.[42]

Railroad YMCAs focused on improving the quality of workers' lives. Many members of the Pennsy branch, for example, cashed their checks at taverns, "compelled to go to such places and spend money in order to get currency for checks as they were not paid till Saturday and most of them in the afternoon when all Banks are closed." For their service, the saloon keepers received a small commission or depended on being able to secure customers. It was not uncommon for a single saloon to cash over $8,000 of payroll checks each month. Unhappy with this arrangement, more than twenty-five trainmen appealed to the Pennsy branch secretary to help them change a system that caused many workers "to take less [money] home and often make there with none and in an intoxicated condition." The secretary succeeded. The railroad company resurrected a long-ignored policy of maintaining check cashing centers in and around the city.[43]

Railroad YMCAs provided housing. In 1893, the Pennsy branch offered ten sleeping bunks for transient railroad workers, the first time any branch of the Baltimore YMCA offered housing. This effort drew new members and provided an extremely important service to the railroad industry. By 1915, the B&O branch, too, entered the housing business with twenty-four beds, the rental of which accounted for 8 percent of its income. That year, the Pennsy branch had eighteen beds, which generated 15 percent of its receipts. Although the number of beds at both branches never exceeded fifty, thousands of men rotated through them each year. In 1923, for example, 7,763 different men roomed in Baltimore's railroad branches. Within six years, that number doubled to 15,780 lodgers per year.[44]

Educational offerings were a component of the railroad branches' programming too. Among the Pennsy branch's classes, some, such as stenography, typewriting, and practical arithmetic, were intended for professional development, while others, including Bible study and music, were for personal enrichment. The YMCA reported, "opportunity is thus afforded any P.R.R. man or his sons to improve themselves intellectually, increase their value and their income." By 1898, the Pennsy branch's class enrollments and membership were second only to the work of the Central branch. Rehabilitation was part of the railroad branches' educational mission too. The B&O branch offered vocational classes that were adapted for workers who lost limbs "in service of the road." In 1893, two injured trainmen made "considerable progress in stenography," which enabled them to "take positions peculiarly adapted to their disabled condition."[45]

The Apprentice School, a partnership between the Baltimore YMCA and the railroad companies, was the most significant educational offering of the railroad branches. Opened in 1911 with 133 young men enrolled, the Apprentice School met in the wee hours of the morning at the YMCA's West branch to instruct railroad apprentices in technical work. Historian Daniel Nelson suggests that to satisfy their need for trained workers, railroads reformed the apprenticeship system to provide a steady supply of thoroughly trained employees, many of whom would ultimately assume managerial positions. The B&O and Pennsy were among several railroads that contracted with the YMCA to teach the academic portion of this important though short-lived program.[46]

Between 1910 and 1920, railroad branch membership increased dramatically. In 1916, a national recruitment campaign resulted in local membership exceeding 1,400, while the total national railroad membership increased by more than 30,000. In 1919, another national membership drive netted 1,012 new members for the B&O branch and 2,001 for the Pennsylvania branch. The military's needs changed the organization of railroad YMCAs, including extending operations to twenty-four hours a day and introducing full restaurant service.[47]

Nationally, expanded recreation and health programming helped railroad membership to peak in the 1920s. It was then typical for a railroad branch to offer bowling, golf, swimming, horseshoe pitching, dances, fishing clubs, glee clubs, orchestras, tennis, gun clubs, hiking, garden clubs, and volleyball, appealing to a wide cross section of railroad employees.[48]

From the beginning, with the notable exceptions of race and gender, the railroad branches were inclusive.[49] In 1895, the Pennsy branch declared that all railroad men were welcome "regardless of POSITION, OCCUPATION, CREED OR RELIGION." Because the B&O branch's rooms at Riverside and Camden Station were so close to the roundhouse and yards, "a large number of men in overalls, coming direct from their trains and work" participated in programs. Attending YMCA activities in work clothes was considered by association leaders to be of "immense practical service to the men" and encouraged the attendance of a variety of railroad men. Although every department of railroad service was represented, many of the Pennsy branch's members were shopmen and clerks in their twenties and thirties. Nearly a third were trainmen or freight and passenger employees. Members belonged to eleven different religious denominations.[50]

By 1930, when railroad branches nationwide became racially inclusive, allowing "no ban of race, position, or creed," YMCAs were hailed by supporters as "the greatest single welfare agency for railroad men in the world." Many observers described the railroad work as the YMCA's most successful effort to establish contact with laborers, as "men of all languages and faiths" were "found in the swelling ranks of this brotherhood."[51] By then, many who had been boys or young men when they joined the railroads as workers (and the railroad YMCA as members) had become railroad officials all over the country: "To many of these men the . . . Railroad Association is what his alma mater is to the graduate of a college or university."[52]

Just as the railroad branches peaked, some met their demise. The effects of the Great Depression caused the Baltimore railroad branches' membership to shrink to 851 in 1932, "the smallest at any time in recent history." In January 1933, the Pennsylvania Railroad Company, itself in dire straits, withdrew its appropriation. The Pennsy branch closed after forty-three years of service.[53] The B&O branch weathered the depression.[54]

Nationally, the Great Depression and changes in railroading, including fewer division points, halved the number of railroad associations.[55] In addition, aging physical plants and changes in American culture largely eclipsed the need for, and attraction of, railroad YMCAs.[56] Yet the legacy of the YMCA within the railroad's corporate culture lingered in monthly prayer services that grew out of discussions between the railroad's agent and workers in the 1930s where it was deemed proper "to ask God's blessing on our undertakings."[57]

By the 1890s, the success of the YMCA's activities for railroad workers spurred other industrial leaders to consider corporate welfare partnerships with the YMCA. In 1892, for example, the Canton Company, an early industrial complex in East Baltimore, wanted "some Christianizing influence at work in its neighborhood and among its employees" and was prepared "to appropriate considerable money to support such work." Meanwhile, the YMCA's leaders, themselves concerned with the spiritual life of industrial workers, wished to increase their programming at industrial sites. Railroad men aside, there were few workingmen among YMCA members, because "not many men who worked all day with their hands

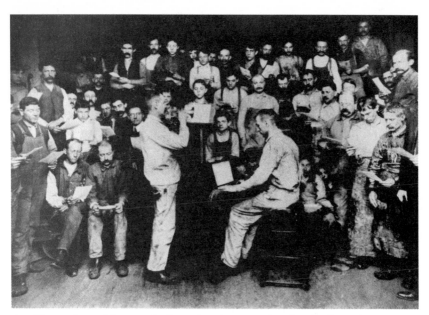

11. To reach workingmen in factories, the YMCA offered religious services at work sites. These shop meetings were the single biggest category of religious work done by the YMCA in the early 1900s. Pictured here is a 1906 shop meeting in a furniture factory conducted by Baltimore's Central YMCA. YMCA Collection, University of Baltimore Archives.

would be likely to care for exercise in the gymnasium." There were some workingmen who participated in the evening classes, but "none were engaged in the distinctively religious work of the Association."[58]

In response, the YMCA devised shop meetings, religious services held under the auspices of the YMCA at work sites, an attempt to augment the role of spirituality in the lives of workingmen while helping corporations to offer a Christianizing environment. Mainly gospel services, shop meetings occasionally featured health and educational talks. Their popularity spread quickly. They were the single biggest category of religious work done by the YMCA in the early 1900s. Some of the shop meetings were led by ministers who volunteered weekly to ensure "the mid-week contact of church people with the great group of industrial men."[59]

Firms participating in YMCA-sanctioned shop meetings ranged from the Maryland Workshop for the Blind, to the McCormick Spice Company, the Detrick and Harvey Machine Company, Carnegie Steel, B&O offices, the Mt. Vernon Mills, the Maryland Biscuit Company, the Bagvy Furniture Company, Evans Marble Works, and Swindell Glass Works.[60] In 1919, shop meetings, "limited only by the number of men and the amount of money available," peaked when they were held at 33 work sites in Baltimore with an annual attendance of 72,250.[61]

The YMCA celebrated the religious content of industrial work: "[T]he fact that special religious meetings have been carried on with the cooperation of industrial leaders and proprietors is the best evidence of the recognized value of the industrial program." In 1925, the YMCA declared that its interest in shop meetings and other religious programming for industrial workers was interpreting "the friendly interest of the church in the lives of men everywhere [which] by its very nature helps to establish mutual understanding, friendly intercourse and unselfish service as part of the daily routine."[62]

Although YMCA shop meetings were intended for industrial workers, managers found spiritual solace there, too. In 1922, H. D. Bush, head of Carnegie Steel in Baltimore and a member of the YMCA's Education Committee, planned his funeral: "I want my funeral services held in the lunch rooms of the shop. The YMCA Secretary who has been talking here is to have charge of my funeral. The song leader is to lead the singing. Select a good hymn. Mr. Whitely can have the room cleaned. The tables ought to be scrubbed."[63] That a high-ranking corporate executive favored the religiosity and company of the YMCA over that of a denominational church is quite remarkable.

Like the railroad branches, the industrial work soon featured recreational programs. YMCA leaders recognized that "if individuals and society are ever to become Christian they will not do so apart from the usual experiences of life. It is in experiences indicant to play and work that attitudes are formed and decisions made. That is the essence of character development."[64] Games at the noon hour became a mainstay of the YMCA industrial work.

After World War I, the YMCA's industrial work was retooled and professionalized. In 1919, the YMCA hired a full-time physical director to develop recreational work in factories and to supervise Saturday afternoon athletic contests at industrial sites. By so doing, the Sabbatarian YMCA "practically eliminated the desire for Sunday baseball by filling Saturday afternoon with supervised athletic sports."[65] That year, the YMCA also hired two secretaries to "devote all their time to developing work in the big industries." F. C. Downs was the new industrial secretary, and L. O. Waters focused on Americanization work, which included finding foreign-born men "who can be taught English, and the meaning of American citizenship. It is a big job, but full of promise and practical results."[66]

The professionalization of industrial work allowed the industrial secretaries to lead a threefold ministry of social, religious, and recreational activities. Initially, thirty-two plants in the Baltimore area were involved, through which 433 foreign students studied English; 40,000 men attended shop meetings; 22,000 men went to social events; and almost 15,000 athletes and onlookers participated in athletic contests involving more than six score corporate teams competing in indoor and outdoor volleyball and baseball. Many workers, like those employed by Hutchinson Brothers, enjoyed the YMCA's on-site athletics. To show their appreciation, Hutchinson Brothers' workers presented the YMCA's director of industrial work with a full set of bathroom fixtures they had made for him.[67]

At its peak in the 1920s, the YMCA's industrial work reached about 20 percent of Baltimore's workers through activities at nearly fifty different industrial sites, most of which were in South Baltimore and the Canton district. In half of these plants, the YMCA's full industrial program was supervised by trained YMCA industrial secretaries.[68]

In 1929, the Baltimore YMCA's industrial work came to include merchant marines when it took over the administration and ownership of the Anchorage, formerly a mission for seamen located at the foot of Broadway in Fell's Point in East Baltimore.[69] The depression severely strained the YMCA's ability to provide relief to needy seamen. In 1934, the relief work there was so big that the Anchorage's Committee of Management leased part of the building to the Federal Relief Administration, Bureau of Transients, and handed them complete responsibility for housing seamen on relief.[70]

In the period from the 1870s through the 1930s, the Baltimore YMCA showed considerable flexibility and alacrity in conceiving and designing services for the city's new industrial proletariat. The YMCA was both "pushed" and "pulled" into its industrial work. Criticism leveled at the churches and the YMCA for their perceived neglect of the needs and interests of workers provided the push. The YMCA's elastic mission was the pull. YMCA leaders, in concert with workers and managers, found common ground in working to impress a structure of spiritual meaning and an improved corporate culture on Baltimore's increasingly industrialized landscape. While this plunge into corporate welfare brought with it a host of challenges—maintaining a delicate coalition between management and labor, dealing with rapidly changing worksites and workforces, adapting and creating programs to meet the needs of transient industrial workers—it also demonstrated the Baltimore YMCA's willingness to broaden its constituency and adapt to changing needs.

7

"Hurry Up and Become Proficient"

The YMCA Schools, 1883–1934

Work, proclaimed Baltimore mayor James H. Preston in 1915, was the "great redeeming trait in human nature." "An industrious nature," he argued, when combined with Christian character was the best way "to fight the devil." A longtime YMCA member and supporter, Preston affirmed the association's ability to train workers and thus shape the civic landscape. In his view, the YMCA and its nonsectarian programs provided the city's young men "a body in which every one who believes may follow in the footsteps of the Master."[1]

Preston equated the YMCA's efforts to educate young men with the critical role he saw playgrounds and recreation programs playing in citizen building and "Divine uplift." The YMCA, in his view, occupied "a unique place in our national, state, and civic life." It was so important to making productive citizens that for Preston there was "no better influence in the community . . . [no] more valuable asset to the municipality of Baltimore than the work that is now being done by Mr. Morriss." A Democrat, Preston reported that "progressive municipalities" were deeply interested in an individual's civic, moral, and religious training, recognizing their "infinite bearing upon the future of the individual citizen" and the "vast influence" they had "upon the aggregate citizenship of the community."[2]

Many YMCA leaders had long shared Preston's commitment to the nobility of work. Religious concerns and modern philanthropic impulses spurred YMCA leaders both black and white to construct an educational and training apparatus to provide ambitious and able men of limited means broad access to civic and commercial authority based on ability and achievement. Believing in the YMCA's potential as an incubator for civic and commercial leadership, they designed and instituted courses reflecting the growth of new technology and the burgeoning of a managerial class. Through its educational offerings, the YMCA became a critical factor in the making of a meritocracy in Baltimore.[3]

By creating educational and training opportunities for working-class and other young men, the YMCA provided a respectable route to civic and commercial leadership based on ability and achievement rather than on accidents of birth.[4] The YMCA schools (and the certificates and diplomas they granted) authenticated the attainments of thousands of otherwise ordinary men and women. This was possible by the 1880s because institutionally the YMCA had gained the attention and approval of both a local and a national audience. Through its schools, the YMCA passed on its institutional authority and legitimacy to thousands of individuals eager to rise in the world.[5]

Self-improvement was an early goal of the YMCA's classes. The vitality of the association's Chatauqua Literary and Scientific Circle (CLSC), which enabled its members to "resume the studies which they were compelled to relinquish when the 'stern reality' was forced upon them," was the germ for a modern education program. Rooted in the classics, the CLSC was often chaired by faculty members from the Johns Hopkins University (JHU) and featured subjects such as Greek, Roman, English, and American history, as well as botany.[6]

By the early 1880s, the white YMCA offered a wider range of courses. Some, like foreign languages, music, and the CLSC offerings, enhanced general knowledge, while others, such as elocution and phonography ("one of the most important and useful acquisitions in this busy nineteenth century"), more directly influenced a young man's employability and earning capacity, reflecting the concern of the YMCA's Committee on Evening Classes: "How to convey . . . knowledge to others, how to assist those who have, in their earlier days, been bereft of the means or opportunity of pursuing their studies . . . advantages which are absolutely necessary in this age of reason, of energy and of close competition. It therefore devolves upon our philanthropic institutions to supply the means, whereby they may be gained at a comparatively small cost."[7]

During the 1880s, education programs were being established by YMCAs nationwide. In 1886, associations in Boston, New York, Brooklyn, and Philadelphia each registered about 1,000 men for their fall classes. Baltimore's enrollment was much smaller. Secretary William H. Morriss, desiring to expand his association's schools, recommended that "special effort be made to secure desks and proper fittings for class rooms, also competent teachers in practical branches of study."[8] Leaders of the Baltimore YMCA saw their niche as providing training for those short on privilege but long on ambition: "That we may furnish to the young man of limited means and opportunities some measure of what his more fortunate brother has at the college and university, general culture as well as direct instruction." The YMCA offered vocational training and more, "for the genius of the YMCA demands broader work, a culture of mind as well as body and spirit, that will fit the young man to adorn whatever station he may be called to occupy."[9]

According to historian Joseph Kett, vocational education at the YMCA "arose without the benefit of advertising and directly in response to the aspirations of its members." It had "job improvement" as its fundamental motive. Although Americans had long aspired to better jobs, not until the 1880s was vocational education identified as a significant avenue of advancement.[10] And the YMCA responded quickly to the demand for vocational training. It is not surprising, therefore, that the most heavily enrolled courses were those designed to improve job prospects. A class in telegraphy was among the white YMCA's first efforts to provide professional training. It met in a specially outfitted room that had wire connections from the Central YMCA to other downtown buildings.[11]

Nationally, the number of stenographers, typists, bookkeepers, cashiers, and accountants ballooned between 1870 and 1900.[12] The YMCA provided the training that enabled many of Baltimore's aspiring young white men to gain access to these new professions and to the middle-class respectability that accompanied them. In 1894, the chairman of the YMCA's Educational Committee reported: "Many of the future leaders of business may be studying in our classes, and it is to the interest of the city and should be desired by every lover of our city that these young men should have good training."[13]

Women, too, were clerical workers. Historian Angel Kwolek-Folland argues that office work became increasingly feminized as more women became clerical workers. Between 1870 and 1930, women's involvement in the clerical workforce increased from less than 2.5 percent to almost 53 percent nationally.[14] Historian Margery Davies reports that women stenographers and typists were extremely plentiful, constituting 40 percent of the field in 1880, 75 percent in 1900, and 95 percent nationwide by 1930.[15] Still, the Baltimore YMCA trained mostly men, and for many years, despite the growing employment of women (trained presumably at the YWCA, among other places), demand for male stenographers in Baltimore exceeded supply. As a result, many men enrolled in the YMCA's stenography classes.[16]

Meanwhile, as Baltimore's managerial sector grew, YMCA leaders recognized that although on-the-job-training was still possible, it was increasingly desirable for young men to master some fundamentals of business before commencing employment. Association leaders contended that "business men are not made in school rooms, but in office, store, or [ex]'change." What was needed for success was "a plain and rapid handwriting, speed and accuracy at figuring, an acquaintance with the principles that underlie business transactions, and the recording of the same." The YMCA school could better prepare a man for his future, as "all these things a young man may obtain before actively entering business pursuits. *They may be taught in school.*"[17]

Desiring to reach many young men, the Baltimore YMCA regularly added new courses to its curriculum, claiming that "where there is any evidence of a real demand for a branch of study, it is our purpose to meet the demand." In 1888, classes in mechanical drawing and civil service were added. The latter ran six months, with units in history, geography, commercial arithmetic, and English grammar, including letter writing, taught by a civil service examiner.[18] Typewriting was a new YMCA course in 1889.[19] Beginning in 1890, the YMCA offered a class in American history, in the hopes that it would "awaken interest in branches a little out of the line of the utilitarian studies hitherto pursued." Influenced by JHU's curriculum, YMCA leaders believed that history, literature, political economy, and "kindred studies" could "wisely be added to the Association curriculum." Meanwhile, JHU faculty considered their students' involvement as YMCA teachers "the most successful educational experiments by Johns Hopkins men."[20]

In 1893, the Central YMCA's course offerings were divided into three divisions, each comprising a two-year sequence of classes. The commercial course included bookkeeping, penmanship, and arithmetic; the technical course included mechanical drawing, phonography, and typewriting; and the language course included German and French.[21] Courses in civil government and American politics were soon added. In 1894, the YMCA's formal educational offerings were dubbed the Evening Institute. Admission was open to any young man at the instructor's discretion.[22] Students came from a variety of vocations. In 1895, 169 clerks, 35 office men, 36 full-time students, 45 mechanics, 48 general tradesmen, and 9 professional men constituted the 342–member student body. Although it was possible to take single classes in subjects such as arithmetic and writing, increasingly the YMCA suggested gaining competence by enrolling in a multiyear series of courses that required attendance at classes three evenings each week for as long as three years.[23]

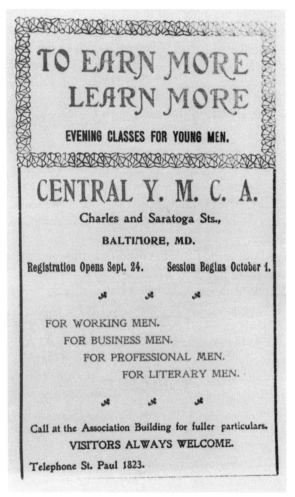

TO EARN MORE LEARN MORE

EVENING CLASSES FOR YOUNG MEN.

CENTRAL Y. M. C. A.

Charles and Saratoga Sts.,

BALTIMORE, MD.

Registration Opens Sept. 24.   Session Begins October 1.

FOR WORKING MEN.
FOR BUSINESS MEN.
FOR PROFESSIONAL MEN.
FOR LITERARY MEN.

Call at the Association Building for fuller particulars.
VISITORS ALWAYS WELCOME.

Telephone St. Paul 1823.

12. Titled "To Earn More, Learn More," this 1900 Education Committee pamphlet reflects the fact that many YMCA students pursued courses to increase their salaries. The committee sponsoring the classes included Herbert B. Adams of Johns Hopkins University. YMCA Collection, University of Baltimore Archives.

In May 1895, the Evening Institute granted its first certificates, five to men in the commercial course, and two others in stenography and typewriting. The next year, six certificates were granted in the commercial course, and three in civil government and American politics. In 1897, there were sixteen graduates, all but one in the commercial course.[24]

Despite the plethora of course offerings, the largest number of students pursued those with the most direct bearing upon job advancement and increased salaries. According to the YMCA, "It is natural that among a class so largely made up, as our membership is, of those who are earning their own living, the desire to qualify for an advanced position in business should be very strong." At first, penmanship was the most popular course offered, with 120 students enrolled. Soon, bookkeeping and civil service rivaled its popularity.[25]

New York oil tycoon and philanthropist Charles Pratt boosted the work of YMCA schools by providing for a national secretary to give his entire time to the work of encouraging and directing Education Departments of associations nationwide. As a result, in 1896 Baltimore's Evening Institute adopted syllabi arranged by the International Committee of the YMCA, a development celebrated by local leaders: "A standard approved by the best educators in this country has been adopted . . . all certificates and awards given to students will be for work that measures up to this international uniform standard." Students benefited from affiliation with the YMCA's International Committee because it gave local YMCA educational work national recognition and portability. By 1898, more than fifty colleges around the country accepted YMCA diplomas in lieu of examination in particular areas of study.[26]

As the content, sequencing, and portability of the Central YMCA's educational offerings were systematized, the branches experimented with formal education.[27] To avoid duplication and to improve quality, the YMCA rationalized all of its class offerings. Individual branches modified courses to reflect local conditions. As early as 1892, for example, the Pennsylvania Railroad branch discontinued classes in penmanship and mechanical drawing, citing financial trouble and the fact that members preferred Central's better and more plentiful offerings. In 1897, the B&O branch closed an isolated classroom at Camden Station because of its location and inferior equipment. That year, the YMCA transferred the mechanical drawing class from Central to the West branch, the locale designated by the YMCA for classes designed to benefit trades apprentices and young men involved in mechanical pursuits. The West branch YMCA then discontinued commercial classes and focused exclusively on technical ones, beginning with a thrice-weekly class in mechanical and architectural drawing.[28] The Druid Hill Avenue YMCA featured an educational program for African-American members with courses in English, first aid, physiology, and Bible studies. Its night school for workingmen had 18 men enrolled in 1905, twice the number of the previous year.[29]

Regardless of venue, well-equipped classrooms and competent teachers were critical to attracting and retaining young scholars. Without them, students in the YMCA's classes cut short their tenure. In 1884, for example, the Baltimore YMCA reported a drop in enrollment due "wholly to the irregularity of teachers and this irregularity is accounted for by our inability to pay a respectable compensation to instructors."[30] By 1887, the YMCA's leaders bolstered the position of the Education Department by securing the best rooms at Central for class work, hiring qualified teachers, and enrolling 430 different students.[31]

The case of elocution classes proves the importance of dynamic, motivated instructors. Public speaking was a part of the YMCA's offerings from the 1880s; its popularity exploded when Dale Carnegie began teaching in 1913. According to the YMCA, public speaking was a "manly art" that gave one "confidence in himself and grants to the possessor equipoise among all classes of people. In this way you may capitalize on the art of Public Speaking as a business proposition." Carnegie first offered a class called "The Commercial and Professional Value of Public Speaking" and soon added a class in salesmanship entitled "Sales Training and Personality." He commuted from New York City each week to conduct the Baltimore course, just one of his six weekly night classes at six different YMCAs along the East Coast. His tenure in the Baltimore YMCA extended through the late 1920s, with an average class enrollment of 50 students per course.[32]

Despite the popularity of instructors like Carnegie, business realities often curtailed class attendance. In October and November 1888, for example, average class attendance was 76 percent. However, with the approach of the Christmas season and the night hours required of clerks, class attendance fell almost 20 percent. Many students dropped out before the end of the term "because of business demands and not lack of interest." In hopes of improving attendance, the association required students to make a deposit upon entering a course. It would be refunded at the term's end if the student attended 75 percent of the class meetings. Encouraging good attendance was critical to the YMCA's mission: "Nothing we can teach him will be of more service to a young man than habits of industry and perseverance."[33]

Enhanced employability remained the most tangible benefit of training at the YMCA's Evening Institute. Better positions were often secured through the YMCA's Employment Bureau or through instructors' business contacts. As early as 1885, the YMCA received a testimonial from a gratified student of phonography, who reported that the lessons, with an hour's study each day for two months, and the influence of his "excellent instructor" had enabled him to secure a position as a stenographer. In

1888, another satisfied student reported that phonography instruction "has been the means, together with your valuable assistance, of securing me a position in one of the best firms of this city as a stenographer." In 1892, a policeman, the father of a young man who gained employment through the YMCA, testified that it was "the best institution in our city for helping young men":

> My boy went to the Charles Street Building some time ago to learn Stenography and Typewriting; after making satisfactory progress for several months, a business firm made application for a young man as a typewriter in their office . . . my boy . . . was accepted and began work for $16 a month and was not long in their employ before they raised him to $50 a month. In December he was taken sick, and was away from the office a month or longer, at the end of which time, they sent him a check for his month's salary, with a request for him to go South and they would pay his expenses. That is what the YMCA has done for *my boy*.

As different career options were recognized by its leaders, the YMCA mobilized to provide appropriate training. Association work itself became a profession, as reflected in the creation of a YMCA Training Center in Baltimore in 1914, offering beginning and advanced courses to those who wished to become association workers. Even fiction writing was professionalizing. A course in short story writing, taught by magazine fiction writers, began in 1919 on the premise that it too could improve students' personal marketability: "Short story writing is a remunerative avocation in which teachers, ministers, clerks and society people may like to engage. The demand for worth-while stories, moving picture scenarios and articles is increasing." In all trades, the YMCA urged its members to "Hurry up and become proficient . . . good places await you."[34]

In 1920, a twenty-year-old streetcar conductor, who "did not expect to be a conductor all his days," visited the Baltimore YMCA for vocational advice. Through the association's Employment Bureau he secured a new position as a stock clerk in a wholesale paper house, with the chance to "learn the stock and trade and then go on the road." After deliberations and despite a salary cut of more than 50 percent (from $15 to $7 weekly), he took the new job and enrolled in the YMCA's night school. In ten months, he was on the road and advancing within the company. Within two years, he became the firm's number two man, drawing an annual salary of $5,000. For his success he credited "the minister who brought him to the YMCA and the organization itself."[35]

Keeping its educational offerings inexpensive was critical. Not only did affordability give the YMCA a competitive advantage over more expensive proprietary business schools, YMCA leaders were mainly concerned with covering costs rather than making a profit: "The YMCA is . . . in business to . . . help young men, that is, helping young men to help themselves."[36] Classes were an important form of self-help:

> The men who study in these classes are not compelled by their parents to attend the Institute, but are Eager for Self-Improvement, and take their leisure moments to equip themselves for higher and better service. Ambitious, energetic and self-reliant, the Association meets these young fellows at the place of their greatest need and provides for them opportunities that will open a world known only to the student, and from which, by no fault of their own, they are now shut out.[37]

For many students, affordability was critical. The Evening Institute, according to alumnus J. Edmund Schueler, filled "the long-felt want of many young men whose ambition is greater than their purse." In six weeks, Schueler's courses at the YMCA allowed him to get a job as a bookkeeper. By the term's end, he secured an even better position keeping the books of six different businesses. A shorthand class alumnus reported: "the heart of many a lad whose sensibilities were being blunted by the roar of machinery at a time when he should have been yet at school, will throb with unwonted gratitude towards the management of the Y.M.C.A. for affording him an opportunity for retrieving that which in his early years was neglected."[38]

The downside of affordable prices was a shortfall of revenue for the YMCA. Often the Evening Institute's income did not cover expenses. In 1900, for example, the institute's work on behalf of 327 students exceeded by $700 what the young men themselves paid. But, the YMCA's leaders claimed (and their personal philanthropy attested), the benefits to society were worth the investment, as it would be "quite impossible to secure such results from such expenditure in any other institution."[39]

Although personal benefactors eased the YMCA's burden, they did not solve the financial problem. The YMCA looked to the business community for patronage to expand the educational work: "There are no doubt hundreds of men thrown on their own resources early in life and forced to work hard all day, who would gladly avail themselves of these evening classes and thus secure the benefits of such practical studies." As early as 1886, the YMCA created a special fund for educational work, "so that teachers and appointments in such departments as Free Hand Drawing, Bookkeeping, Penmanship, etc. . . . can be permanently secured." When general pleas failed, the YMCA attempted to instill a kinship between their students and business leaders: "If the business men of Baltimore, many of whom have struggled up from just such conditions as many of our students are now in, could come into closer contact with our work, and appreciate what it means in the moral and economic welfare of the city, we should not have to wonder whether we are to have the $100 worth of electrical apparatus so sadly needed." Realizing they might woo industrial and mercantile supporters by catering to workplace needs, in 1895 the YMCA's Education Committee spent the summer canvassing the large manufacturers and mercantile houses "with a view of learning the educational needs of the men employed and the possibility of meeting the same."[40]

To meet the needs of industry, in 1911 the YMCA inaugurated the Apprentice School at the West branch, where 133 B&O Railroad employees "were entrusted to the Association for instruction for technical work." By 1916, local businesses engaged in employer-sponsored tuition remission programs at the YMCA schools. As late as 1920, the YMCA initiated a course in foremanship after several firms expressed interest.[41]

The growth of other schools, public and private, affected enrollments in the YMCA schools. In 1895, for example, matriculation in YMCA technical classes fell off when Baltimore Polytechnic Institute, a public high school created to train engineers, relocated near Central.[42] Sometimes, though, the Evening Institute augmented offerings elsewhere. For example, in 1899 a YMCA student reported that because he was also enrolled at Baltimore City College (another public high school for white boys), he had not yet been able to bring to practical use his training in stenography and looked to the YMCA to provide that opportunity.[43]

The YMCA schools attracted many students who realized their need for a better education only after they had "reached an age when they are not willing to attend the free city schools." In 1897, the YMCA cited its crowded classrooms as "prima facie evidence that this field is not otherwise occupied, and that we meet an existing demand; also, that the public schools do not furnish the same facilities." According to YMCA statistics, public night schools reached only 20 percent of the nation's boys and young men, yet "the best Association educational work is carried on in cities where free public night schools are conducted." The YMCA's "upbuilding of young men" resulted.[44]

"Christian influence" suffused the classes, which were designed to attract new members who might become practicing Christians. Although most students opportunistically used the YMCA for a single program, for some the association proved spiritually important:[45] "I have attended the German and penmanship classes during the winter, and have experienced much good from them. I joined the Y.M.C.A. for the benefit of the classes, taking a two dollar ticket as an associate. I have been so well pleased that when I renew my ticket it will be a six dollar one, and as I have joined a church, it will be active also."[46] Phonography lessons enabled another student to take a synopsis of his pastor's sermons.[47]

Despite their evangelizing impulses, YMCA leaders opened the Evening Institute to all white men (and during World War I and again during the Great Depression, women too) regardless of faith. A young man did not have to be a Christian to attend YMCA schools: "Because he is not a Christian he is none the less welcome. His personal rights in the way of opinion or belief are never encroached upon."[48]

Christian concern and market demand motivated YMCA leaders to extend educational programs to younger scholars. Until 1895, matriculation in the Evening Institute required a minimum age of sixteen. In response to increasing interest from younger scholars, the YMCA began an evening preparatory division designed for boys under sixteen as well as for "young men who have grown rusty in the common school branches." Classes met two evenings a week. The YMCA invited employers to "send us your office boy. We think we can put some improvements on him that will not be out of place. We will be interested in the boy."[49] The continued employment of child laborers in Baltimore caused the YMCA's leaders to redouble their educational efforts on behalf of boys:

> So long as such a large proportion of boys are forced into the ranks of the wage-earners at 14 years of age, so long will the Christian Church be expected to see that these boys and young men have a fair chance in evening schools to equip themselves for their life work. Nor is the city night school an adequate solution of this problem. Young men at this age need a sympathetic hand, and a chance themselves to elect the studies that will best fit them for their fight with the world.[50]

In 1914, through the Franklin Day School, the YMCA initiated a day division, offering boys and young men courses in commerce, stenography, and academic subjects. Pitching itself to "Backward Boys," "Ambitious Boys," and "Boys Who Want to Prepare for Business or College," the Franklin Day School became an important facet of the YMCA's educational work, growing from 48 to 237 students in a year. In 1916, a state examination accepted its standards for professional schools' entrance examinations.[51] In 1918, again in response to child labor, the YMCA created the Employed Boys' Night Grammar School, which catered to boys ten to thirteen years old. "So long as the majority of boys are compelled to leave school before they have adequate education, organizations such as ours, with easily adaptable programs, must render supplementary service."[52]

In addition to boys, the YMCA began serving Baltimore's burgeoning foreign-born population, which numbered 77,043 by 1910. Classes in Americanization and English for foreigners constituted much of the YMCA's work among immigrants. In 1908, the YMCA began extension work with foreign-born young men "carried on in neighborhoods where the largest number of such men live or work." YMCA representatives met boats and welcomed new immigrants to Baltimore while assisting those going farther afield. By 1911, work with foreigners was such an important part of the Baltimore YMCA's operations that an industrial secretary was added to "promote work among foreign-speaking men and study the industrial problems incident to a large manufacturing city." In service to the YMCA and as a way of gaining experience working with immigrants, JHU students taught English to foreign-born men. Enrollment of non-English-speaking men in YMCA English classes was 214 in 1914 alone.[53]

In 1915, the YMCA began offering "Naturalization," a course to teach immigrant men the fundamentals of American history, civics, and English in preparation for the citizenship examination. Of all the YMCA's course offerings, only "Naturalization" and "English for Foreigners" were available to nonmembers.[54] After World War I, the YMCA hired new staff to run a special section of Industrial Work, which included a basic English course and lectures on the meaning of American citizenship: "It is a big job, but full of promise and practical results."[55]

Recognizing the limitations of its facilities and income, the YMCA didn't see itself as a college ("we leave that to the 'Hopkins'") until 1914. Until then, the YMCA schools were appropriate "if a man wants to know how something in business is done, how some mechanical work is done, how drawing is done, some language, or some science; busy all day earning his living; here is his school in the evening: a good one."[56] But, in response to the needs of modern business practice, and YMCA leaders' perceptions of the increasing importance of college training, in 1908 YMCA leaders created a professional accounting curriculum at the Baltimore YMCA's Accountancy Institute (later called the Baltimore School of Commerce and in 1914 the Baltimore College of Commerce [BCC]). BCC offered instruction in professional accountancy (CPA), business administration, fundamentals of accountancy, cost accounting, and law for businessmen. "The man who is trained for these positions," claimed the YMCA, "does not have to worry about a position and salaries. Business firms worry about getting and holding him."[57]

BCC's enrollment increased steadily, going from 237 students in 1913 to 306 in 1915. Courses in business administration, accountancy, and banking and finance were offered with the three-year course in accountancy being the most popular major. YMCA leaders believed that BCC would be "of equal rank with the Wharton School at the University of Pennsylvania and the schools of Commerce at New York, Boston and Chicago." It had the backing of a "large number of the wealthiest employers of the city."[58] In 1915, the State of Maryland gave BCC authority to grant the Bachelor of Commercial Science (BCS) degree, only the second time an American YMCA earned that privilege. In 1920, the YMCA conferred its first six BCS degrees on students who completed the four-year course in accountancy, business administration, real estate, advertising and salesmanship, banking and finance, foreign trade, or teaching commercial subjects.[59]

The accountancy course at BCC was one of two from which standards were created for use in other YMCA night schools nationally. Those who taught accountancy for the Baltimore YMCA were "leading accountants, lawyers, and professors of economics. . . . If one cannot learn from them, then he must indeed be hopeless." Success in accountancy was measured in the increase of students' annual salaries measured against tuition payments. In 1918, "dividends from 25 to 300 per cent have been obtained on the original [tuition] investment."[60]

The onset of World War I had a great impact on the YMCA course offerings and the makeup of its student body. The federal government's employment of hundreds of cost accountants for the war coupled with "necessity" created increased opportunities for BCC's accounting graduates to work for manufacturers "who had no adequate systems to install cost accounting systems to obtain correct data for fixing the prices of their products." In the postwar period, world manufacturers used accountants to modernize their business operations, a fact the YMCA used as a springboard for selling accountancy classes to students with business aspirations: "In the colossal readjustment which will be made the Accountant must play a big part. . . . Already, every man in our courses beyond the first year has obtained a better position or larger salary as a result of his knowledge. The future is golden with opportunities." The implementation of a federal income tax also spurred the need for accountants. According to the YMCA, "Some of those men who hesitated a few years about taking up this study now realize that they made a big mistake by not enrolling then. They would be occupying good positions today."[61]

In addition, in 1918, as a result of the war effort's personnel needs and the federal government's urging, the YMCA's Education Department offered both men and women intensive training in typewriting and stenography, promising: "the demand from Government officials and business men for typists enables us to guarantee a position to everyone who completes the course. Young girls, 17 or 18 years old, who have never worked before are able after five weeks' training to secure positions paying at least $95 a month. Such opportunities were undreamed of a few years ago." These classes began in 1918 under the auspices of the YMCA's Franklin Day School. Several hundred YWCA members were among the women who matriculated to take advantage of stenographic, typewriting, and civil service training. During the 1918–19 school year, 718 students enrolled in courses related to the war effort, and 539 graduated.[62]

Other more traditional YMCA classes were retooled for the war effort. The YMCA's telegraphy programs received commendation from the Department of Commerce's Navigation Service, whose officers recommended the YMCA Radio School, because "without exception" its graduates had "passed the examinations conducted in this office for radio operator's licenses." The school, they reported, was "thoroughly equipped with radio apparatus for practical demonstration purposes," and the teachers were "men of ability, capable of making the students familiar with the technical phase of radio."[63]

In 1918, the YMCA also created an Evening Technical School with course offerings such as plan reading for shipbuilders, and physics, chemistry, and electricity laboratories. Instructors were men employed in the steel and shipbuilding plants. The war's end, coupled with the need for reconstructing building operations and manufacturers curtailed by the war, generated great interest in the evening technical classes, particularly in structural engineering and mechanical drafting.[64]

In 1920, enrollment in the YMCA schools peaked with more than 2,100 students in day and evening classes, ranging from remedial elementary school courses to advanced professional and technical ones. (In 1920, the YMCA initiated an Evening Law School that offered "law courses for personal and business needs. Exceptionally strong faculty.")[65] Among the five YMCA schools (the College of Commerce, Franklin Day School,

Evening High School, Commercial School, and the YMCA School of Law), there were 69 teachers and receipts were $61,462.[66]

Enrollment in the Baltimore YMCA schools started slipping in 1921 when the YMCA National War Work Council rescinded free tuition offers for some veterans. That same year, the Baltimore association excluded women students.[67] Meanwhile, the city's Public Improvement Commission undertook an extensive survey of the public schools, resulting in $7 million of improvements and an enhanced reputation. Despite falling enrollments, leaders of the YMCA schools still innovated. For example, Taylorism and scientific management were recognized by the YMCA educational programs as important new concepts and a course in "Efficiency" was offered.[68]

Still enrollment fell. By 1925, total matriculation in all five YMCA schools was down to 746 students. The establishment that year of the University of Baltimore with its co-ed Law and Business Schools hurt enrollment as did the 1928 founding of an accounting program operated by the Strayer, Bryant and Stratton College, a proprietary business school.[69]

The falling enrollment troubled YMCA leaders, calling into question the efficacy of their self-help agenda and their obligation to serve. In 1924, the YMCA reported that only half of American boys finished elementary school, while 10 percent graduated from high school, and just one in a hundred graduated from a college or university. In the field of adult education, the association saw itself as a pioneer. Its leaders worried that if they could not help young men "equip themselves so as to take their rightful place in the community, bear family responsibilities and develop their largest capacities" then they were "failing" in their "largest field of usefulness."[70]

The onset of the Great Depression forced the streamlining of the Baltimore YMCA's educational offerings. The Men's Elementary School closed in 1932, and the Evening High School met its demise in 1934.[71] Although competition from the public schools forced the YMCA out of its Evening High School niche, concomitantly the YMCA started a summer school in 1933 to replace the public schools' discontinued summer program. The summer school effort alone buoyed the YMCA's educational enrollment in 1933 to 1,073 students, a quarter of whom were women.[72]

Overall, the depression had "a stimulating effect" on the YMCA's educational work because, due to lack of jobs, "Young men and young women have turned with a deeper interest to the practical aspects of education." Enrollment in the Baltimore YMCA schools (as in schools across the country) increased by 10 percent in 1934. It was not depressed business conditions alone that increased enrollment. The re-inclusion of women and lowered fees helped as well.[73]

During the 1930s, BCC attracted high school and college graduates.[74] Its mission was "to provide business education of the college level to young men and women who were employed by day, of limited financial means, and whose prospects could be improved by the training." In the view of many of its students, BCC was "uniquely successful in its mission. The students were devoted to it and to their personal objectives. Many became highly successful in their professional work and developed into real leaders in accounting and financial fields."[75]

Without the infusion of energy, interest, and enrollment generated by the Great Depression, the YMCA might have retreated from the educational arena. Instead, the depression revived a community need for streamlined YMCA schools to provide affordable and high-quality training for men and women, a legacy that lasted until 1973.[76] The schools, like the YMCA, aimed to "help people to help themselves; to assist them in becoming self-reliant, self-supporting, Christian citizens, prepared for and desirous of contributing to the advancement of a better world order." Their courses emphasized "business" because they recognized that "the vast majority of our students will ultimately earn their livelihood in the field of business and that a stabilized social order is predicated upon economic security."[77]

In developing a multifaceted educational apparatus to train men (and sometimes women) at a variety of economic and skill levels, the YMCA did more than simply celebrate an emerging culture of merit, mobility, and professionalism. It helped to reconstruct these concepts and to reshape the social order predicated thereon. With its emphasis on serving the educational needs of ambitious men of even meager means, with its enthusiastic embrace of new technologies such as the typewriter and the telegraph, and with an awareness of the importance of other new institutions such as the civil service system, the YMCA opened new paths to commercial and civic authority, power, and leadership for a broad range of people. Through its educational programs, the YMCA became a critical force in the democratization of commercial and civic opportunity in Baltimore.

Beginning in the 1880s, then, the Baltimore YMCA helped to create a merit-based social order increasingly predicated on training and ability rather than on family privilege. A logical outgrowth of the American penchant for associationalism identified by Alexis de Tocqueville in the

1830s, the YMCA's educational programs and facilities were schools for democracy.[78] They were literally, in the words of Sara Evans and Harry Boyte, "free spaces" where generations of Baltimore's civic leaders participated in political discourse that would shape the city for much of the twentieth century. Through them, ordinary people became "participants in the complex, ambitious, engaging conversation about democracy." The YMCA schools succeeded as places that fostered "new opportunities for self-definition, for the development of public and leadership skills, for a new confidence in the possibilities of participation, and for wider mapping of the connections between the movement members and other groups and institutions."[79]

8

"The Art of Living with Others"

The YMCA as Homemaker and Caretaker, 1908–1933

Associational life appealed to young men of the urban middle class and those aspiring to become middle class because, according to historian Howard Chudacoff, it helped young men adrift to compensate "for their social isolation." Membership in groups such as the YMCA framed bachelorhood, "a period in which single men were torn between a desire for independence, which often involved release from family restraints and obligations on the one hand, and a need for social interaction along with the emotion and financial support that, on the other hand kinship could provide." The interest of YMCA leaders (themselves married men) in working with young bachelors reflects an American reverence and dependence on the family "as the chief institution for promoting citizenship and social order."[1] In an effort to prevent young, unattached men from being marginalized as outcasts by living in rooming houses and other settings outside the family, YMCA leaders established their organization to serve *in loco parentis*, with an interesting gendered twist whereby men consciously and deliberately nurtured and made homes for other men.

The culmination of YMCA bachelorhood-framing activities occurred early in the twentieth century as the YMCA itself literally began making homes while continuing its campaign of moral stewardship especially in the area of father-son relationships. For some young men, the Baltimore YMCA became a "near total institution" as a result of these endeavors coupled with the association's ongoing vocational, educational, athletic, and spiritual initiatives.[2] In its actions, if not always in its rhetoric, the YMCA developed as a contender for the roles and functions served by established institutions such as the Protestant churches and schools and portended the purpose of corporate welfare programs. This chapter explores the YMCA's efforts to fill a void in critical urban services of homemaking and caretaking.

13. The desire to provide housing was a major impetus for building a new Central Building. The Baltimore YMCA's new Central, at Franklin and Cathedral Streets, opened in 1908 and featured 124 dormitory rooms on three floors. YMCA Collection, University of Baltimore Archives.

In response both to the demise of idealized boardinghouses and to the economic opportunity provided by the increasing popularity of lodging (or rooming) houses, the Baltimore YMCA's leaders zealously embraced homemaking as they planned for the second Central Building, which opened in 1908 and featured 124 dormitory rooms. In addition to expanded facilities, the new building, unlike the original Central, featured three full floors of residential rooms and excluded street-level commercial space, thus allowing the building to be "entirely devoted to the purposes of the Association." By then, dorm rooms in YMCA buildings had "come to be recognized as one of the most practical features that can be incorporated in an Association building." Nationally, nearly all other post-1895 YMCA buildings featured dorm rooms, and "the universal verdict is that they wish they had more."[3]

In Baltimore, the YMCA's first foray into housing was at the railroad branches. In 1893, with the introduction of sleeping bunks for trainmen on layovers, the YMCA initiated a new kind of housing at its Pennsylvania Railroad branch. The provision of housing attracted new members and generated new revenue.[4] That homemaking generated income caused no discomfort. YMCA leaders were unconcerned with the stricture of a pious home rightfully existing outside the marketplace.

Central's dorms, located on the fifth, sixth, and seventh floors of the building at Franklin and Cathedral Streets, were "an ideal place for young men to room." They were "not intended for old men," nor were they "designed for 'the down and out class,' but for young men with a purpose in life." The dorms were to provide a running start to ambitious young men of modest means. The YMCA went so far as to say that young men of independent means were ineligible to use the dorms: "The Dormitory rooms are for young men earning their own livelihood on a salary basis." The rooms (at least in the estimation of the YMCA promoters) were attractive and desirable: "No better place in Baltimore for a young man to live. Café open all the winter. Think of bachelor quarters—furnished to meet a man's notion of comfort and located right in a great building with Shower Baths, plenty of hot water, excellent service. Then add the finest Swimming Pool in the city and a great Gymnasium down stairs."[5]

The dorms proved quickly popular with middle-class men who became resident members of the YMCA. The dormitory at Central was in such great demand that in 1914 the House Committee doubled up some of the single rooms to accommodate more men at lower rates, making the YMCA a more attractive option to younger men with smaller salaries. The 124 rooms held 145 beds. Of the 700 men served annually, about 300 stayed at least a month. The rest were short-term transients.[6] Commenting on the "practical character" of Central's dormitory, in 1916 the YMCA reported that the rooms were "100 percent efficient. . . . there is never a time when there is not a waiting list. This is a practical form of service to young men and at the same time a paying investment of the Association." An increase in density continued. In 1931, most of the dorm rooms at

14. These 1908 photos show the homelike qualities of the new Central YMCA's dorm rooms. The top photo shows an occupied room, the bottom a room awaiting young men. YMCA Collection, University of Baltimore Archives.

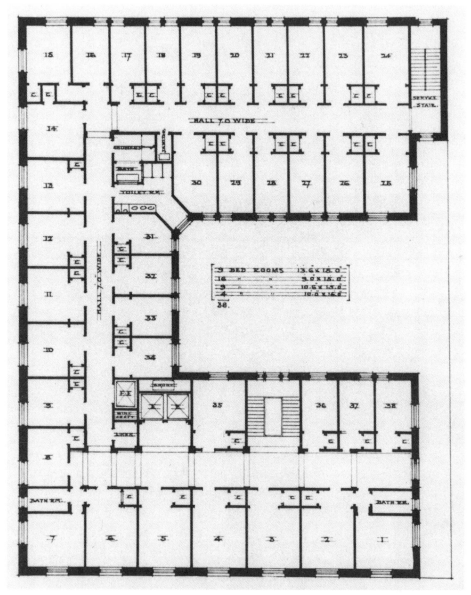

15. Central's fifth, sixth, and seventh floors contained single and double dormitory rooms, communal showers, and toilets. The rooms were both lodgings for young men and a source of income for the YMCA. YMCA Collection, University of Baltimore Archives.

Central had been doubled to house 225 men at one time, men who were "establishing their first contacts in the city." Rent was paid weekly.[7]

The presence of the myriad resident members enhanced the "home atmosphere of the Association building" and minimized the "institutional feeling" so dangerous in such a large building. The resident members "brought a strong group of men available for volunteer workers into the building and . . . [threw] safeguards around many a man in the time of his need."[8] Even the restaurant provided an "added attraction of the home atmosphere."[9]

Secretary William H. Morriss spoke for many YMCA leaders when he reported that dormitory life was "one of the greatest services that men cooperatively can render to each other." The rooms at Central had dual functions. They were "permanent lodgings for young men who are regularly employed in this city." In addition, they were "the endowment feature of the building, and every room means two things—a source of income to aid in maintaining the work and a pleasant congenial home for some young man."[10] In 1915, total receipts for the Central branch were $84,484, of which $23,679 was dorm rents. The Druid Hill Avenue YMCA, sponsored by Julius Rosenwald, was also designed with housing. It opened in 1919 with a dorm capacity of 71 young men in 52 rooms. So successful was the revenue-generating capacity of these dorms that in 1920, when association leaders contemplated erecting a building largely devoted to boys' work to make "as fine a contribution as could be made to the moral and religious welfare of our city," by including three or four floors for dormitories, they imagined that "the expense of maintenance would be largely solved."[11]

The demand from young men for housing far exceeded the YMCA's own supply. As a result, the association continued to provide referrals elsewhere. In 1919, for example, the YMCA housed 125,000 soldiers, 95,000 in Central's dorm and an annex next door; 25,000 more on cots in Central and the annex; and another 5,000 in the Mt. Vernon Methodist Church several blocks away. In 1923, the YMCA placed 4,406 men into approved boardinghouses. Three years later, the YMCA referred 2,766 men elsewhere because its own facilities were full. During the depression, the number of men referred to approved rooms and lodgings increased to nearly 8,000 annually. The YMCA communicated with all places where men could be lodged and prided itself on never turning any man away to walk the streets.[12]

Through federal census data and the YMCA's own records, it is possible to create a snapshot of the men who lived at Baltimore's Central

YMCA in 1910 and again in 1920.[13] In addition, through the personal reminiscences of long-term residents, a portrait of Central in the 1930s emerges. The vast majority of residents were American (by birthplace and parental nativity).[14] Most were single.[15] Although a sizable minority were Maryland born, men came to the YMCA from a range of places.[16]

The average age of the YMCA's residents was thirty-two in 1910 and twenty-eight in 1920.[17] Most residents were in their twenties. Men in their thirties were also an important age cohort. There were small groups of men in their forties, fifties, and sixties, but their relative importance declined from 14 to 5 percent of the total resident population by 1920.[18]

The occupational profile of the YMCA residents is revealing. In 1910 and 1920, the five most popular occupations were sales, engineering, accounting, clerking, and being a student. In 1910, these five occupations involved 44 percent of the YMCA's residents; and in 1920, 52 percent. Very few of the YMCA's residents were manual laborers. Most held semi-skilled or skilled jobs, the majority of which were white collar. The fields in which these men worked were, like the jobs they held, relatively consistent from 1910 to 1920. Both years, the top three employers were the government (local, state, and federal), factories, and schools. In 1910, these three fields employed 22 percent of the residents, while in 1920, 30 percent were employed by them. Certain changes can be seen, however. For example, in 1910 there were no YMCA residents involved in the nascent auto industry, but by 1920, reflecting the increasing popularity of the automobile industry nationally, 7 percent of Central's residents were thus engaged. The relative importance of the construction and banking industries also increased during these years, while the percentage of men involved in wholesaling declined by 50 percent.[19]

Although replicating an idealized Christian family life was important to the YMCA's leaders, most residents had no formal church connection. In 1913, only 89 of Central's 504 different occupants (less than 18 percent) were members of Protestant churches, perhaps revealing the ongoing struggle between the organizers' intentions to lead men to church affiliation, and the fact that the YMCA itself offered a comforting religious presence that for many men appears to have sufficed.[20]

While the average tenure of YMCA residents is not known, a majority of men for whom information is available (thirteen of twenty-one) were bachelors who left the YMCA's dorm between 1913 and 1916 for marriage. Others left for work and school. Some left for military service in World War I.[21] Only two men appeared as YMCA residents in both the 1910 and 1920 census. Howard Cassard, a widower, was a chemist with a drug company. Harry Hanscher was single and a pressman with a printing office. Both men were native-born Marylanders, and both were over the age of fifty in 1910. Unlike the younger men, for Cassard and Hanscher the YMCA was a permanent and final home.

The reminiscences of men who lived at Central in the 1930s help to reveal the experience of YMCA life. In 1938, Paul Noble, a native of Maryland's Eastern Shore, followed in his older brother's footsteps by moving to Baltimore and living at the Central YMCA.[22] A high school graduate, Noble lived in the dorms for four years while attending Strayer's Business College. For him, life at Central was "like a home away from home." He participated in religious services with Pop Harvey, a retired minister. At Central, the Christian ideal "wasn't something you talked about or wore there on your sleeves. It was something you lived in your day to day activities." Noble left his home at Central to marry a women he had met at a rooftop dance at the YMCA.

In November 1939, nineteen-year-old Robert S. McCandliss of Los Angeles was offered, via telegram, a job as a clerk at Social Security in Baltimore for which he had qualified through a civil service test. McCandliss, a secretarial school graduate, traveled cross-country by train. In Baltimore, he rented a room at Central for $16 per month. His work at Social Security was tedious, but his coworkers included lots of other young people who had also relocated, "glad to be able to accept . . . a steady job and regular paychecks." Harold Claussen, McCandliss's roommate, from Newport, Kentucky, also worked as an evening clerk at Social Security. Each man earned $1,250 per year, which allowed them to take meals in cafes, cafeterias, and restaurants, eating to their "unstinted satisfaction for about $1.25 per day." Their wash was done by "numerous and cheap Chinese laundries nearby."[23]

McCandliss describes Central's accommodations as "spare but adequate. Our narrow room held two beds, . . . two dressers, and a lounge chair with reading lamp. There was no radio. A large walk-in closet met our storage needs. A wash basin was in the corner, but the floor's showers and toilets were at the end of the corridor." Life at Central was comfortable: "Beds were made and fresh towels delivered daily by the chambermaids, young black women supervised by an older one, all neatly dressed in white, starched uniforms." The YMCA's recreational facilities were available—swimming pool, gym, handball courts, workout rooms, as well as a large lounge with "over-stuffed chairs, reading tables, writing desks, and a piano."[24]

McCandliss developed a coterie of friends at the YMCA, including Joe

Hargreaves, a devout Catholic from Rhode Island, and Bob Byrd, "a South Carolinian with a thick southern accent and strong racial prejudices he made little effort to conceal." These young men eased their homesickness by doing things together. The city was new to them, and they often went out exploring. Sometimes they took the trolley to the end of the line, walked in the woods, and then got back on and rode back into town. Hargreaves often attended Mass in Baltimore's main cathedral, just across the street from the YMCA. Sometimes McCandliss went, too. Leisure-time activities included trips across the street to the main public library.[25]

The YMCA's professional staff took a personal interest in the residents' well-being, especially those who worked evenings and "had considerable time . . . during daytime hours." YMCA staffers helped evening workers form the Allstate Club, which met weekly for lunch and featured speakers such as Theodore McKeldin, Baltimore's mayor and Maryland's future governor. The Allstate Club also sponsored tours, which McCandliss and his friends augmented by organizing their own sight-seeing trips to other eastern cities.[26]

McCandliss's gang socialized with young women: "One of the most productive sources was a residence hall for young Catholic women located nearby. . . . Sponsored by an adjoining convent, its residents were able to come and go at will and also to entertain male visitors in the hall's parlor." In addition, the house mothers who oversaw the Catholic young women's hall "had no objection to liquor being served at parties . . . held there," which was not the case at dances sponsored at the YMCA (or for that matter, those held another block down Franklin Street at the YWCA).

McCandliss moved from Central after a year. He and two fellow YMCA residents (both former Pennsylvania coal miners) left for Loyola College, moving to a boardinghouse nearer campus, where Virginia Biggs provided them with breakfast and dinner for nine dollars per week. The three men attended college while working the afternoon shift at Social Security. McCandliss stayed in contact with friends at Central. For Thanksgiving, he persuaded his landlady to allow "five additional West Franklin orphans to join us for her feast."[27]

For long-term residents, the YMCA's housing provided an environment that was comfortable, nurturing, and spiritually infused.[28] For these residents, Central was a "home away from home" where friendship, safety, opportunity, and ritual were found. Reflecting back on his experience at the Central YMCA from a distance of more than half a century, McCandliss reported, "the Baltimore Y was a haven for me and many other young fellows who were drawn to the city in those days by the promise of a reliable sustenance and with the opportunity for personal development. I have always been grateful for the kind and insightful support we received from the Y's professional staff, and, in turn the entire community that supported the Y."[29]

Residents' recollections of the YMCA's housing initiatives suggest the need for a reexamination of the role of gender in homemaking and caretaking. Describing the work of Chicago's Eleanor Clubs (boardinghouses for women), for example, Lisa M. Fine writes that "in the midst of unsettling changes the leaders of the Eleanor Association created a home-like refuge . . . and perhaps functioned as surrogate mother figures." These residential clubs, she argues, "stood as a haven, or 'way station' between the security of family, home, and traditional values, and a changing new world." Fine's argument is based on the assumption that there was something distinctively feminine about the fact and function of homemaking. The experience of the men of the Baltimore YMCA suggests that this gender-based understanding of homemaking could just as well be extended to men.[30]

Assuming the experiences of Noble and McCandliss were typical, the YMCA's leaders proved themselves to be extremely competent and nurturing homemakers. And for many of the residents, it appears that the Central YMCA was a sort of way station between youth and marriage. Like the women residents of the Eleanor Clubs, the male residents of the YMCA "ultimately abandoned . . . an independent life for marriage." And, again, like Fine's women, it appears that these young men "did not do so unthinkingly."[31]

The Baltimore YMCA, in a sense, appropriated what historians have since identified as distinctively feminine elements of the experience and language of housing and melded it with unabashedly male characteristics and rhetoric:

I am a moulder of manhood.

I take boys and young men in the plastic impressionable period and enlighten them in the art of living—fit them for success by teaching them how to be clean, strong, efficient.

I am a trellis to which the tendrils of youth can cling in healthy, happy, well-ordered growth, avoiding snarls and tangles due to ignorance, idleness, neglect.

In an age notable for powerful allurements of the forces of evil, I constantly present virtue in its true attractiveness. I mix morality with mirth, flavor discipline with fun, and exalt always the glory of strength—physical, intellectual, spiritual. . . .

I am a grain of mustard seed which a man took and cast into his garden, and it grew and waxed a great tree, and the fowls of the air lodged in the branches of it.

I am at work in every land thoroughly equipped and organized for the service of young men and boys.

I am the Young Men's Christian Association.[32]

By reworking the gendered language of housing, the YMCA's leaders articulated a vision of the proper Christian home for urban America. The YMCA's program in moral stewardship cinched the YMCA's role as an institutional parent, a corporate "Father Knows Best" that supported nurturing activities in an idealized (if institutional) Christian home.

In addition to sheltering thousands of young men new to the city, the YMCA worked to enhance and define masculinity in the modern city by modeling what its leaders believed was desirable social, emotional, and political comportment of men as husbands and fathers. Unlike the housing initiative, these activities were geared primarily to local men and boys. Starting in 1910, the YMCA promoted the Father and Son movement, which culminated in an annual father and son banquet. Although YMCA leaders supported mothers as the "guardian angel of the daughter," they argued that the "protection of the son against the many perils of the city life primarily rests with the father." The Father and Son movement sought to persuade men to "lead the son with a firm hand through the days of boyhood, he ought to make a companion and a friend of him as he grows to manhood." Calling into question the ability of mothers to train sons about modern life, YMCA leaders claimed, "Infinite misery, and unhappiness are frequently caused by nothing else but the fact that the father neglects to gain the confidence of the son and thereby misses the opportune time to warn him against besetting dangers." The role of the annual banquet was to "bring about a sound family relationship, a community of interest, and strengthening of family ties to combat the perils of city life and appreciate its advantages, and will inculcate broader conceptions of good citizenship in the midst of the next generation."[33] The father and son banquet was popular, attracting more than 400 fathers and sons each year. It was the only event that compelled the YMCA to use its gymnasium as a banquet room.[34]

The YMCA expanded the father and son banquet into a citywide event. In 1918, the YMCA Boys' Department worked with churches to create twelve dinners in various parts of the city. The idea of "bringing fathers and sons together in this special manner is of inestimable service to all," reported the YMCA's chroniclers.[35] In 1919, the national YMCA planned a National Father and Son Week. In Baltimore, an enthusiastic committee of laymen and clergy promoted it throughout the city to churches, boys' organizations, men's clubs, and related agencies. The Baltimore YMCA maintained an information bureau that provided help in planning father-son dinners and church sermons. Baltimore mayor James H. Preston wholeheartedly endorsed the idea of National Father and Son Week, writing "I believe that no other influence is so helpful as that of the guiding hand of the father, and I believe this to be an interdependence, for the father's obligation to and love for the boy also elevates the father."[36]

The father and son programs fell under the Boys' Department of the YMCA and combined boys' work with issues of comportment and propriety,[37] "to bring to the attention of fathers a new and larger responsibility to their boys . . . [and] to challenge fathers and sons to realize as never before their joint relationship to the home, church, school, community, state, nation, and the world for a Christian Democracy."[38] The YMCA used a variety of approaches to reach boys, including a Business Boys' Bible Study Group, a Boys' Orchestra, formal schoolwork, and High "Y" Clubs, among others. Many boys and their parents attested to the success of the YMCA boys' work, especially in bridging the perennial generation gap. As one father, himself a minister, wrote about his relationship to his son: "We were estranged and did not even have the desire to understand each other. Your help has brought us together again and we are pals. If the YMCA never did another thing but this it has been worth all that it ever cost."[39]

Boys' work was a principal concern of the YMCA during the 1920s. More than 1,400 boys were members, and more than 2,600 participated in programs. The range of boys' work included "talks on vocational, cultural, and sex problems." By 1930, the YMCA offered sex education for young men and their parents. The father and son programs continued throughout the 1930s, and by 1933, recognizing that women would continue to nurture their sons, the YMCA introduced mother and son activities. The boys' program included "careful instruction in sex education for older boys and parents . . . as a natural part of the programs." A program in child psychology for parents of boys was embraced by the YMCA in

1930 so that the boys' work done there might be supplemented at home.[40] At the same time, the association's moral stewardship programs focused on "Marriage and the Home," by means of a lecture series dealing with "Sex and Marriage," "Psychology of Marriage," "The Legal Side of Marriage," and "Spiritual Factors of Marriage."[41]

YMCA leaders also developed their ability to intervene in times of crisis. By the 1920s, the YMCA's buildings were open around the clock. Often, boys who had "missed the way" were befriended by YMCA workers after Baltimore had "gone to bed." The YMCA's door never closed to youth, and its light never went out. As a result, about 500 young men, many of whom were runaways and thus at risk, were helped each year.[42]

Starting in 1908, when the YMCA literally began serving as homemaker, and continuing with the father and son initiative of 1910, for decades the paid and volunteer staff of the YMCA framed the bachelorhood of thousands of young men. Residents as well as civic and YMCA leaders lauded the housing initiative: "Probably no other service which the Association is rendering has such a high value as maintaining a home for young men in the heart of a great city where they can find wise counsel and a safe and economical place to live during their period of social and economic adjustment."[43] That this was done by men for men confounds the gendered idea of housing mores and manners. The YMCA's activities in both homemaking and caretaking blurred (or, more accurately, melded) the neat divisions of the prevailing rhetoric: "I constantly present virtue in its true attractiveness. I mix morality with mirth, flavor discipline with fun, and exalt always the glory of strength—physical, intellectual, spiritual."[44]

The YMCA's ability to rework the gender-based language of the domestic sphere underscores both the attraction and the shortcomings of gender as a category for historical analysis. Gender alone is not a sufficient tool to understand a complex organization like the YMCA. Given the spaces that the YMCA sought to occupy, and the realms it sought to claim (and reclaim), the YMCA and its plethora of programs in religion, education, vocation, homemaking, and caretaking are better understood as a programmatically broad-based but single-mission institution that sought to bring young men to Jesus, or perhaps more aptly, worked to keep young men adrift from the modern city's immoral clutches. By repeatedly ignoring the gendered distinctions between the public and private spheres, the Baltimore YMCA leaders and members fundamentally reshaped public culture by focusing creative and corporate energy on the business of training men for "the art of living with others."[45]

Notes

Any unattributed *Annual Reports, Baltimore Men, Weekly Bulletin, Association Bulletin,* Survey Commission, YMCA Survey, Executive Minutes, or Minutes of the Board of Directors are publications of the Baltimore YMCA and are part of the Baltimore YMCA collection in the University of Baltimore Archives (UBA). Unless otherwise attributed, box, folder, and file numbers refer to these archives.

A Flexible Vessel: The Baltimore YMCA and Community Change

1. Fraser and Gerstle, eds., *The Rise and Fall of the New Deal Order, 1930–1980.*

2. According to Barry Karl and Stanley Katz, the Great Depression of the 1930s launched the federal government into areas previously dominated by private philanthropy and local government. Karl and Katz, "The American Private Philanthropic Foundation and the Public Sphere, 1890–1930."

Thoughtful work on these larger themes includes Hall, *Inventing the Nonprofit Sector*; Kaus, *The End of Equality*; Dawley, *Struggles for Justice*; and Sealander, *Private Wealth and Public Life.*

3. Putnam, "Bowling Alone."

4. The YMCA's leaders were very much a part of the Social Gospel and reflect themes discussed by Hopkins in *The Rise of the Social Gospel in America Protestantism*; and Carter, *The Decline and Revival of the Social Gospel,* among others.

5. The first two associations in North America were started in 1851 in Montreal and Boston. Hopkins, *History of the YMCA,* 3–8, 16.

6. For information on the adaptability of the Chicago YMCA, see Zald, *Organizational Change.*

7. Because of the Civil War, the building, located at Peirce and Schroeder Streets, was used as a YMCA for only a handful of years. It was then occupied by a series of churches. New Union Baptist Church, an African-American congregation, bought the building in 1931 and occupied it until the late 1960s, at which time the building was demolished to make way for Interstate 70 (which, incidentally, was never completed). *Baltimore Sun,* 22 January 1928, 2 December 1929.

The mission statement for the YMCA of Central Maryland currently reads: "The YMCA is dedicated to enriching the spiritual, mental, and physical well-being for all people in our community."

8. For another perspective on JHU's role within Baltimore, see Bender, *Intellect and Public Life,* 6, 42–43, 130.

9. See Crooks, *Politics and Progress*, 3–12.

10. Kemp, *Housing Conditions in Baltimore*.

11. 1919 *Annual Report*, 14; 1921 *Annual Report*, 7–8; 1922 *Annual Report*, 13.

12. Skocpol, "Unravelling from Above," 4.

13. Ibid., 11.

14. Hall, *Inventing the Nonprofit Sector*, 3. See also Dawley, *Struggles for Justice*; Hawley and Critchlow, eds., *Federal Social Policy in Modern America*.

15. As a result of the white flight of the 1950s and 1960s and the increasing availability and affordability of both city apartments and suburban housing, the character of the YMCA's housing programs changed considerably, becoming predominantly a provider of housing of last resort, a landlord for people down on their luck and without other housing options.

16. Salamon, *Partners in Public Service*, 11–12.

17. Lasch, *The Revolt of the Elites and the Betrayal of Democracy*, 7–8.

18. Olasky, *The Tragedy of American Compassion*, 222–27.

19. Peter Dobkin Hall reminds us that despite both Tocqueville romanticism and the rhetoric of conflict, in reality the majority of funds for nonprofit organizations have long come not from private donations but from government grants and contracts, public financing, and investment income. *Inventing the Nonprofit Sector*, 1.

1. The YMCA and Baltimore's Faith Community, 1858–1900

1. Williams, *Reminiscences of a Pastorate of Thirty-Three Years*, 6; 1854 *Annual Report*, 17.

2. Nancy Cott argues that as early as the mid-seventeenth century, women outnumbered men in the New England churches. What was new in the nineteenth century, according to Cott, was just how conspicuous the "feminization" of Protestantism had become. See Cott, *The Bonds of Womanhood*, 126–32.

3. Barbara Welter coined the term "feminization of religion" in "The Feminization of Religion in Nineteenth-Century America." For other examples of scholars concerned with the feminization of Protestantism, see Smith-Rosenberg, "The Cross and the Pedestal," in *Disorderly Conduct*, 129–64; Ryan, *Cradle of the Middle Class*, 60–144; Bederman, "'The Women Have Had Charge of the Church Work Long Enough'"; Douglas, *The Feminization of American Culture*.

4. *Baltimore American*, 21 October 1859; Wroth, "Churches and Religious Organizations in Baltimore," 678. For a good overview of Christianity in Baltimore in the period before 1850, see Bilhartz, *Urban Religion and the Second Great Awakening*.

5. Wilson, *The Life Story of Franklin Wilson as Told by Himself in His Journals*; 1854 *Annual Report*, 4–5; original notice for the formation of the YMCA of Baltimore, 12 November 1852 (emphasis in original), Wilson Papers, MS 833, Box 3, Maryland Historical Society, Baltimore (hereafter cited as MHS).

6. Only eight clergymen attended the meeting. In addition to Williams, John Chester Backus of First Presbyterian, Joseph T. Smith, D.D., of Second Presbyterian, John Henry Van Dyke of Christ Church, and the ministers from Westminster Presbyterian, First German Reformed, and Methodist Episcopal churches were present. 1854 *Annual Report*, 16–17.

In its early years, the YMCA distinguished between members of evangelical and non-evangelical churches, allowing only the former to be "active" members, while the latter were "associate" members. By 1869, as a reflection of its increased emphasis on nondenominationalism, the association removed this disparity in membership status, reasoning that if any young man was "willing to work with us in saving young men, and persuading them to give up their evil habits and associations, why not let them do so without stopping to inquire what their particular views are in regard to abstruse questions of theology or what theological teachings they believe in." 1869 *Annual Report*, 6.

7. Franklin Wilson. Original notice for the formation of the YMCA of Baltimore, 12 November 1852, Wilson Papers, MS 833, Box 3, MHS. See also Haltunnen, *Confidence Men and Painted Women*, esp. chap. 1.

8. 1854 *Annual Report*, 19–20.

9. 1921 *Annual Report*, 1–2.

10. 1854 *Annual Report*, 8, 19, 20.

11. Ibid., 3.

12. Excerpt from 1858 Constitution; 1858 *Annual Report*, 14.

13. 1857 *Annual Report*, 4.

14. Paul Boyer and Allan Stanley Horlick in their work on young men in the city have largely accepted the YMCA's rhetoric identifying itself as "auxiliary to the churches." The YMCA, however, did not represent a nostalgic form of middle-class social control borne of status anxiety and xenophobia, as Boyer and Horlick argue. The YMCA was instead a harbinger of American modernity that actually challenged the monopolistic role of the churches in the shaping of urban religiosity by presenting a masculine, nondenominational option separate and distinct from traditional congregations. Boyer, *Urban Masses and Moral Order in America*, 108–20; Horlick, *Country Boys and Merchant Princes*, 226–43.

15. 1858 *Annual Report*, 6.

16. 1857 *Annual Report*, 3. Earlier attempts at interdenominational work in Baltimore were short lived. 1854 *Annual Report*, 3; Steiner, "Maryland's Religious History," 12–13.

17. In 1854, Rev. William I. Hoge served on the YMCA's board and on its Committee on Publication, Rev. J.W.M. Williams was also a member of the board and served on the Committee on Lectures, and Rev. Franklin Wilson was the board's recording secretary and served on the Committee on Lectures. 1854 *Annual Report*, 4–5, 17; 1858 *Annual Report*, 18–19.

18. Bell, *Crusade in the City*.

19. 1858 *Annual Report*, 8–9. Several historians have claimed that the YMCAs

were "the chief motivating force and promotional agency of the nation-wide revivals" that followed the Panic of 1857. Hopkins, *History of the YMCA*, 45; Bremner, *The Public Good*, 11; Bell, *Crusade in the City*, 182–83.

20. Baltimore YMCA, "Mirror of the Festival," 24 May 1859, Box 74, Folder 5.

21. 1858 *Annual Report*, 3–4.

22. Baltimore YMCA, Notice, 19 April 1859, Box 7, File 1; "Mirror of the Festival," 24 May 1859, Box 74, Folder 5; Open Letter from J. Dean Smith, 1 July 1859, Box 7, File 1.

23. The leadership of the YMCA resolved "to take no part in any political question." Minutes of Board of Managers, 19 October 1854, Box 7, File 1.

Unlike the neutral stance of the YMCA, many of Baltimore's churches were Union or Confederate. For more information on sectional church ties, see Steiner, "Maryland's Religious History," 8, 18–19.

24. No records for the Baltimore YMCA survive for the period between May 1860 and 1866.

25. Cannon, "The United States Christian Commission"; Hopkins, *History of the YMCA*, 89–92.

26. 1859 *Annual Report*, 14; 1868 *Annual Report*, 3, 5, 22–23.

27. 1868 *Annual Report*, 6; 1869 *Annual Report*, 23; 1871 *Annual Report*, 7.

28. In 1868, the association leaders declared, "We have nothing in the world to do with sectional or political differences, and take no part." 1868 *Annual Report*; 1871 *Annual Report*, 5–6.

29. In 1877, the YMCA reported: "Our organization is one composed of Christian Workers, from the various denominations, banded together to work for 'The Master.' We hold to our respective churches, and consider our first duty belongs there, but in the many intermediate hours of leisure, we can find plenty of time to engage in YMCA work." *Weekly Bulletin,* 25 November 1877, Box 70.

30. "Mirror of the Festival," 24 May 1859, Box 74, Folder 5. When the Young Women's Christian Association (YWCA) was founded in Baltimore in 1883, its leaders wanted it to be visible in the city's churches. The YWCA's leaders, however, never called their work auxiliary to the churches. Instead, the YWCA proposed that interested churches could win the right to claim that they were auxiliary to the YWCA if at least a dozen women congregants declared interest in the YWCA's work. Although the YMCA used handmaiden rhetoric when discussing its relationship to the churches, it appears that association leaders saw the YMCA as an increasingly viable alternative to and not an auxiliary of the churches. Adams, "Work among Workingwomen in Baltimore," 6–7.

31. *Weekly Bulletin,* 25 November 1877, Box 70 (emphasis in original).

32. 1868 *Annual Report*, 4, 10.

33. In 1867, for example, twelve men went "out from the Association during the year to study for the Ministry." 1868 *Annual Report*, 5.

34. The hostility between some rabbis and Baltimore's Young Men's Hebrew Association (YMHA) was more overt and therefore instructive. Established in 1854, the Baltimore YMHA was the first YMHA founded in the United States, the inspiration coming, no doubt, from the successful model provided by the Baltimore YMCA. The YMHA engendered opposition from rabbis who saw it in direct competition for the loyalty and membership of young men. In 1870, for example, Rabbi David Philipson was amazed at another rabbi's opposition to Friday night YMHA meetings, explaining "all the preaching and reformed divine sermon on a sabbath will have very little effect on the young men, as they mostly never visit the temple on a sabbath, chained (as they are) to their stores and various offices." Years later, despite much enthusiasm from the Jewish community at large, Rabbi William Rosenau voiced opposition to the YMHA: "I am opposed to the formation of a [YMHA] in this city or anywhere else because these deflect the interests of young people from the synagogue." Letters of David Philipson, 24 January 1870; letter from Rosenau to William Levy, 15 January 1917, cited in Fein, *The Making of an American Jewish Community*, 132, 219.

35. Moore, *The Story of the Railroad "Y,"* 68–69, 137.

36. In 1868, members of the YMCA became involved in "Street and Park Preaching." Executive Committee Reports, 15 September 1868, Box 11, Folder 3; 1869 *Annual Report*.

37. In 1874, the YMCA's secretary commented that the open-air meetings would remain a program of the YMCA because both laymen and clergy saw them as being "of immediate importance" and something from which neither group could be absolved. Solving the problems endemic to this neighborhood required the cooperation of all concerned citizens. 1874 *Annual Report*, 7, 17; *Weekly Bulletin*, 2 December 1877, Box 70.

38. 1869 *Annual Report*, 10; 1871 *Annual Report*, 17.

39. Moody himself was part of the migration from farm to city. He arrived in Boston in 1854 and joined the YMCA soon after. Born in rural Massachusetts in 1837, Moody, a "nominal Unitarian" before his conversion to Congregationalism, joined the association for social rather than religious reasons. An aspiring merchant, in 1856 Moody moved to Chicago where he again joined the YMCA and soon became involved in its administration. After volunteering for the Christian Commission, Moody served as president of the Chicago YMCA. He earned a national reputation for his work in the YMCA and in the Sunday school movement. In 1870, Moody, a successful wholesaler and committed Christian, gave up his business enterprises and formal YMCA leadership to become a full-time evangelist, holding numerous revivals throughout Great Britain and the United States. Findlay, *Dwight L. Moody*, 46–47, 63, 92–118.

40. During his Baltimore revival, Moody attended many YMCA meetings and preached some 270 sermons, each with an average attendance of 1,500 to 1,800 men, at churches throughout the city. Beadenkopf and Stricklen, *Moody in Balti-*

more, 6; Findlay, *Dwight L. Moody*, 344; Garrett, "Address by John W. Garrett, Delivered on the 30th of January, 1883, before the YMCA of Baltimore on the Occasion of Their Thirtieth Anniversary"; Hopkins, *History of the YMCA*, 344.

According to his granddaughter, Emma Moody Fitt Powell, Moody settled in Baltimore in 1878–79 because his wife was expecting their third child in April 1879 and because he was invited to hold meetings. The time in Baltimore was "one of the happiest years of the Moody family records. . . . Will Moody [a son] says it became a second home to him and there was no city he ever visited where he was assured of a more cordial welcome." D. L. Moody Papers, Yale Divinity School, New Haven, Conn., Series 28, I, Box 8, Folder 98.

41. *Weekly Bulletin*, 2 December 1877, Box 70, 6–8; Beadenkopf and Stricklen, *Moody in Baltimore*, 27; Hopkins, *History of the YMCA*, 188.

42. Baltimore YMCA, 27 June 1879, Letter to Ministers from YMCA Committee, James Carey Thomas, Chairman, Box 7, File 1.

43. *Weekly Bulletin*, 18 June 1881.

44. 1921 *Annual Report*, 5–6.

2. The YMCA, Housing, and Moral Stewardship, 1858–1890

1. Blackmar, *Manhattan for Rent*, 113.

2. Ibid., 63, 129.

3. 1869 *Annual Report*, 20. Betsy Blackmar's study of New York housing in the period from 1800 to 1840 suggests that the feelings of New Yorkers presaged those of the Baltimore YMCA leaders by about thirty years, which is not surprising given the greater density of New York and earlier onset of housing shortages. *Manhattan for Rent*, 129.

4. 1869 *Annual Report*, 20.

5. Not all boardinghouses were desirable. Those in New York suffered censure from their association with sailors and wharf-district epidemics. Blackmar, *Manhattan for Rent*, 134.

6. Peel, "On the Margins," 814. For more information on the differences between lodgers and boarders, see Harris, "The End Justified the Means."

7. Wolfe, *The Lodging House Problem in Boston*, 1.

8. Ibid., 4–6.

9. Minutes, 4 March 1858, Box 7; 1868 *Annual Report*, 16; *Weekly Bulletin*, 6 May 1882, 3, Box 44.

10. Peel, "On the Margins," 814.

11. Although fictional, the novel is based on the experiences of a Mrs. Townsend, a women who served for many years as housekeeper of a boardinghouse for students at Johns Hopkins Medical School. Tucker, *Miss Susie Slagle's*, 15–16.

12. Ibid., 13–14, 23–24, 25.

13. 1874 *Annual Report*, 5.

14. Ibid.

15. 1883 *Annual Report*, 12–13 (emphasis in original).

16. 1885 *Annual Report*, 8.

17. By 1869, the News Boys' Home was incorporated as a separate organization. 1869 *Annual Report*, 26–27.

18. *Baltimore Men*, 5 November 1914; 1869 *Annual Report*, 25; 1868 *Annual Report*, 5–6.

19. In its first full year, the Friendly Inn furnished 14,015 meals and helped 291 men get jobs. In 1879, it gave away or subsidized more than 50,000 meals. That year, poor men slept in the 70 single beds nearly 19,000 times, 250 men took free baths, 63 men received clothing, 101 religious meetings were held, and 175 men got help finding employment. The Friendly Inn represented a major financial commitment for the YMCA. In 1877, total YMCA expenditures were $7,820, and the inn absorbed nearly 50 percent of that. Like the News Boys' Home, the Friendly Inn was short lived as a YMCA endeavor. 1883 *Annual Report*, 15–17; Minutes, Executive Committee, 12 January 1880; *Weekly Bulletin*, 11 November, 23 December 1877, Box 70.

20. *Weekly Bulletin*, 11 November, 23 December 1877, Box 70.

21. For more information on tramps in Baltimore, see Gould, "How Baltimore Banished Tramps and Helped the Idle," and Gould, "Transients and Tramps in July," 14–15.

22. Even during the Great Depression, the YMCA did not take on the hard-core destitute. In 1931, the YMCA provided several hundred men with clothing, and provided 6,000 free meals and 7,700 nights of sleeping accommodations. Still, the YMCA "cooperated closely with the established charitable agencies by referring all homeless men to them." 1931 *Annual Report*, 2.

23. Minutes, Board of Directors, 1 September 1896, Box 17.

24. Minutes, Board of Directors, 5 February 1895, Box 16.

25. Concern about social purity and illicit sexual relations led the Church of England, in 1883, to form the White Cross Society. Then, in 1885, under the auspices of the Episcopalian Church, the White Cross movement came to the United States when the first American branch was formed at New York's St. John the Evangelist Church. David Pivar reports that the general public received the White Cross Society favorably. The adoption of the White Cross Society by the YMCA resulted in spectacular membership gains for the White Cross. Pivar, *Purity Crusade*, 111, 189.

26. Epstein, *The Politics of Domesticity*, 126–27. See also Bordin, *Women and Temperance*.

27. "The Third Anniversary of the White Cross Society," *Philanthropist*, April 1887, 3.

28. Ibid.

29. Blaikie, "Personal Purity," 3.

30. 1890 *Annual Report*, 37.

31. By the turn of the century, membership was still strong at 432. 1887 *Annual Report*, 28; 1890 *Annual Report*, 37; 1891 *Annual Report*, 36.

32. Pivar, *Purity Crusade*, 188.

33. Blaikie, "Personal Purity," 4.

34. Pivar, *Purity Crusade*, 112–14.

35. Scully, *A Scarlet Pansy*. The issue of homosexuality in the YMCA is also addressed by Wrathall in *Take the Young Stranger by the Hand* and by Chauncey in "Christian Brotherhood or Sexual Perversion?"

36. 1885 *Annual Report*, 7–8.

3. Faith, Science, and YMCA Leaders, 1880–1920

1. Trachtenberg, *The Incorporation of America*; Chambers, *The Tyranny of Change*; Chandler, *The Visible Hand*; Mills, *White Collar*; Zunz, *Making America Corporate*.

2. Charles Sheldon's best-selling 1897 novel *In His Steps* presented a picture of what could happen in a community torn by social dissension if Christians would ask themselves at every moment, "What would Jesus do?" Noll, *A History of Christianity in the United States and Canada*, 305–7; White and Hopkins, *The Social Gospel*, xi–xii; Curtis, *A Consuming Faith*.

3. Baltimore YMCA, *YMCA News*, January 1940, William Morriss Obituary File, MHS.

4. Executive Committee Minutes, 30 June 1882, Box 8.

5. 1922 *Annual Report*, 1–2.

6. Abbott, *Religious Life in America*, 4.

7. 1921 *Annual Report*, 1–2.

8. Ibid.

9. Ibid.

10. Brown University Archives, Margaret Shove Morriss File, "Deaths"; Baltimore YMCA, *YMCA News*, January 1940, William Morriss Obituary File, MHS.

11. In 1893, having observed inadequate bathing facilities in the homes of his working-class parishioners, Thomas M. Beadenkopf, a Baltimore native, JHU graduate, and minister of the Canton Congregational Church in southeast Baltimore, asked Morriss, Thomas, and Levering to help secure permanent public baths. By 1898, the Free Public Bath Commission was lobbying for the establishment of year-round baths. Surprisingly, although reformers controlled the municipal government between 1895 and 1910, they were not responsive to the demands for municipal baths. Though rebuffed by the city government, the Bath Commission aroused the support of Henry Walters, son of a Baltimore merchant prince, who erected three indoor bathhouses. Williams, *Washing "The Great Unwashed,"* 110–13; Beadenkopf, "The Baltimore Public Baths and Their Founder, the Rev. Thomas M. Beadenkopf."

12. YWCA, 1915 *Annual Report*; Baltimore YMCA, *YMCA News*, January 1940, William Morriss Obituary File, MHS; *Baltimore Sun*, 15 March 1951.

13. An early and effective advocate of the view that society has a responsibility to enable women to use their education outside the home, Peggy Morriss also championed women's ability to accept leadership positions in society. She believed women would be happier if they did not confine themselves to the home. Women, she asserted, had a responsibility to use their education: "I don't think society is just in giving all this training to women if it's not going to be used," she said, echoing Jane Addams's famous lament, "After college, what?" Dr. Morriss was a member of the League of Women Voters and the Consumers' League. She served as national president of the American Association of University Women from 1937 to 1944. *Baltimore Sun*, 15 March, 5 August 1961; Baltimore YMCA, *YMCA News*, January 1940, William Morriss Obituary File, MHS; Mitchell, *Encyclopedia Brunoniana*, 396; Brown University Archives, Margaret Shove Morriss File, "Deaths."

14. Mary died in 1951. Peggy lived until 1975. *Baltimore Sun*, 15 March 1951, 5 August 1961; Baltimore YMCA, *YMCA News*, January 1940, William Morriss Obituary File, MHS; Mitchell, *Encyclopedia Brunoniana*, 396; Brown University Archives, Margaret Shove Morriss File, "Deaths."

15. Although outvoted, Thomas favored coeducation at JHU. Both he and his cousin Francis King, another YMCA leader, were also Bryn Mawr College trustees. Both men were won over to the higher education of women by their daughters. Flexner, *A Quaker Childhood*, 197; Flexner, *An American Saga*, 126, 148, 234.

16. While M. Carey Thomas was one of a group of celebrated women who founded Baltimore's Bryn Mawr School in the 1880s, Mary Whitall Thomas herself was also keenly interested in improving educational opportunities for girls. In the early 1870s, she established the "Friends School," which was short lived. Mary's father, John Whitall, sent $500 to meet the defunct school's debt, admonishing his daughter for stepping out of the "province of women." Flexner, *An American Saga*, 169; Dobkin, *The Making of a Feminist*, 310. For an in-depth biography of M. Carey Thomas, see Horowitz, *The Power and Passion of M. Carey Thomas*, esp. chaps. 1–5.

17. Flexner, *Abraham Flexner*, 59.

18. After the revival, Moody asked Mrs. Thomas to lead the women's activities at future meetings. Although she declined, she imagined gaining international fame by being part of the trilogy of "Moody, Sankey, and Thomas." (Ira Sankey was Moody's musical accompanist and an integral part of his team.) Letter from Mary W. Thomas to her daughter Helen, 3 July 1885, quoted in Flexner, *An American Saga*, 164–65.

19. Son Henry's wife, Zoe Carey Thomas, was a YWCA manager. Daughter Margaret C. Thomas was chairman of the YWCA's Northwestern branch and also served on the Library and Provident Savings Bank Committees. Daughter M. Carey helped found the Bryn Mawr Summer School for Women Workers, in which

the national YWCA was a major participant. Flexner, *A Quaker Childhood*, 107; 1892 *Annual Report*, 4, 6–7, 16; Horowitz, *The Power and Passion of M. Carey Thomas*, 434–35.

20. Flexner, *A Quaker Childhood*, 108–9.

21. *White Ribbon Herald*, Memorial Number . . . Mary Whitall Thomas, WCTU of Baltimore, 1888. Quoted in Flexner, *An American Saga*, 195. A Memorial Union for the Rescue of Homeless and Friendless Girls was founded in Mary Thomas's memory. Headquartered at, and auxiliary to, the WCTU, it worked to secure proper homes for girls new to Baltimore who lacked family and other support networks. The Memorial Union had six rooms in private homes throughout the city where girls were placed until suitable homes and work were found for them. Unlike the YWCA, the Memorial Union required no references for extended stays. *Directory of the Charitable and Beneficent Organizations of Baltimore and of Maryland*, 22.

22. Joshua Levering was actively involved in Baptist activities both locally and nationally. He was a member and Sunday school superintendent of the Eutaw Place Baptist Church. Later he was a founder of the University Baptist Church, near JHU's Homewood campus. He was vice president of the Foreign Mission Board of the Southern Baptist Convention and the American Baptist Publication Society, and president of the Southern Baptist Theological Seminary, then the largest theological school in the country. Beginning in 1898, Joshua Levering was president of the Maryland Baptist Union Association. He also served as president of the Southern Baptist General Convention. *Sunday American*, 6 October 1935; Steiner, *Men of Mark in Maryland*, 1:248–51.

23. Two of Joshua Levering's seven children became missionaries. *Baltimore Sun*, 6 October 1935; Steiner, *Men of Mark in Maryland*, 2:46–50.

24. Gould, in his study *The Housing of the Working People*, 401–2, argues that "the only lodging house that can bear comparison with those found in Great Britain, is that recently opened in Baltimore by the well known philanthropist, Mr. Eugene Levering." Gould goes on to describe the facility as a "workingman's residential club, where isolated sleeping apartments may be hired by the night or the week." Moderately priced meals and bath were available, and smoking, reading, and games were allowed, giving workingmen "most of the conveniences and accessories of a gentleman's ordinary club." Levering was hoping for a commercial return on his investment, which provided accommodations for eighty lodgers nightly.

25. French, *A History of the University Founded by Johns Hopkins*, 361; Steiner, *Men of Mark in Baltimore*, 1:248–51.

26. Beadenkopf, "The Baltimore Public Baths and Their Founder, the Rev. Thomas M. Beadenkopf."

27. Eugene Levering's involvement in the YMCA continued long after Levering Hall was built. In 1906, he led the YMCA's building campaign by raising $500,000 for the new Central Building, and before his death in 1928 he spearheaded the

fund-raising campaign that built a new Levering Hall on JHU's Homewood campus. Baltimore YMCA, *"Y" News*, 1928, Enoch Pratt Free Library (hereafter EPFL), Vertical File.

28. *Baltimore Sun*, 4 August 1928.

29. Ann Walker Levering, Joshua and Eugene's mother, served as first vice president of the YMCA's Ladies' Auxiliary for more than twenty-five years, and then as an honorary vice president for several years more. She was also involved in the YWCA from its beginning in 1883 and continuing for more than twenty years as a manager (and later honorary manager) and member of the Lunch and Lodging House Committees. Like her mother-in-law, Mrs. Joshua Levering also had ties to the YMCA's Ladies' Auxiliary, where she helped organize the 1886 Grand Bazaar, and to the YWCA, where by 1903 she had become a manager and a member of the Employment Bureau, Entertainment, Second Branch, and Nominating Committees.

30. His grandfather, Miles White, Sr., a Quaker, came to Baltimore from North Carolina in 1849, after amassing great wealth from real estate investments. He made more money in Baltimore real estate on which he built homes to let for the city's growing population. Miles Sr. was a stockholder and manager of Greenmount Cemetery and president of the Baltimore Cemetery. He also served as president of the People's Bank. In his will he left $100,000 to found the "Miles White Beneficial Society of Baltimore City," for the promotion of piety and Christianity.

Miles's son Francis (F. A.'s father), powerful in the financial world, became a major real estate owner in Baltimore. He had a "generous and thoughtful disposition," which resulted in a constant "waiting list of would-be tenants for his houses, wherever located, as people were always ready to move into one of his houses the very day it became vacant." Francis White was an original trustee of both JHU and the Johns Hopkins Hospital, having been appointed by Johns Hopkins himself. He was also an executor of Hopkins's will. Francis White was also a director of the National Farmers' and Planters' Bank, the Eutaw Savings Bank, the Safe Deposit and Trust Company, the Georges Creek Coal and Iron Company, and the Peabody Fire Insurance Company, and a manager of the Maryland State Insane Asylum, the Maryland Historical Society, and Haverford College. In 1904, the Francis White Chair of Greek was established at JHU and was first held by Basil Gildersleeve, who was an active member of Levering Hall. French, *A History of the University Founded by Johns Hopkins*, 146.

31. Three generations of Whites made generous financial contributions to the YMCA. Francis White was a major YMCA contributor, giving at least $100 a year, and gifts of $1,000 or $2,000 for special appeals. In his will he left $35,000 to a variety of charitable and religious purposes including the YMCA and YWCA, the Manual Labor School, Shelter of Aged and Infirm Colored Persons, Baltimore Eye, Ear, and Throat Hospital, Boys' Home Society, Home of the Friendless, Maryland Prisoners' Aid Association, Society for the Protection of Children from Cruelty

and Immorality, Union Protestant Home for the Incurable, the Friends, and Port Mission for Seamen.

The Miles White Beneficial Society also made annual contributions of $100 in the 1880s and 1890s. Francis A. White began contributing in 1889. By 1901, he was giving $200 annually. His brother, Miles White, Jr., was a modest YMCA benefactor. 1883 *Annual Report,* 23–30, 32; 1885 *Annual Report,* 26–27; 1886 *Annual Report,* 32–33; 1887 *Annual Report,* 34; 1889 *Annual Report,* 49; 1890 *Annual Report,* 53; 1893 *Annual Report,* 24; 1896 *Annual Report,* 34; 1900 *Annual Report,* 36; 1901 *Annual Report,* 49; 1906 *Annual Report,* 16.

32. 1887 *Annual Report,* 5; 1889 *Annual Report,* 3; 1892 *Annual Report,* 3; 1893 *Annual Report,* 3; 1898 *Annual Report,* 2; 1900 *Annual Report,* 28; 1922 *Annual Report,* 4.

33. Steiner, *Men of Mark in Maryland,* 408–9; *Baltimore Sun,* 20 February 1930.

34. Bremner, *The Discovery of Poverty in the United States,* 52–57; Trattner, *From Poor Law to Welfare State,* 86–97.

4. The YMCA and the Coming of Modern Philanthropy, 1880–1900

1. Bremner, *The Discovery of Poverty in the United States,* 124–25.

2. *Weekly Bulletin,* 8 April 1882, Box 70.

3. Ibid.

4. Letter from Eugene Levering to JHU Trustees, 1 May 1889, R.G. 13.030, Series 2, Box 1, Ferdinand Hamburger, Jr., Archives (hereafter JHU); Hawkins, *Pioneer,* 279.

The aims of the Levering Lectures were "the defence of the fundamental doctrines of Christianity," or "the promotion of an interest in Biblical studies," or "the promotion of Christian life by biological, historical, or ethical studies." These lectures were delivered annually from 1890 to 1900. JHU *Handbook,* 1903–4, 11, JHU.

5. Tucker, *It Happened at Hopkins,* 1.

6. French, *A History of the University Founded by Johns Hopkins,* 4–5, 7–8.

7. Butts and Cremin, *A History of Education in American Culture,* 392–93; Wheatley, *The Politics of Philanthropy,* 13–15.

8. Steiner, *Men of Mark in Maryland,* 1:156–59; and Flexner, *Daniel Coit Gilman,* 50–51, 54–55, 66, 82.

9. Daniel Gilman, quoted in Hawkins, *Pioneer,* 3, 21–23.

10. See Hawkins, "History and Political Economy," in *Pioneer,* 169–86.

11. Flexner, *Daniel Coit Gilman,* 50–51, 54–55, 66.

12. Bremner, *The Discovery of Poverty in the United States,* 46–47, 51, 52, 124.

13. Gilman first learned about COS work from an account he heard of the London COS at a meeting of the American Social Science Association. By the time the Baltimore COS was established, similar societies had already begun in Buffalo,

Boston, Brooklyn, and Philadelphia, and they served as models for the Baltimore group. Steiner, *Men of Mark in Maryland*, 1:156–59; Hirschfeld, *Baltimore, 1870–1900s*, 137–38.

14. Constitution of the COS (1885), in Hirschfeld, *Baltimore, 1870–1900*, 139–40.

15. Hirschfeld, *Baltimore, 1870–1900*, 135. It is interesting to note that Hirschfeld's work itself was published as part of the series Studies in Historical and Political Science under the direction of the Department of History, Political Economy, and Political Science.

16. This was a different Friendly Inn than the one begun in the 1870s by the YMCA and discussed in chap. 2.

17. In 1892, lodging or a meal cost fifteen cents, which could be paid by cash, chit, or work in the wood yard. Sawing and splitting four sticks bought a meal, ten sticks bought a lodging. *Directory of the Charitable and Beneficent Organizations of Baltimore and of Maryland*, 21.

18. Born in 1829, Glenn was a Baltimore native. With his wife, a Miss Smith, Glenn had two children. His daughter married Charles Biddle of Philadelphia. His son, John Glenn, Jr., served as a director of the Friendly Inn and the Maryland School for the Blind, and as a trustee for JHU, from which he graduated in 1885. He worked as a lawyer in the Baltimore law office of his cousin, John M. Glenn. Like his uncle, John M. Glenn was concerned with public affairs and scientific philanthropy. He left Baltimore and his law practice to become a managing director of the Russell Sage Foundation in New York, where he was responsible for its model housing program, Forest Hills Gardens. *Baltimore: Its History and Its People*, 3:735–36.

19. Hirschfeld, *Baltimore, 1870–1900*, 142.

20. According to the Maryland Bureau of Industrial Statistics, in December 1893, 10,000 men (11 percent of the labor force) were unemployed. A study of trade unionists in January 1894 showed that 38 percent were out of work, and the number of unemployed unskilled workers was undoubtedly higher. Crooks, *Politics and Progress*, 167. Hirschfeld estimated that 30,000 men or one-half of the labor force were unemployed during the worst months of the depression. Hirschfeld, *Baltimore, 1870–1900*, 54–55, 149.

The efforts of the COS affected public policy. The impulse to reform municipal charitable policy in Baltimore came after the election of 1895 when Mayor Alceaus Hooper appointed "a board of trustees of the Poor who believed in the principles of the COS," three of whom, including the president of the board, were COS managers. In addition, the COS surveyed the entire field of municipal charities. Their recommendations were incorporated into the city's 1898 Charter. Hirschfeld, *Baltimore, 1870–1900*, 151–54.

21. Watson, *The Charity Organization Movement in the United States*, 326–27.

22. In 1882, the COS had no volunteer visitors. Hirschfeld, *Baltimore, 1870–1900*, 141, 145.

The relationship between the YMCA, COS, and Hopkins was symbiotic. For example, the COS reported that a mother was worried about her fourteen-year-old son, Tommy, whom she had put out to work. As a messenger boy, Tommy was sent to dangerous places, and the mother feared the consequences. The COS sent a visitor, likely a JHU student, through whom Tommy secured a better position. The visitor called on Tommy and then had Tommy and his friends visit him. The mother thanked the COS for their efforts, reporting that the boys had become "all so much more self-respecting." She reported, too, that it was "their ambition" to save enough money to join the YMCA so that they could study in the evening. Baltimore Charity Organization Society, 1903 *Annual Report*, 23.

23. JHU YMCA, 1893–94 *Student Handbook*, 4, JHU; *New York Christian Advocate*, 18 April 1889.

24. Hawkins, *Pioneer*, 297.

25. Herbert Baxter Adams, Commemoration Address, 12 June 1890, as reported in 1890–91 *Student Handbook*, 4, JHU.

26. *New York Christian Advocate*, 18 April 1889.

27. Through his work with the Baltimore COS, Commons met John M. Glenn (John Glenn's nephew), who, as director of the Russell Sage Foundation, financed Commons's work on the Pittsburgh Survey, an aggressive effort in 1906–7 to document that city's abysmal environment and social services landscape. Commons, *Myself*, 42–43.

28. JHU YMCA, 1893–94 *Student Handbook*, 15–16, 38, JHU.

29. Ibid., 15–16, 38; 1894–95 *Student Handbook*, 23, JHU; and Letter from Dr. Marion Dexter Learned, Professor of German and President of Levering Hall, to Daniel Gilman, JHU President, 4 May 1890, MS 1, JHU.

30. Adams, Ely, and Remsen were all German-trained Ph.D.'s. Adams and Remsen were both at JHU when it opened in 1876, Adams in history, and Remsen in chemistry and physics. Marion Dexter Learned earned the first Ph.D. in German at JHU in 1887 and stayed on the faculty until 1895 when he went to the University of Pennsylvania. He served as president of Levering Hall for much of his time at JHU. Hawkins, *Pioneer*, 47–48, 162, 172–78, 279, 297.

31. French, *A History of the University Founded by Johns Hopkins*, 328.

32. Lawrence came to Baltimore in 1889 from Poughkeepsie, New York, where he had known and worked with William Morriss. In his condolence letter to Lawrence's mother, Morriss wrote "In September, 1875 [your son] and I commenced work together in Poughkeepsie, NY, he as pastor of the Congregational Church, and I as secretary of the [YMCA]. By a singular coincidence, we reached the city on the same day. . . . For seven years we worked side by side." Lawrence helped to found Poughkeepsie's COS. According to Morriss, "These were the early days of social economics, and a broad-minded and warm-hearted leader was needed, and Mr. Lawrence proved just the man to direct and control. Until the time

of his leaving Poughkeepsie, he was at the head of the Charity Organization." Morriss described Lawrence as "broad in his sympathies, catholic in spirit, every good enterprise appealed to him, and his hand and heart were always at the service of his fellows." When Lawrence moved to Baltimore, he and Morriss renewed their friendship and cooperated together through the COS, the JHU, and the YMCA, on behalf of social welfare work in the city. Letter from W. H. Morriss, in Margaret Woods Lawrence's detailed account of her son's work, *Reminiscences of the Life and Work of Edward A. Lawrence, Jr.*, 341–42; Adams, *The Church and Popular Education*, 61–67.

33. Lawrence, *Reminiscences of the Life and Work of Edward A. Lawrence, Jr.*, 347–50, 441–68; JHU YMCA, 1894–95 *Student Handbook*, 22–23; 1896–97 *Student Handbook*, 32, JHU; French, *A History of the University Founded by Johns Hopkins*, 327.

34. Lawrence, *Reminiscences of the Life and Work of Edward A. Lawrence, Jr.*, 441–68.

35. Dorothy Ross described the work of both Adams and Ely in terms of the model of historico-politics pioneered by Francis Lieber, which she described as the "foundation for most Gilded Age political science." Adams read Lieber as an undergraduate at Amherst and studied both political science and history in Germany. When Adams applied for a job at JHU, he wrote that he wanted to "pursue historical research and to contribute something to Political Science." Ross, *The Origins of American Social Science*, 64, 68.

The influence of the Scottish moral philosophy curriculum, adumbrating philosophy, history, political science, and economics can also be detected in the name selected and inquiries pursued by the JHU Department of History, Political Science, and Political Economy.

36. Ibid., 109–10.

37. Flexner, *Daniel Coit Gilman*, 74–75, 92, 94; Furner, *Advocacy and Objectivity*.

38. Letter from John Glenn to D. C. Gilman, 13 July 1888, Gilman Papers, MS 1, Ferdinand Hamburger, Jr., Archives, JHU.

39. Gilman, *Recollections of the Life of John Glenn*, 11.

40. Of the nearly 100 men that James Crooks identified as reform leaders in Baltimore, almost a quarter attended the arts and sciences portion of JHU either as undergraduate or graduate students and another quarter taught either at JHU or at the Hopkins medical school. Of these 50 men, more than half were at some point members of Levering Hall. Crooks, *Politics and Progress*, 202–3.

41. *Report of a Conference on Charities*.

42. Gilman, *Recollections of the Life of John Glenn*, 17.

43. Letter from John Glenn to D. C. Gilman, 31 May 1890, Gilman Papers, MS 1, Ferdinand Hamburger, Jr., Archives, JHU.

44. Whereas the trustees of the university had succeeded in opening JHU in 1876, less than three years after its benefactor's death, it took the hospital's trust-

ees until 1889 to make the hospital operational. A combination of falling stock prices (the majority of Hopkins's estate was in the form of B&O Railroad stock) and the trustees' commitment to upholding the proviso in Hopkins's will that required that buildings be paid for with interest income caused the delay. Tucker, *It Happened at Hopkins*, 3.

45. French, *A History of the University Founded by Johns Hopkins*, 4–8.

46. From the beginning, as a result of the terms of its original endowment, medical school admissions were ostensibly open equally to men and women. The medical school had its own endowment of more than $500,000, which was separate and distinct from both JHU and JHH. The endowment had begun in 1890 when committees of women in many American cities together contributed $111,000 to the medical school on condition that women be freely admitted. The terms were accepted by JHU. An additional gift of $200,000 for professorships was transferred to the medical school's endowment from JHH. Finally, Mary Elizabeth Garrett, the daughter of John Work Garrett, president of the B&O Railroad, was an extremely important benefactor, alone giving more than $300,000 to the endowment. JHU YMCA, 1893–94 *Student Handbook*, 6, JHU.

47. Clinical opportunities were supplied by JHH. In addition, the amphitheater and clinical laboratories were located at the hospital. Physiology was taught in the biology laboratory at JHU. JHU YMCA, 1893–94 *Student Handbook*, 6–7, JHU.

48. The medical school's YMCA offered social activities, a reading room in the administration building, housing assistance, religious meetings, Bible study, and "outside work," in which "a large number of men" participated in the work of the COS. French, *A History of the University Founded by Johns Hopkins*, 328; JHU YMCA, 1906–7 *Student Handbook*, 32–34, JHU.

49. Gilman, *Recollections of the Life of John Glenn*, 8.

50. Mencken, quoted in Flexner, *Daniel Coit Gilman*, 13, 101–2.

51. Choate et al., *Elgin Ralston Lovell Gould*, 3–4, 33.

52. Flexner, *Abraham Flexner*, 24, 29.

53. Trattner, *From Poor Law to Welfare State*, 102.

54. Howard, *Biographical Sketch of Amos Griswold Warner*, 8–10; Hirschfeld, *Baltimore, 1870–1900*, 159–60.

55. JHU YMCA, Record Group 13.030, Series 2, "The Association," 1890–91; JHU; Hirschfeld, *Baltimore, 1870–1900*, 151–54, 159–60.

56. Commons, *Myself*, 38–62.

57. For more information on Richmond, see Lederman, "From Poverty to Philanthropy."

Upon the establishment of the Russell Sage Foundation in 1907, Daniel Gilman was named one of its trustees. Franklin, *The Life of Daniel Coit Gilman*, 268.

5. Baltimore's Black YMCA, 1885–1925

1. Before 1890, there was no predominantly African-American residential area in Baltimore. Rather, blacks lived throughout the city. In 1880, blacks constituted

more than 10 percent of the city's population in 15 of its 20 wards, yet no single ward was more than one-third black. Karen Olson, "Old West Baltimore: Segregation, African-American Culture, and the Struggle for Equality," in Fee, Shopes, and Zeidman, *The Baltimore Book*, 57–78.

2. Wilson, "Druid Hill Branch, Young Men's Christian Association"; "The Druid Hill Branch YMCA: The First One Hundred Years, 1885–1985" (brochure), YMCA Vertical Files, Maryland Room, EPFL, Baltimore.

3. The standard history of the YMCA is Hopkins, *History of the YMCA*.

4. For information on Baltimore's black community in the antebellum period, see Phillips, *Freedom's Port*; Paul, "The Shadow of Equality," 14–30; Clayton, *Black Baltimore, 1820–1870*. Olson, "Old West Baltimore," in Fee, Shopes, and Zeidman, *The Baltimore Book*, has information on the making of community on the west side in the postbellum period.

5. Mjagkij, *Light in the Darkness*, 1.

6. The two men were George D. Johnston and Henry Edwards Brown. Ibid., 3.

7. Ibid., 37–38, 50–51, 109.

8. Graham, *Baltimore*, 201.

9. Wilson, "Druid Hill Branch"; "Baltimore YMCA, Druid Hill Avenue Branch: The YMCA and Negro Youth," 26 February 1944, Box 53, File 2.
Those active in the early work of the Colored YMCA included W. T. Greenwood (the first president), F. C. Lewis, Milton N. White, M. B. Mayfield, J. H. Murphy, Sr., R. Mattell, M. Williams, T. H. Smith, R. Hall, and T. Alexander Date.

10. Attempting to ensure that no such request would again arise, in 1883, the Central YMCA's board of directors set room rental fees at an astronomical minimum of fifteen dollars per night. In 1895, when Booker T. Washington, president of Tuskegee Institute, applied to rent the Central YMCA's hall for a lecture, the room rental issue was revisited. James Carey Thomas and Daniel Gilman endorsed Washington's application. The board of directors, hoping that Washington would use rooms elsewhere (which in fact he ultimately did), gave Secretary Morriss discretionary power to respond to Washington's application. Minutes, Executive Committee, 27 November 1883, Box 8; Minutes, Board of Directors, 30 October 1895, 1 October 1899.

11. Mjagkij, *Light in the Darkness*, 49.

12. The 1891 convention followed one held in Nashville in 1890. Ibid., 137; Minutes, Board of Directors, 7 April 1891.

13. The clergymen were W. M. Alexander, Patterson Avenue Baptist; Harvey Johnson, Union Baptist; W. Brown, Knox Presbyterian; E. F. Eggleton, Grace Presbyterian; J. W. Norris, Trinity AME; and I. I. Thomas, Centennial AME. Minutes, Board of Directors, 5 April 1892, Box 16.

14. Charity Organization Society, *Directory of the Charitable and Beneficent Organizations of Baltimore and Maryland*, 103–5.

15. Minutes, Board of Directors, 5 April, 4 October 1892, Box 16; William A.

Hunton, "The Association among Colored Men," *Men*, 18 December 1897, 249, as cited in Mjagkij, *Light in the Darkness*, 41.

16. Minutes, Board of Directors, 6 September 1892, Box 16.

17. *Baltimore Afro-American*, 16 November 1912; 1893 *Annual Report*, 10.

18. Many in the black community considered only initiatives from the mid-1890s on as part of the history of the Druid Hill branch. At the dedication of the new building, older men who had helped to start the work more than twenty years earlier told the real history of the association. *Baltimore Afro-American*, 20 December 1918.

19. *Association Bulletin*, January 1896, Box 70.

20. Minutes, Board of Directors, February 1898.

21. *Baltimore Afro-American*, 16 November 1912.

22. *Association Bulletin*, January 1899, Box 70.

23. Osofsky, *Harlem*, 15, 80, 151, 219n.70.

24. *Baltimore Afro-American*, 2 July 1898. The literature on muscular Christianity is important to this discussion.

25. *Association Bulletin*, January 1899, Box 70.

26. *Baltimore Afro-American*, 25 June 1898.

27. *Association Bulletin*, February 1899, Box 70.

28. *Association Bulletin*, September 1899, 5, Box 70; Minutes, Board of Directors, 6 June 1899.

29. *Association Bulletin*, September 1899, 5, Box 70.

30. 1900 *Annual Report*, 36; Minutes, Board of Directors, 6 June 1899, August 1900.

31. *Baltimore Afro-American*, 16 November 1912; Wilson, "Druid Hill Branch," 139.

32. W. Edward Williams to J. E. Moorland, 3 November 1900, as cited by Mjagkij, *Light in the Darkness*, 56.

33. Minutes, Board of Directors, December 1900, 3 January 1901. Goines came to Baltimore from Atlantic City at Moorland's recommendation. He left the Druid Hill YMCA about 1908 to become the colored secretary at Orange, New Jersey. He was succeeded by W. F. Bardeleben, who was there through the 1912 fund-raising campaign. S. S. Booker followed as Druid Hill's secretary and presided over the opening of the new building in 1919.

34. Minutes, Board of Directors, 5 December 1893, 5 June 1894, 5 February 1895, 6 June 1899, 4 December 1900.

35. For information on the sports program of the Colored YMCA/Druid Hill Avenue branch, see Coates, "Recreation and Sport in the African-American Community of Baltimore, 1890–1920," 89–118.

36. By late 1904, a bathroom was fitted up featuring two showers and complete toilet accommodation. That, combined with twenty secondhand lockers, sufficed. Minutes, Board of Directors, 6 June 1899, 30 September 1904.

37. Survey Commission, 1924, Part II, 26, Box 3.

38. In 1924, the Baltimore YMCA undertook a survey of the immediate needs of the boys and young men of Baltimore to ascertain what kind of expansion the Central branch required. The compilation of much useful and disturbing information about Baltimore's African-American community was an important by-product. Problems of housing, health, and recreation in black areas were reported and put at the disposal of other groups of people who might be influential in having the problems met. John R. Cary, a board member of the Druid Hill YMCA, brought the issue of the high levels of tuberculosis in West Baltimore to the attention of the nascent Urban League, which in turn advocated for a much larger study of the African-American community and, ultimately, for the razing of the area known as the lung block. Survey Commission, 1924, Box 3; Druid Hill Avenue Branch: The YMCA and Negro Youth, 26 February 1944; The Interracial Situation and the YMCA, Box 53.

For more information on tuberculosis and Baltimore's African-American community, see Samuel K. Roberts, Jr., dissertation, Princeton University, forthcoming.

39. *Baltimore Men*, 3 June 1915.

40. During September 1904, boardinghouse information was provided to eight young men. Two months later, the branch sent four other men to boardinghouses. Minutes, Board of Directors, September, November 1904.

A second black YMCA opened on Carlton Avenue in Brooklyn, Maryland. *Baltimore Afro-American*, 28 September 1912.

41. Minutes, Committee of Management, Druid Hill Avenue Branch, 13 December 1927, Box 53.

42. A classroom to accommodate workingmen featured used desks and blackboards bought from Mrs. Pendleton's school on Charles St. near Read. Students ranged in age from sixteen to fifty-seven years old. The enrollment of workingmen in night school classes was relatively small in the early years, totaling eighteen in 1904. *Association Bulletin*, September 1899, 5, October 1899, Box 70; Board of Directors, August 1900, 30 September 1904.

43. Minutes, Board of Directors, 31 May 1904.

44. *Association Bulletin*, October 1899, Box 70; 1901 *Annual Report*, 24; 1906 *Annual Report*, 34.

45. Minutes, Board of Directors, 30 November 1904.

46. Minutes, Board of Directors, 7 January 1900.

47. For more information on Rosenwald's philanthropy, see Sealander, *Private Wealth and Public Life*, 69–72; Mjagkij, *Light in the Darkness*, 76–77; *Baltimore Afro-American*, 16 November 1912.

48. *Baltimore Afro-American*, 16 November 1912.

49. Ibid., 9, 16, 30 November 1912. The district captains were T. A. Date, Walter S. Emerson, P.D.G. Pennington, Thomas J. Smith, Dr. Albert O. Reid, Dr. J. C. Robinson, W. T. Greenwood, Samuel E. Young, and Dr. T. S. Hawkins. The original pledge list survives and is quite instructive. The pledge book is in Box 53.

50. For more information on the *Afro-American*'s history and advocacy, see Farrar, *The Baltimore Afro-American, 1892–1950*.

51. *Baltimore Afro-American*, 23 November 1912.

52. Ibid.

53. Ibid., 30 November, 14 December 1912, 12 July 1918.

54. Ibid., 23 August 1918.

55. "Y Fund Growing," ibid., 22 December 1917.

56. *Baltimore Men*, 3 June 1915.

57. *Baltimore Afro-American*, 30 August, 20 September 1918.

58. For insights into the YMCA's military work, see Shillinglaw, *An American in the Army and YMCA, 1917–1920*.

59. In April 1918, 2,261 soldiers visited, 198 stayed overnight, and 3,642 were directed to services such as restaurants, barbershops, railroad stations, homes, and churches. *Baltimore Afro-American*, 29 December 1917, 24 May 1918.

60. Ibid., 9 February 1918.

61. S. S. Booker, a graduate of Virginia Union University class of 1910 and an accomplished athlete and outdoorsman, joined the Druid Hill YMCA as secretary in 1912 after working for YMCAs in Chattanooga and in Indianapolis. *The First Colored Directory of Baltimore City*, 96.

62. For this campaign, there had been a contest. J. D. Lewis, who brought in 148 members, won first place and a pair of gold cuff links. Desmond Lynch, in second place with 82 members, won a gold scarf pin. Benjamin P. Dixon won third place and a leather ticket case. An incentive for joining were dues of one dollar for boys and men, which for men doubled to two dollars following the close of the contest. *Baltimore Afro-American*, 1 March 1918.

63. Ibid., 12 April, 10 May, 13 September, 11 October 1918.

64. Ibid., 3 May 1918.

65. Ibid., 23 August 1918.

66. Ibid., 20 September, 11 October 1918.

67. Ibid., 3 January 1919.

68. Ibid., 10 January 1919.

69. Ibid., 27 December 1918; *Baltimore Men*, 9 January 1919.

70. *Baltimore Men*, 9 January 1919; 1919 *Annual Report*, 13–14; *Baltimore Afro-American*, 10 January 1919.

71. 1918 *Annual Report*, 3–4.

72. *Baltimore Men*, 9 January 1919.

73. Data was drawn from the *Fourteenth Census of the United States*, 1920, Manuscript Population Schedules, Baltimore City, Enumeration District 240, Sheet 11B, Ward 14, p. 23A. Five of the men were between the ages of twenty-eight and thirty-three, another six were between thirty-five and thirty-nine. There were also three each in their forties and fifties and one man who was seventy-six. More than one-quarter were employed as waiters. Three men each worked as elevator operators and chauffeurs. Two men each were employed as clerk, bellboy, laborer,

cook, porter, tailor, and YMCA staff. Hotels employed more than a third of the borders. Four men worked for private families. Three men were employed by restaurants. Other industries employing one or two Druid Hill residents were the post office, an apartment house, railway, music conservatory, schools, shop, factory, construction, a bank, a department store, a bakery, clubs, and the YMCA itself.

74. 1921 *Annual Report*, 10; 1926 *Annual Report*, 7; Survey Commission, 1924, Part I, 47, Box 3, File 3.

75. Of these, 8,198 were public school students between the ages of five and twenty-one, all but 619 in elementary school. An additional 6,900 young men were between eighteen and twenty-four years old. In the age group twenty-four to forty-nine, there were 23,354 men. Survey Commission, 1924, 18, 39, 42.

76. 1921 *Annual Report*, 10; 1922 *Annual Report*, 14.

77. YMCA Survey, 1924, Part II, 25, Box 3, File 3.

78. A year after its opening, at a cost of $7,500, the Druid Hill YMCA was retrofitted with a swimming pool. William Morriss, the Baltimore YMCA's secretary and a member of the City Public Bath Commission, received credit for seeing the pool to fruition as a great public service for the community. 1920 *Annual Report*, 8.

79. YMCA Survey, 1924, Part II, 25–26, Box 3, File 3.

6. The Railroad and Industrial Work of the YMCA, 1879–1933

1. Abbott, *Religious Life in America*, 4, 12–13, 15–16.

2. *Association Bulletin*, January 1890, 15, Box 70.

3. Chambers, *The Tyranny of Change*, 24. Between 1881 and 1905, a total of 36,757 strikes involving more than six million workers erupted across the nation. See also Adams, *Age of Industrial Violence, 1910–1915*.

4. May, *Protestant Churches and Industrial America*, 92, 99–100, 110.

5. In 1916–17, the federal government first studied corporate welfare. Findings were reported in February 1919 by the U.S. Bureau of Labor Statistics (BLS) in Bulletin 250, *Welfare Work for Employees in Industrial Establishments in the United States*, which reported that although welfare work began at the cotton mills of Lowell with company housing, it had only recently occurred at worksites. The BLS surveyed 431 different establishments to assess the state of corporate welfare, which it defined as: "Anything for the comfort and improvement, intellectual or social, of the employees, over and above wages paid, which is not a necessity of the industry nor required by law." Those business establishments doing the most along welfare lines were superior in pay scale, length of work day, and working conditions. BLS, Bulletin 250, February 1919, 1–8.

A more personal account of corporate welfare work is found in Gilson's *What's Past Is Prologue*. Zahavi's *Workers, Managers, and Welfare Capitalism* offers an account of one company's corporate welfare programs. Gittleman provides an overview of corporate welfare in "Welfare Capitalism Reconsidered."

6. Brandes, *American Welfare Capitalism, 1880–1940*, 5–6.

7. Fine defines welfare capitalism as "a management approach popular during the second and third decades of the twentieth century, characterized by an array of services and benefits bestowed upon the workers designed to evoke workers' loyalty and preempt unionization." Fine, "'Our Big Factory Family,'" 280–81, 283.

8. Olson, *Baltimore*, 194–97.

9. Gillett, "Camden Yards and the Strike of 1877."

10. Ibid. By 1880, the B&O had instituted an Employees' Relief Program that, in exchange for employee-paid premiums, included paid sick and accident leave and death benefits. In 1884, the B&O also established the nation's first pension plan. Both programs became models for the industry.

11. Moore, *The Story of the Railroad "Y,"* 18–20, 76, 255; Hicks, *My Life in Industrial Relations*, 20–21.

In *Trade Union Gospel*, Fones-Wolf conflates the industrial work of the YMCA and YWCA and mistakenly labels the approach "conservative." See 122–44.

12. *Weekly Bulletin*, 20 January 1878, Box 70; Heald, *The Social Responsibilities of Business*, 11.

In 1872, the Cleveland YMCA was the first to formalize its work with railroad men by providing a room in the railroad station for employee rest, recreation, and prayer meetings. Hopkins, *History of the YMCA*, 227–29.

13. Hicks, *My Life in Industrial Relations*, 20–21. The first B&O YMCAs were organized in 1877 at Keyser and Grafton, West Virginia. *Weekly Bulletin*, 11 November 1877, Box 70.

14. Moore, *The Story of the Railroad "Y,"* 68–69; Garrett, "Address by John W. Garrett, Delivered on the 30th of January, 1883, before the YMCA of Baltimore on the Occasion of Their Thirtieth Anniversary"; Baltimore and Ohio YMCA, Riverside, Baltimore, *1904 Prospectus*.

15. 1883 *Annual Report*, 11; *Baltimore Men*, 19 February 1914, Box 70; Moore, *The Story of the Railroad "Y,"* 68–69.

16. Brandes, *American Welfare Capitalism*, 14–15. Zahavi argues that the strike wave of 1877 and the labor struggles that ensued were the impetus that led many industrialists to experiment with industrial reforms, including corporate welfare. Zahavi argues that underlying management's paternalistic solutions was the fear of class conflict. "The emergence of corporate paternalism was ultimately a product of conflict, at once a result of and a response to the struggle for control of the means and fruits of industrial capitalism." Zahavi, *Workers, Managers, and Welfare Capitalism*, 2.

17. Andrews, *Corporation Giving*, 24–25.

18. Garrett, "Address by John W. Garrett, Delivered on the 30th of January, 1883, before the YMCA of Baltimore on the Occasion of Their Thirtieth Anniversary."

19. Moore, *The Story of the Railroad "Y"*, 259.

20. So important were the railroad YMCAs to the establishment of corporate

philanthropy that in the 1920s a study of Community Chests (the forebears of the United Way) claimed them as the antecedents of corporate giving to philanthropic enterprises. Ibid., 34.

21. Riebenack, *Railway Provident Institutions in English-Speaking Countries*, 253–55.

22. Abbott, *Religious Life in America*, 37–38.

23. *Weekly Bulletin*, 15 January 1881, December 1882, Box 70; Minutes, Executive Committee, 8 September 1879, Box 8; Minutes, Board of Directors, 6 November 1894, Box 16; 1902 *Annual Report*, 29–30.

24. Abbott, *Religious Life in America*, 37–38.

25. In 1897, Vanderbilt contributed $215,000 for the erection of a Railroad YMCA Building in New York City. In Wanamaker's case, his influence and support persuaded Thomas Scott, president of the Pennsylvania Railroad, to become interested in Christian work for railway men. Moore, *The Story of the Railroad "Y"*, 72, 73.

26. Moore, *The Story of the Railroad "Y,"* 257–58.

27. In *Employing Bureaucracy*, Jacoby argues that "despite its pledge of neutrality, the YMCA's industrial programs were intended to benefit, and were controlled by, corporate sponsors." Jacoby questions the YMCA's commitment to neutrality: "Although it met regularly with employers, never once did the YMCA hold a meeting with union representatives." See 56–59.

28. Moore, *The Story of the Railroad "Y,"* 167.

29. Andrews, *Corporation Giving*, 24–25; Abbott, *Religious Life in America*, 39.

30. *Association Bulletin*, 1 January 1888, July 1894, Box 70.

31. In 1889, the branch's members were just about evenly divided between railroad men (103 members) and neighborhood men (102 members). Minutes, Board of Directors, 29 April, 5 November 1889, Box 16.

32. Minutes, Executive Committee, 2 February 1889; Board of Directors, 29 April 1889, Box 16; *Association Bulletin*, July 1894, Box 70. See also Baltimore and Ohio YMCA, Riverside, Baltimore, *1904 Prospectus*.

33. The Church of the Covenant met at the branch for three years before establishing a permanent church, and the German Lutheran Church met there before it located elsewhere. Moore, *The Story of the Railroad "Y"*, 68–69, 137; 1883 *Annual Report*, 32–33; *Association Bulletin*, 1 January 1888, July 1894, Box 70.

34. The estate of bookseller Humphrey Moore provided about $30,000 for this acquisition. The trustees of his estate determined in 1890 to use the proceeds to erect a building that would then be turned over to the YMCA to manage. The building at Baltimore and Carey Streets was rented to the YMCA for five dollars a year for twenty years. Unfortunately, despite having a gymnasium, this branch did not receive the expected neighborhood support. In 1916, it was closed and the building returned to the trustees of the Humphrey Moore Institute. Meanwhile, the old West branch/B&O branch was rented to a Republican Club. Minutes,

Board of Directors, 2 September 1890, 26 June 1891, 3 November 1896, Box 16; 1916 *Annual Report*, 4.

H. L. Mencken wrote about this branch in "Adventures of a YMCA Lad." At the urging of his father, the fourteen-year-old Mencken joined the West branch YMCA in 1894 and hated it: "All that the YMCA's horse and rings really accomplished was to fill me with an ineradicable distaste, not only for Christian endeavor in all its forms, but also for every variety of calisthenics, so that I still begrudge the trifling exertion needed to climb in and out of a bathtub, and hate all sports as rabidly as a person who likes sports hates common sense." Mencken, *Heathen Days*, 19.

35. Minutes, Board of Directors, 4 November 1890, 5 May 1891, Box 16; 1898 *Annual Report*, 14; 1900 *Annual Report*, 13.

36. Baltimore and Ohio YMCA, Riverside, Baltimore, *1904 Prospectus*.

37. *Baltimore News*, 18 May 1908, 12.

38. Jennie Smith also held meetings at the B&O YMCA in 1881. In 1882, she continued her work in western Maryland where, on average, more than 100 men professed conversion in each town. *Weekly Bulletin*, 10 December 1881, 20 May 1882; *Association Bulletin*, 1 June 1888, Box 70.

39. *Association Bulletin*, January 1894, Box 70; 1891 *Annual Report*, 10; Minutes, Board of Directors, 2 June, 2 September 1890, Box 16; 1891 *Annual Report*, 10.

40. Of these, there were 148 shopmen, 62 clerks, 22 warehousemen, 21 firemen, 16 enginemen, 13 agents, 12 brakemen, 12 sons of employees, 10 foremen, 9 brakemen, 8 company officials, and 4 conductors. 1901 *Annual Report*, 16.

41. *Association Bulletin*, January 1894, March 1895, March 1897, February 1900, Box 70.

42. 1891 *Annual Report*, 10; 1901 *Annual Report*, 16; 1902 *Annual Report*, 11; 1916 *Annual Report*, 3; 1919 *Annual Report*, 11, 13; 1920 *Annual Report*, 11; 1922 *Annual Report*, 16; 1923 *Annual Report*, 9.

43. In February 1895, seven Baltimore saloons cashed checks issued to about 1,200 trainmen for $40,000. Minutes, Board of Directors, 7 November 1893, 5 February, 5 March 1895, Box 16.

44. In 1915, the Pennsy branch referred 59 men to reputable boardinghouses nearby, in addition to housing 3,059 different men in its dormitory. That year, the B&O branch housed 5,405 different men in its dormitory. 1895 *Annual Report*, 11; 1924 *Annual Report*, 10–11; 1929 *Annual Report*, 17; *Baltimore Men*, 3 June 1915, Box 70.

45. *Association Bulletin*, July 1894, October 1897, March 1898, Box 70; 1893 *Annual Report*, 44; 1894 *Annual Report*, 44; 1902 *Annual Report*, 29–30.

46. By the third year, the Apprentice School had eighty students. 1912 *Annual Report*, 7; 1915 *Annual Report*, 2. See also Nelson, *Managers and Workers*, 97.

47. 1917 *Annual Report*, 4; 1919 *Annual Report*, 13.

48. In 1929, the combined membership of the Baltimore branches was 2,079.

That year, the B&O Railroad's YMCA branches were so popular that more than 20,000 of its 35,000 employees were involved in the YMCA's health and recreation program. 1923 *Annual Report*, 9; 1924 *Annual Report*, 10–11; 1929 *Annual Report*, 17.

49. One railroad company that had many African-American employees ran a company club on the principles of the YMCA but financed and managed by the company, in which club facilities were provided on separate floors of the club building for black and white employees and their families. Alice L. Whitney, "Welfare Work for Employees in Industrial Establishment in the U.S.," BLS Bulletin 250, 1919, 75–76.

50. Although Heald argues in *The Social Responsibilities of Business*, 12, that in its railroad work the YMCA's orientation "seems to have been toward the aristocracy, the skilled mechanics and trainmen, rather than the common workers," that appears to have been less true in Baltimore.

At the Pennsy YMCA in Baltimore, there were 110 members in 1891, of which there were 40 shopmen, 23 clerks, 5 engineers, 3 conductors, 1 each telegraph operator and roundhouse man, and 30 other men in positions such as agent and messenger. Nine of the men were under twenty; 30 were between the ages of twenty and thirty; 34 were from thirty to forty; 23 were from forty to fifty; and 7 were over fifty. *Association Bulletin*, December 1890, August 1891, February, March 1898, Box 70.

51. 1931 *Annual Report*, 6; Moore, *The Story of the Railroad "Y"*, 192, 228, 268.

52. *Association Bulletin*, January 1890, 15, Box 70.

53. 1933 *Annual Report*, 8.

54. By the late 1930s, membership drives and increases in railroad employment led to a daily attendance at the B&O branch of about 700 men, with the beds used 11,846 times annually. In 1944, R. B. White, president of the B&O Railroad, reported that the YMCA buildings on his line were "old and although we have tried to improve and adapt them to changing conditions they nevertheless offer rather difficult problems in administration and operation." Even so, the YMCAs "meant much to the railroad men using them . . . it has been a good thing for our railroad employees using these Ys to come under the influence of their leaders." 1934 *Annual Report*, 11; 1937 *Annual Report*, 6; Letter from R. B. White, president, B&O Railroad Company, to Hamilton Davis, vice president, Baltimore YMCA, 26 May 1944, Box 75, File 1.

55. Hopkins, *History of the YMCA*, 571.

56. The B&O branch in Baltimore closed in the early 1950s. The exact date is not known. In October 1953, the Baltimore YMCA reported about the railroad branches, "After substantial service, conditions changed and the special branches were no longer needed," suggesting that it had been some time since it had operated. Baltimore YMCA, *Of Time and a Triangle*, 15 October 1953, 7, Box 75A.

57. Twenty years later, some company officials attributed the site's near perfect

safety record to the prayers: "Fifteen months . . . without a reportable accident, No wonder." "Workmen Who Pray for Safe Guidance," *Baltimore Sun*, 28 March 1953.

58. Minutes, Board of Directors, 7 June 1892, Box 16.

59. In 1901, Abbott reported that there was one preacher in Baltimore who was universally popular among workingmen but that even he "had probably not a single workingman in his church. . . . It was apparently only from the newspapers, in which his sermons often appeared, that the workingman had any knowledge of him, and on his newspaper reputation his popularity among them almost wholly rested." Abbott, *Religious Life in America*, 46; 1919 *Annual Report*, 8.

60. The single most popular shop meeting was that held on the eighth floor of the B&O office building, where an average of 130 men attended. The Maryland Biscuit Company and Carnegie Steel tied for second with average attendance of 100 men. *Baltimore Men*, 4 March 1915, Box 70.

61. In 1909, 253 YMCA shop meetings had a total attendance of 19,000. In 1913, 15 industrial sites hosted 350 meetings. In 1916, there were 905 meetings with attendance of 54,750. In 1921, 63 volunteer clergy and lay leaders ministered to more than 36,000 industrial workers with 6,000 to 8,000 men reached monthly through shop meetings. Seven ministers spent between two and six years leading shop meetings, with the Revs. John Clarke Finney and Edward Niles leading the group. In 1926, there were 16 lay and 39 clergy volunteers. *Baltimore Men*, April 1921, Box 70; 1909 *Annual Report*, 4; 1914 *Annual Report*, 8; 1919 *Annual Report*, 8; 1921 *Annual Report*, 7; 1927 *Annual Report*, 6–7.

62. 1924 *Annual Report*, 4; 1925 *Annual Report*, 5.

63. 1922 *Annual Report*, 19–20.

64. 1927 *Annual Report*, 8–9.

65. 1919 *Annual Report*, 7; 1920 *Annual Report*, 8; 1925 *Annual Report*, 5; 1929 *Annual Report*, 6–7.

66. English-language classes for foreign-born men were begun before these secretaries were hired. In 1918, courses in "thrift" and "Americanization" attracted 789 students. The YMCA was successful with newly arrived industrial workers from Poland, Greece, Russia, and Serbia. 1919 *Annual Report*, 14.

The YMCA discontinued industrial Americanization programs in 1921 when Baltimore's public schools took them over. 1922 *Annual Report*, 13.

67. 1921 *Annual Report*, 7–8; 1922 *Annual Report*, 5.

68. Survey Commission, 1924, 63, Box 3.

69. In 1920, the YMCA undertook work for the nearly 100,000 merchant seamen who came to Baltimore in connection with the growing shipping interests of the port. That year, in cooperation with the Anchorage, the YMCA offered "all the privileges of an up-town club." *Baltimore Men*, 23 September 1920, Box 70.

70. Minutes, Board of Trustees, 21 February 1934, Box 13. For information on how the YMCA dealt with seamen during the New Deal, see Argersinger, *Toward a New Deal in Baltimore*, esp. chap. 5.

7. The YMCA Schools, 1883–1934

1. *Baltimore Men*, 4 March 1915, Box 70. Preston served as mayor from 1911 to 1919. During his administration, many public improvements occurred, the most notable of which was the annexation (Baltimore's last) that took place in 1918, which nearly tripled Baltimore's size and increased the population by almost 100,000 people to 700,000. Under Preston's administration, a form of civil service for city employees was approved, as was a race segregation ordinance that aimed to separate black and white residential areas. Coyle, *The Mayors of Baltimore*, 219–28.

2. *Baltimore Men*, 4 March 1915, Box 70.

3. The 1890 YMCA's *Annual Report* claimed, "No department of the Association's activities appeals so strongly to the sympathy of all classes of men as the educational class work. It is in line with the best philanthropic thought, as well as with the most practical Christianity."

4. Although unusual when compared to other northern cities of the same era, for much of the period under discussion Baltimore was led by men born into an "upper class." For example, in assessing the efficacy of boss rule in the city, James B. Crooks argues, "The mayor was frequently a member of Baltimore's upper class and popular with both ward workers and civic leaders. Such was the case with Ferdinand C. Latrobe, who served seven terms between 1875 and 1895. Latrobe's father was general counsel for the Baltimore and Ohio Railroad, and his grandfather had helped to design the nation's capitol." Crooks, *Politics and Progress*, 11–12.

According to Burton Bledstein, higher education was the seminal institution within the culture of nineteenth-century American professionalism. By 1860, commercial pursuits had risen dramatically as a professional choice of college graduates, only slightly below the law and ministry in popularity. Bledstein, *The Culture of Professionalism*, 121, 198.

The making of a professional middle class is also discussed by Gilkeson, *Middle-Class Providence*; Wiebe, *The Search for Order*; Zunz, *Making America Corporate*; Mills, *White Collar*; Blumin, *The Emergence of the Middle Class*, among others.

5. As early as 1854, the YMCA's Board of Managers considered "the propriety of forming classes for mutual mental improvement, such as the reading of original essays, debates . . . and the forming of classes in Biblical literature [and] for the study of language [and] bookkeeping." Soon after the YMCA was reconstituted after the Civil War, foreign language classes were "revived." Minutes, Board of Managers, 9 March 1854, Box 7; Minutes, Executive Committee, 22 September 1868, Box 11.

6. *Weekly Bulletin*, 12 February 1881, 21 September 1883, Box 70.

7. Ibid., 12 February 1881.

8. Minutes, Executive Committee, 16 January 1886, Box 8.

9. *Association Bulletin*, May 1896, 5, Box 70.

10. Kett, *The Pursuit of Knowledge under Difficulties*, 242–43.

11. Minutes, Executive Committee, 26 February 1884, Box 11.

12. Bledstein reports that the number of stenographers and typists nationally grew from 154 in 1870 to 112,364 in 1900, while the number of bookkeepers, cashiers, and accountants increased from 38,775 to 254,880 during the same years. Bledstein, *The Culture of Professionalism*, 37.

13. *Association Bulletin*, June 1894, 11, Box 70.

14. *Association Bulletin*, May 1900, 8, Box 70; Kwolek-Folland, *Engendering Business*, 4–5.

15. Davies, *Woman's Place Is at the Typewriter*, 79–80.

16. Beginning at its founding in 1883, the Baltimore YWCA offered free educational classes to its members in a variety of subjects including bookkeeping (which in its second year attracted 50 scholars), arithmetic, reading, writing, and spelling. Even a course in knitting was offered to "12 little cash girls who greatly desired to learn this womanly industry." 1884 *Annual Report*, 12; 1885 *Annual Report*, 7.

17. *Association Bulletin*, July 1895, 6, Box 70 (emphasis in original).

18. In 1883, the Federal Civil Service Act became law, a response to President Garfield's assassination at the hands of a disgruntled worker.

19. The typewriters were a gift of A. G. Seal, general agent of the Remington Company, which had marketed the first commercial machines in 1874. *Association Bulletin*, October 1888, 4, October 1889, 8, May 1896, 5, Box 70.

20. 1891 *Annual Report*, 33; and Adams, *Public Educational Work in Baltimore*, 12.

Initially, the American history class was jointly sponsored by the YMCA and JHU. Readings included Benjamin Franklin's autobiography, about which JHU's Herbert Baxter Adams, wrote, "Many a young man has received a life-incentive from reading that entertaining and wholesome book." According to Adams, the course, featuring "interesting reading and class discussions of some of our best American authors, and some of the most important topics in the history of the American political and economic development," was "an entirely new feature in the educational work of the YMCA [that] will tend to promote habits of good reading and an intelligent use of the library facilities of Baltimore, besides giving definite instruction in the literature and history of our own country." Letter from Adams to W. H. Morriss, in *Association Bulletin*, September 1890, 7, Box 70.

After Adams's untimely death at the age of fifty-one in 1901, Richard T. Ely memorialized him: "Everywhere in our broad land we find university men working . . . to promote good citizenship; and for this condition of affairs a great deal is due to the [JHU] Studies in Historical and Political Science." Ely, *Herbert B. Adams, Tributes of Friends*, 36.

21. *Association Bulletin*, May 1893, 6–7, Box 70.

22. This is typical of the pattern where, through the use of entrance screenings, formalized courses of study, publishing textbooks, standardizing examinations, and awarding degrees, higher educators convinced the public that objective prin-

ciples determined competence in American life: "Intelligence prevailed over family inheritance as a requisite for accomplishment in society. Educators successfully advocated that the proliferation of schools in America prevented any privileged social class, any closed guild, or any preferential apprenticeship system from monopolizing the services of an occupation or from angling the truth according to the private perceptions of a few men." Bledstein, *The Culture of Professionalism*, 124.

23. *Association Bulletin*, July 1894, 7, August 1894, 3, May 1895, 3, Box 70.

The YMCA's mechanical drawing course met three evenings a week for a period of three years. The YMCA described it as "second to none in the City, not in the spirit of competition, simply because we believe there is the demand to be met."

In 1892, the YMCA made arrangements with the Maryland Institute to provide the best evening student with a scholarship for technical classes there. "We believe there is a hint in this educational department of that opportunity which is before the Association for coming into touch with the great movements of the day which tend to the education of the masses." 1893 *Annual Report*, 13.

24. *Association Bulletin*, May 1896, May 1897, 4, Box 70.

25. Ibid., May 1897, 6; 1887 *Annual Report*, 25; 1890 *Annual Report*, 33.

26. 1893 *Annual Report*, 13; 1897 *Annual Report*, 8; 1898 *Annual Report*, 10; *Association Bulletin*, May 1897, 6, May 1898, 3, Box 70.

27. In 1889, the B&O and West branch offered classes in penmanship, phonography, arithmetic, vocal music, and mechanical drawing to forty-six students, and in 1890 enrollment increased to fifty-five. In 1893, with sixty-two students, the West branch eliminated vocal music and mechanical drawing but added bookkeeping. When classes ceased in 1896 because of declining enrollments caused by the opening of public night schools nearby, the nineteen remaining students transferred to Central's Evening Institute. 1893 *Annual Report*, 13; 1894 *Annual Report*, 32; Minutes, Board of Directors, 3 November, 1 December 1896, Box 17.

The German branch's evening classes in English, penmanship, and freehand drawing were among the branch's principal attractions until the advent of public night schools hurt enrollments. Many of the German students were hard hit by the depression of 1893, making it impossible for them to buy the YMCA membership then mandatory for course enrollment. The branch's closing in 1896, the result of a culture clash between its members and Central's leadership, precluded the revival of educational work. 1893 *Annual Report*, 33; 1894 *Annual Report*, 37; 1895 *Annual Report*, 15.

28. Minutes, Board of Directors, 2 April 1895, Box 16; 1893 *Annual Report*; 1898 *Annual Report*, 10, 11, 22, 28.

29. 1906 *Annual Report*, 34.

30. 1884 *Annual Report*, 7.

31. By 1890, the Education Department employed fourteen instructors. 1888 *Annual Report*, 11; 1891 *Annual Report*, 13.

32. In addition to Carnegie, Henry J. Sutton, an instructor in memory training,

also commuted from New York City to teach at the Baltimore YMCA's Evening Institute. *Baltimore Men*, 22 January 1914, 1; 15 October 1914, 1; 14 October 1915, 5; 28 November 1918, 2; 6 February 1919, 2.

Despite the familiarity of Dale Carnegie's name (after leaving the Baltimore YMCA schools, he changed the spelling from "Carnagey" to suggest ties to Andrew Carnegie) and his work, especially his 1936 book *How to Win Friends and Influence People*, he has been largely ignored by scholars.

33. 1889 *Annual Report*, 13; *Association Bulletin*, June 1894, 10, April 1895, May 1896, 5, Box 70.

34. 1887 *Annual Report*, 26; *Association Bulletin*, 1 April 1888, 2, December 1889, 3, April 1892, 9, Box 70; *Baltimore Men*, 1 January 1914, 2, 20 March 1919, 2, 27 January 1921, 1, Box 73.

35. 1922 *Annual Report*, 9.

36. *Association Bulletin*, August 1895, 6, Box 70.

37. 1897 *Annual Report*, 8.

38. *Association Bulletin*, 1 April 1888, 2, May 1898, 5, Box 70.

39. On 6 March 1897, for example, the *New York Times* reported a $10,000 gift from Esther Herrman to the New York Young Men's Hebrew Association, the income from which was to be used for educational classes. Mrs. Herrman, the widow of a textile manufacturer, explained her largesse: "Many years ago, when one of my sons was developing into manhood and required wise counsel to guard him from the temptations of a large city, I advised him to join the evening classes of the Young Men's Christian Association. The benefit he gained therefrom impressed me so favorably that I hoped to see similar advantages extended to young men of our own race, with branches established in various quarters of the east side of our city, where the unfortunate, born in ignorance and poverty, could be trained to be useful and self-supporting citizens." As reported in *Association Bulletin*, May 1897, 6–7, Box 70.

At his death in 1899, John V. L. Graham, Baltimore YMCA treasurer for twenty-five years, left $12,000 in ground rents to the "Graham Education Fund," which he hoped would yield $600 or $700 annually for the Evening Institute. 1900 *Annual Report*, 18; *Association Bulletin*, May 1900, 8, Box 70.

40. 1886 *Annual Report*, 10; 1887 *Annual Report*, 9–10; *Association Bulletin*, April 1895, May 1897, 6–7, Box 70.

41. Firms including Consolidated Gas, Electric Light and Power Company, Maryland Casualty, L. Grief and Bros., Smith, Lockhart & Co., Southern Rome Co., Baltimore Maryland Engraving Co., State Bank of Maryland, Mercantile Trust Co., Charles E. Falconer, Max Gans, and others were paying employees' tuition. 1912 *Annual Report*, 7; *Baltimore Men*, 26 October 1916, 2, 27 January 1921, 2, Box 70.

42. In 1884, the Baltimore City Public Schools established the Baltimore Manual Training School on Courtland Street. In May 1893, its name was changed to Baltimore Polytechnic Institute. From its founding, the school was under the

influence of U.S. Naval Academy graduates. By 1921, the school tried "to give its students something more than fundamental instruction in applied science. It aims to prepare for intelligent service in the engineering professions—the professions to which the world is indebted for all the conveniences of life and for the economic production of its necessities." Despite Poly's popularity during this period (largely due to a dearth of public school options for white boys), fewer than 25 percent of the students who entered ever graduated. Of these, half went on for additional schooling. Strayer, *Report of the Survey of the Public School System of Baltimore, Maryland*, 3:5–6, 266–67.

43. Minutes, Board of Directors, 30 October 1895, Box 16; *Association Bulletin*, June 1899, 7, Box 70.

44. 1898 *Annual Report*, 10–11.

45. Educational classes were an important recruiting tool for attracting new members. In 1886, 111 of the 399 men attending classes joined the YMCA solely for the educational benefits. In 1888, nearly 20 percent of the YMCA's 2,304 members failed to renew. "This loss of so large a portion of our membership is due to the fact that many join for the advantages of the gymnasium and classes, and having enjoyed these allow their membership to lapse." Yet for Morriss and his band of volunteer leaders, the constant turnover was considered an evangelical opportunity. 1887 *Annual Report*, 11–12; 1888 *Annual Report*, 9.

46. The ticket this young man referred to was his YMCA membership. Because he had become a member in good standing of an evangelical Protestant church, he was eligible for an "active" membership in the YMCA. *Association Bulletin*, 1 April 1888, 2–3, Box 70.

47. 1890 *Annual Report*, 33.

48. The same tolerance was not extended to African Americans, whose only educational opportunity through the YMCA was limited to the handful of classes at the Druid Hill branch. *Association Bulletin*, August 1895, 7, Box 70.

49. *Association Bulletin*, May 1895, 3, October 1895, 7, Box 70.

50. 1902 *Annual Report*, 4.

51. 1915 *Annual Report*, 2; *Baltimore Men*, 28 January 1915, 4, Box 70.

52. *Baltimore Men*, 26 December 1918, 1, Box 73; 1919 *Annual Report*, 6.

53. 1909 *Annual Report*, 3; 1912 *Annual Report*; 1915 *Annual Report*, 5.

54. Forgoing the need for YMCA memberships for students in the English language class developed only after classes at the German branch fell apart because of the inability of students there to pay membership dues during the depression of 1893. *Baltimore Men*, 11 March 1915, 2, Box 70.

55. Ibid., 6 March 1919, 1, Box 73.

56. *Association Bulletin*, September 1898, 7.

57. *Baltimore Men*, 24 September 1914, 1, Box 70.

58. Ibid., 22 January 1914, 1, 9 March 1916, 3, 20 March 1919, 2, Box 73.

59. Ibid., 9 September 1915, 3, Box 70.

60. Ibid., 10 October 1918, 1, Box 73.

61. Ibid., 21 November 1918, 2, 9 January 1919, 2, 6 February 1919, 2, Box 73.

62. The cost of the "Intensive Typewriting" course was fifteen dollars. Ibid., 21 November 1918, 2, 12 December 1918, 1, Box 73; 1919 *Annual Report*.

63. *Baltimore Men*, 7 March 1918, 1, Box 73.

64. Ibid., 10 October, 28 November 1918, 2, Box 73. The issue of the YMCA's relation to wartime planning and reconstruction is worthy of additional study. In *American Problems of Reconstruction*, Friedman examines many aspects of the economic and financial issues American businesses and associations faced after the war.

65. The YMCA's involvement in legal education began in 1898, when Ward B. Coe, a member of the Baltimore bar, offered a course of lectures on commercial law. *Association Bulletin*, May 1898, 3; *Baltimore Men*, 23 September 1920, 1, Box 73.

66. 1921 *Annual Report*, 3.

67. BCC's admission policy for women varied. Two women received degrees in 1921, and one in 1922. Four women received degrees in 1928, and then it was not until 1937 that the next women graduated. University of Baltimore (hereafter UB), *Graduates of the Baltimore College of Commerce*, 1918–1948, Registrar's Office, UB; 1922 *Annual Report*, 8.

68. Strayer, *Report of the Survey of the Public School System of Baltimore Maryland*; *Baltimore Men*, 21 October 1920, 2, Box 73.

69. 1926 *Annual Report*, 4. In 1935, also under the auspices of the Strayer, Bryant and Stratton College, the Mt. Vernon School of Law was established. Soon after, the Maryland School of Accounting and the Mt. Vernon School of Law were incorporated as a nonprofit under the name of Eastern University. In 1970, these schools merged into the University of Baltimore. UB, *Eastern University Bulletin*, 1941–42, 6, Registrar's Office, UB.

70. 1924 *Annual Report*, 5–6; 1926 *Annual Report*, 4.

71. The Franklin Day School held its last graduation in 1939. The Commercial School became the YMCA Business College and claimed 1884 as its founding date. It became the Secretarial Science Division of the Baltimore College of Commerce in 1961 as part of the reorganization of the YMCA Schools as a corporation separate from the Baltimore YMCA. The Evening High School had received state accreditation in 1925. 1934 *Annual Report*, 6.

72. Ibid.

73. 1936 *Annual Report*, 3.

74. For example, in January 1930, Elwood Powell, a University of Michigan graduate with a degree in business administration, came to live at the Central YMCA. A full-time worker, he studied accounting at night. He graduated from BCC in 1933 and later passed the CPA exam. For forty years, Powell was employed as an accountant. Baltimore YMCA, Letter from Elwood Powell to the author, 11 May 1995, Box 124.

Clinton C. Emich entered BCC in 1935 from Baltimore Polytechnic Institute. He "could have got into any engineering college . . . including MIT, in the second year and hence earned an engineering degree in three years." But because "engineering jobs were almost nonexistent and the few available paid very little," he decided to pursue a degree in business. BCC, like the Wharton School, offered a cooperative business administration program with six months of school and six months of work for each of five years. At BCC, Ed Shipley, a CPA who audited the state race tracks, was one of Emich's instructors. Not only did Emich date his instructor's daughters, he also worked for Shipley at income tax time. But it was his work at Riggs Distler and Company, mechanical and electrical contractors, that determined his future. First hired in 1934 as an electrical draftsman and then rehired in accounting after his enrollment at BCC, Emich worked for the firm for nearly fifty years, becoming the company's secretary-treasurer, vice president, and finally president and chairman of the board. Emich reported that as a result of the YMCA's emphasis on leadership, he served as an officer of many boards including the following: YMCA Schools, Baltimore Jaycees, Maryland chapter of the Mechanical Contractors of America, the Building Congress and Exchange of Baltimore, and the Baltimore Rotary Club. Baltimore YMCA, Letter from Clinton C. Emich to the author, 24 May 1995, Box 124.

75. Baltimore YMCA, Letter from Marshall Davis, BCC 1939 to the author, 19 May 1995, Box 124.

76. In 1973, the Baltimore College of Commerce, the last YMCA school still in operation, closed. Financial problems, falling enrollment, the lack of accreditation, and an ill-advised relocation from the Central YMCA downtown to the campus of the defunct St. Agnes College in Mt. Washington (seven miles from downtown and then not easily accessible by public transportation) caused the demise of the sixty-three-year-old school. The college's 525 students, library, and alumni were then absorbed by UB.

77. UB, Registrar's Office, *YMCA Business College, Secretarial Science Division, Baltimore College of Commerce, Bulletin,* 1964–67, 28.

78. Alexis de Tocqueville, *Democracy in America*; see esp. chap. 29, "Of the Use to Which the Americans Make Public Associations in Civil Life," 198–202.

79. The YMCA schools also support Evans and Boyte's contention that free spaces are most likely to grow within the voluntary sector of civil society. Evans and Boyte, *Free Spaces*, viii, xix.

8. The YMCA as Homemaker and Caretaker, 1908–1933

1. Chudacoff, *The Age of the Bachelor*, 146–47, 4.

2. See Goffman, *Asylums*; and Elkins's assessment of the extrapolation of this theory to the study of slavery in *Slavery*, esp. 246–47.

3. 1906 *Annual Report*, 9–10.

4. Minutes, Board of Directors, 5 December 1893, 6 February 1894, Box 16.

5. Baltimore YMCA, *Progress-Manhood*, Annual Prospectus, 1912, 5, MHS.

6. Many of the short-term transient residents were visiting members from other YMCAs. Some local members also used the transient rooms. Letting rooms on a short-term basis was justified in 1912 as "a matter of large social and moral advantage." 1912 *Annual Report*, 5.

7. 1915 *Annual Report*, 4; 1916 *Annual Report*, 5; "Making the Most of Life: A Program for Men and Boys," 1931–1932, 4.

In 1931, Central's occupancy rate was 93 percent and Druid Hill's was 79 percent. Those rates fell off as the depression dragged on. In 1932, Central's occupancy rates averaged 75 percent while Druid Hill's was at only 50 percent.

The last component of the YMCA's housing program was the Anchorage branch for seamen at Fell's Point in 1929. In its first year under the YMCA's auspices, the Anchorage housed 14,656 men in its roughly 150 beds. The next year, that number increased more than 50 percent to 21,864 different men sheltered because of the number of rooms that were converted into free dorms. 1930 *Annual Report*, 4; 1931 *Annual Report*, 4; 1933 *Annual Report*, 5; 1939 *Annual Report*, 10.

8. As late as 1940, the YMCA received scores of letters each day from parents and friends "requesting our personal interest in young men coming to Baltimore." In addition, other letters praised the YMCA's helpfulness and cooperation: "In hundreds of instances we have been able to provide that counsel and help—unhurried and personal—that a parent would give under exactly the same circumstances." 1940 *Annual Report*, 10.

9. 1912 *Annual Report*, 5; 1914 *Annual Report*, 9.

10. 1906 *Annual Report*, 9–10; 1923 *Annual Report*, 8–9.

11. The boys' building was never built. 1915 *Annual Report*, 4, 5; 1919 *Annual Report*, 14; 1920 *Annual Report*, 15.

12. 1919 *Annual Report*, 3; 1924 *Annual Report*, 4; 1926 *Annual Report*, 3; 1930 *Annual Report*, 4; 1931 *Annual Report*, 4.

13. Data were drawn from the *Thirteenth Census of the United States*, 1910, and *Fourteenth Census of the United States*, 1920, Manuscript Population Schedules, Baltimore City. Entries for the YMCA in the 1910 census are found on reel 556, Enumeration District 159.

14. In 1910, the census reports 76 men living in the Central YMCA, while in 1920 the number of residents was 189. In 1910, 96 percent (73) of the men were native born and 79 percent (60) had two native-born parents. Ten years later, 93 percent (175) of the residents were native born, while 84 percent (158) had two native-born parents.

15. In 1910 and 1920, 92 percent of YMCA residents were single, 4 percent were married, 3 percent were widowed, and 1 percent were divorced.

16. In 1910, Maryland was the birthplace of 41 percent of the residents, and in 1920, 29 percent claimed it as their original home. Pennsylvania, with 11 percent in 1910 and 13 percent in 1920, was the second most popular home state. Virginia

was third, with 7 percent of the residents claiming it as their birth state in 1910 and 8 percent in 1920.

In 1910, men came to the Baltimore YMCA from 18 different states and one each from Italy, Canada, and England. By 1920, the YMCA was more diverse, with residents hailing from 33 different states and 12 foreign countries, with one each from 11 foreign countries and 3 from Italy. The percentage of foreign-born residents increased from 3.9 percent in 1910 to 7.4 percent in 1920. Divided by region (excluding Maryland), in 1910, 24 percent of the YMCA's residents hailed from New England and the Mid-Atlantic states, 16 percent came from the South, and 15 percent were born in the western states and territories. In 1920, 30 percent of the residents were born in the Northeast, while 20 percent came from the South, and 14 percent were born out west.

17. By 1913, the average age of the lodgers was twenty-eight, and the weekly room rental was three dollars. 1914 *Annual Report*, 9.

18. In 1910, the youngest residents were twenty, but ten years later they were only seventeen years old. In 1910, men in their twenties made up 53 percent of the YMCA's residents. That figure increased to 66 percent in 1920. Men in their thirties made up 34 percent of the residents in 1910 and 23 percent ten years later.

19. In the late 1930s, YMCA residents worked for employers as diverse as Social Security, downtown banks, the Douglas aircraft plant, and Sparrows Point steel mill. Baltimore YMCA, Letter from Robert S. McCandliss to the *Baltimore Sun*, 28 November 1993, Box 124.

20. 1914 *Annual Report*, 9.

21. Entries in the YMCA's periodical *Baltimore Men* (Box 72) give information on when and why twenty-one men moved out. Of these, thirteen left for marriage, five left for work or school, two died in military service during World War I, and one died in the Central YMCA Building.

22. Reminiscences of Paul Noble, video, "YMCA of Greater Baltimore 140th Anniversary Celebration," March 1994, WMAR TV, Box 124.

23. Baltimore YMCA, Letter from Robert S. McCandliss to the *Baltimore Sun*, 28 November 1993, Box 124.

24. Ibid.

25. Ibid.

26. Ibid.

27. Ibid.

28. In 1942, eighteen-year-old Jim Ellington came to Baltimore to work for Martin Marietta. He moved into room 610 at the Central YMCA, his home for the next eight years. Ellington invested much of his free time in the YMCA. He was elected "mayor" of Dorm City, a club for residents, and he wrote the *Y News*, the dorm's newspaper. He also participated in the Co-Ed Club, a group that met each Thursday night and through which he met his wife. Even after marrying, he and his wife served for years as advisers and chaperones for YMCA activities. His involvement in the association continued through matriculation at the Baltimore College

of Commerce, from which he graduated in 1958. Reminiscences of Jim Ellington, video, "YMCA of Greater Baltimore 140th Anniversary Celebration," March 1994, WMAR TV, Box 124.

29. Baltimore YMCA, Letter from Robert S. McCandliss to the *Baltimore Sun*, 28 November 1993, Box 124.

30. Fine, "Between Two Worlds."

31. Ibid.

32. *Baltimore Men*, 18 April 1918, 2, Box 73.

33. Ibid., 29 January 1914.

34. 1915 *Annual Report*, 5; *Baltimore Men*, 27 January 1916, Box 73.

35. 1919 *Annual Report*, 10.

36. *Baltimore Men*, 30 January 1919, Box 73.

37. Formal work with youth began in 1885 when a Junior branch of the YMCA was created for boys from twelve to eighteen. Older men were excluded from the regular meetings, "as it would embarrass the speakers, and the boys would not feel free to express their opinions of the subject in hand." The function of the Junior branch was to "do for the boy what the regular Association does for the man. . . . When a boy reaches twelve he is apt to get restless, and to begin to go out at night. This is just the place needed to counteract the evil which he is bound to meet with at this time of his life." *Association Bulletin*, May 1890, 2–3, Box 70.

38. *Baltimore Men*, 30 January 1919, Box 73. For more information on the YMCA boys' programs, see Macleod, *Building Character in the American Boy*.

39. 1922 *Annual Report*, 12.

40. 1924 *Annual Report*, 2–4; 1930 *Annual Report*, 12, 21; 1934 *Annual Report*, 9.

41. Baltimore YMCA, "Making the Most of Life: A Program for Men and Boys, 1931–1932," 3, UBA. Marriage returned as the topic of a series of Levering Hall YMCA lectures in 1957. So popular were these talks that it was "impossible" to accommodate all the students who wanted to attend. The next year, as part of a lecture series on "Living Religions of the World," the Levering Hall YMCA offered programs on "Marriage for Moderns (Sex, Love, and Marriage)," "The Significance of Sex in the Marriage Relationship," and "The New Society: The Family and Friends of Your Mate." Levering Hall YMCA, "The JHU Branch, 1956–57," Series 2, Box 2; and "The JHU Branch, 1958–59," Series 2, Box 4, JHU, Office of the Chaplain/YMCA Collection, 13.030.

42. 1927 *Annual Report*, 10.

43. 1928 *Annual Report*, 10.

44. *Baltimore Men*, 18 April 1918, 2, Box 73.

45. Baltimore YMCA, "Making the Most of Life," 3, UBA.

Bibliography

Archival Collections

Brown University Archives, Providence, R.I. Margaret Shove Morriss Files.
Goucher College, Towson, Md. Alumnae Records. Margaret Shove Morriss Files.
Johns Hopkins University, Baltimore, Md. Records of Office of the Chaplain/ YMCA and Office of the President (Levering Hall); and Family and Children's Society (Charity Organization Society of Baltimore) Records.
Maryland Baptist Society, Columbia, Md.
Maryland Historical Society, Baltimore, Md. Franklin Wilson Papers. MS 833.
Northfield Mount Hermon School, E. Northfield, Mass. D. L. Moody Archives.
University of Baltimore. YMCA of Greater Baltimore Collection.
Yale Divinity School, New Haven. D. L. Moody Papers.
YWCA of Greater Baltimore. Historic Collections.

Books

Abbott, Ernest Hamlin. *Religious Life in America: A Record of Personal Observation*. New York: Outlook Company, 1902.
Adams, Graham. *Age of Industrial Violence, 1910–1915: The Activities and Findings of the United States Commission on Industrial Relations*. New York: Columbia University Press, 1966.
Adams, Herbert B. *The Church and Popular Education*. Baltimore: Johns Hopkins University Studies in Historical and Political Science, 1890. Series 18.
———. *Public Educational Work in Baltimore*. Baltimore: Johns Hopkins University Studies in Historical and Political Science, 1899. Series 17.
Ahlstrom, Sydney E. *A Religious History of the American People*. New Haven: Yale University Press, 1972.
Andrews, F. Emerson. *Corporation Giving*. New York: Russell Sage Foundation, 1952.
Argersinger, Jo Ann E. *Toward a New Deal in Baltimore*. Chapel Hill: University of North Carolina Press, 1988.
Atwood, J. Howell. *The Racial Factor in YMCA's: A Report on Negro-White Relationships in Twenty-Four Cities*. New York: Association Press, 1946.
Baltimore: Its History and Its People. 3 vols. New York: Lewis Historical Publishing Co., 1912.

Barker-Benfield, Ben. "The Spermatic Economy: A Nineteenth-Century View of Sexuality." In *The American Family in Social-Historical Perspective*, ed. Michael Gordon. New York: St. Martin's Press, 1973.

Beadenkopf, Thomas M., and W. Raymond Stricklen. *Moody in Baltimore*. Baltimore: A. S. Abell, 1879.

Bell, Marion L. *Crusade in the City: Revivalism in Nineteenth-Century Philadelphia*. Lewisburg, Pa.: Bucknell University Press, 1977.

Bender, Thomas. *Intellect and Public Life: Essays on the Social History of Academic Intellectuals in the United States*. Baltimore: Johns Hopkins University Press, 1993.

Bilhartz, Terry D. *Urban Religion and the Second Great Awakening: Church and Society in Early National Baltimore*. Rutherford, N.J.: Fairleigh Dickinson University Press, 1986.

Binfield, Clyde. *George Williams and the YMCA: A Study in Victorian Social Attitudes*. London: Heinemann, 1973.

Blackmar, Elizabeth. *Manhattan for Rent, 1785–1850*. Ithaca: Cornell University Press, 1989.

Bledstein, Burton. *The Culture of Professionalism: The Middle Class and the Development of Higher Education in America*. New York: Norton, 1976.

Blumin, Stuart M. *The Emergence of the Middle Class: Social Experience in the American City, 1760–1900*. Cambridge: Cambridge University Press, 1989.

Bordin, Ruth. *Women and Temperance: The Quest for Power and Liberty, 1873–1900*. Philadelphia: Temple University Press, 1981.

Boyer, Paul. *Urban Masses and Moral Order in America, 1820–1920*. Cambridge: Harvard University Press, 1978.

Boylan, Anne M. *Sunday School: The Formation of an American Institution, 1790–1880*. New Haven: Yale University Press, 1988.

Brandes, Stuart D. *American Welfare Capitalism, 1880–1940*. Chicago: University of Chicago Press, 1976.

Bremner, Robert H. *The Discovery of Poverty in the United States*. New Brunswick, N.J.: Rutgers University Press, 1992.

———. *The Public Good: Philanthropy and Welfare in the Civil War Era*. New York: Alfred A. Knopf, 1980.

Browne, Gary Lawson. *Baltimore in the Nation, 1789–1861*. Chapel Hill: University of North Carolina Press, 1980.

Butts, R. Freeman, and Lawrence A. Cremin. *A History of Education in American Culture*. New York: Holt, Rinehart and Winston, 1953.

Carnegie, Dale. *How to Win Friends and Influence People*. 1936.

Carnes, Mark C., and Clyde Griffin, eds. *Meanings for Manhood: Constructions of Masculinity in Victorian America*. Chicago: University of Chicago Press, 1990.

———. *Secret Ritual and Manhood in Victorian America*. New Haven: Yale University Press, 1989.

Carter, Paul A. *The Decline and Revival of the Social Gospel: Social and Political Liberalism in American Protestant Churches, 1920–1940*. Ithaca: Cornell University Press, 1954.

———. *The Spiritual Crisis of the Gilded Age*. DeKalb: Northern Illinois University Press, 1971.

Chambers, John Whiteclay. *The Tyranny of Change: America in the Progressive Era, 1900–1917*. New York: St. Martin's Press, 1980.

Chandler, Alfred D. *The Visible Hand: The Managerial Revolution in America*. Cambridge, Mass.: Belknap Press, 1977.

Chauncey, George. *Gay New York: Gender, Urban Culture, and the Making of the Gay Male World, 1890–1940*. New York: Basic Books, 1994.

Chayes, Abram. "Introduction." In *Corporations: A Study of the Origin and Development of Great Business Combinations and of Their Relation to the Authority of the State*, ed. John P. Davis. New York: Capricorn Books, 1961.

Choate, Joseph H., et al. *Elgin Ralston Lovell Gould: A Memorial*. Norwood, Mass.: Plimpton Press, 1916.

Chudacoff, Howard. *The Age of the Bachelor: Creating an American Subculture*. Princeton: Princeton University Press, 1999.

Clawson, Mary Ann. *Constructing Brotherhood: Class, Gender, and Fraternalism*. Princeton: Princeton University Press, 1989.

Clayton, Ralph. *Black Baltimore, 1820–1870*. Bowie, Md.: Heritage Books, 1987.

Commons, John R. *Myself: The Autobiography of John R. Commons*. Madison: University of Wisconsin Press, 1964.

Cott, Nancy F. *The Bonds of Womanhood: "Woman's Sphere" in New England, 1780–1835*. New Haven: Yale University Press, 1977.

Coyle, Wilbur F. *The Mayors of Baltimore, Illustrated from Portraits in the City Hall*. Baltimore: Baltimore Municipal Journal, 1919.

Crooks, James B. *Politics and Progress: The Rise of Urban Progressivism in Baltimore, 1895 to 1911*. Baton Rouge: Louisiana State University Press, 1968.

Curtis, Susan. *A Consuming Faith: The Social Gospel and Modern American Culture*. Baltimore: Johns Hopkins University, 1991.

Davies, Margery. *Woman's Place Is at the Typewriter: Office Work and Office Workers, 1870–1930*. Philadelphia: Temple University Press, 1982.

Dawley, Alan. *Struggles for Justice: Social Responsibility and the Liberal State*. Cambridge: Harvard University Press, 1991.

Dedmon, Emmett. *Great Enterprises: 100 Years of the YMCA of Metropolitan Chicago*. New York: Rand McNally, 1957.

Directory of the Charitable and Beneficent Organizations of Baltimore and of Maryland. Baltimore: Charity Organization Society, 1892.

Dobkin, Marjorie Housepian, ed. *The Making of a Feminist: Early Journals and Letters of M. Carey Thomas*. Kent, Ohio: Kent State University Press, 1979.

Dodge, Cleveland E. *"YMCA": A Century at New York (1852–1952)*. New York: Newcomen Society, 1953.

Doggett, Laurence L. *History of the Young Men's Christian Association*. New York: Association Press, 1922.

Douglas, Ann. *The Feminization of American Culture*. New York: Alfred A. Knopf, 1977.

Doyle, Don H. *New Men, New Cities, New South: Atlanta, Nashville, Charleston, Mobile, 1860–1910*. Chapel Hill: University of North Carolina Press, 1990.

Elkins, Stanley. *Slavery*. 3d ed. Chicago: University of Chicago Press, 1976.

Ely, Richard T. *Herbert B. Adams, Tributes of Friends*. Baltimore: Johns Hopkins University Press, 1902.

Epstein, Barbara Leslie. *The Politics of Domesticity: Women, Evangelism, and Temperance in Nineteenth-Century America*. Middletown, Conn.: Wesleyan University Press, 1981.

Evans, Sara M., and Harry Boyte. *Free Spaces: The Sources of Democratic Change in America*. Chicago: University of Chicago Press, 1992.

Farrar, Hayward. *The Baltimore Afro-American, 1892–1950*. Westport, Conn.: Greenwood Press, 1998.

Fee, Elizabeth, Linda Shopes, and Linda Zeidman, eds. *The Baltimore Book: New Views of Local History*. Philadelphia: Temple University Press, 1991.

Fein, Isaac M. *The Making of an American Jewish Community: The History of Baltimore Jewry from 1773 to 1920*. Baltimore: Jewish Historical Society of Maryland, 1971.

Fields, Barbara Jeanne. *Slavery and Freedom on the Middle Ground: Maryland during the Nineteenth Century*. New Haven: Yale University Press, 1985.

Filene, Peter G. *Him/Her/Self: Sex Roles in Modern America*. Baltimore, Johns Hopkins University Press, 1986.

Findlay, James F. *Dwight L. Moody: American Evangelist, 1837–1899*. Chicago: University of Chicago Press, 1969.

First Colored Directory of Baltimore City. Baltimore: R. W. Coleman Publishing Co., 1916.

Fisher, Galen M. *Public Affairs and the YMCA: 1844–1944*. New York: Association Press, 1948.

Flexner, Abraham. *Abraham Flexner: An Autobiography*. New York: Simon & Schuster, 1960.

———. *Daniel Coit Gilman, Creator of the American Type University*. New York: Harcourt, Brace, 1946.

Flexner, Helen Thomas. *A Quaker Childhood*. New Haven: Yale University Press, 1940.

Flexner, James Thomas. *An American Saga: The Story of Helen Thomas and Simon Flexner*. Boston: Little, Brown, 1984.

Fogarty, Robert S. *All Things New: American Communes and Utopian Movements, 1860–1914*. Chicago: University of Chicago Press, 1990.

Folsom, Burton W. *Urban Capitalists: Entrepreneurs and City Growth in Pennsylvania's Lackawanna and Lehigh Regions, 1800–1920.* Baltimore: Johns Hopkins University Press, 1981.

Fones-Wolf, Ken. *Trade Union Gospel: Christianity and Labor in Industrial Philadelphia, 1865–1915.* Philadelphia: Temple University Press, 1989.

Franklin, Fabian. *The Life of Daniel Coit Gilman.* New York: Dodd, Mead, 1910.

Fraser, Steve, and Gary Gerstle, eds. *The Rise and Fall of the New Deal Order, 1930–1980.* Princeton: Princeton University Press, 1989.

French, John C. *A History of the University Founded by Johns Hopkins.* Baltimore: Johns Hopkins Press, 1946.

Friedman, Elisha M., ed. *American Problems of Reconstruction.* New York: E. P. Dutton, 1918.

Furner, Mary O. *Advocacy and Objectivity: A Crisis in the Professionalization of American Social Science, 1865–1905.* Lexington: University Press of Kentucky, 1975.

Gilkeson, John. *Middle-Class Providence, 1820–1940.* Princeton: Princeton University Press, 1986.

Gillett, Sylvia. "Camden Yards and the Strike of 1877." In *The Baltimore Book: New Views of Local History*, ed. Elizabeth Fee, Linda Shopes, and Linda Zeidman. Philadelphia: Temple University Press, 1991.

Gilman, Daniel C. *Recollections of the Life of John Glenn.* Baltimore: Charity Organization Society, 1896.

Gilson, Mary Barnett. *What's Past Is Prologue.* New York: Harper, 1940.

Goffman, Erving. *Asylums: Essays on the Social Situations of Mental Patients and Other Inmates.* Chicago: Aldine, 1946.

Gould, E.R.L. *The Housing of the Working People.* Washington, D.C.: Government Printing Office, 1895.

Graham, Leroy. *Baltimore: Nineteenth-Century Black Capital.* Washington, D.C.: University Press of America, 1982.

Griffin, Clifford S. *Their Brothers' Keepers: Moral Stewardship in the United States, 1800–1865.* New Brunswick: Rutgers University Press, 1960.

Hall, Peter Dobkin. *Inventing the Nonprofit Sector and Other Essays on Philanthropy.* Baltimore: Johns Hopkins University Press, 1992.

Haltunnen, Karen. *Confidence Men and Painted Women: A Study of Middle-Class Culture in America, 1830–1870.* New Haven: Yale University Press, 1982.

Harper, W. A. *Character Building in Colleges.* New York: Abingdon Press, 1928.

Hartman, Mary, and Lois Banner, eds. *Clio's Consciousness Raised.* New York: Harper Torch Books, 1973.

Hawkins, Hugh. *Pioneer: A History of the Johns Hopkins University, 1874–1899.* Ithaca: Cornell University Press, 1960.

Hawley, Ellis W., and Donald T. Critchlow, eds. *Federal Social Policy in Modern America: The Historical Dimension.* University Park: Pennsylvania State University Press, 1988.

Heald, Morrell. *The Social Responsibilities of Business: Company and Community, 1900–1960.* Cleveland: Press of Case Western Reserve University, 1970.

Hicks, Clarence J. *My Life in Industrial Relations: Fifty Years in the Growth of a Profession.* New York: Harper, 1941.

Hirschfeld, Charles. *Baltimore, 1870–1900: Studies in Social History.* Baltimore: Johns Hopkins Press, 1941.

Hopkins, C. Howard. *History of the YMCA in North America.* New York: Association Press, 1951.

——. *John R. Mott, 1865–1955: A Biography.* Grand Rapids, Mich.: William B. Eerdmans, 1979.

——. *The Rise of the Social Gospel in American Protestantism.* New Haven: Yale University Press, 1940.

Horlick, Allan Stanley. *Country Boys and Merchant Princes: The Social Control of Young Men in New York.* Lewisburg, Pa.: Bucknell University Press, 1975.

Horowitz, Helen Lefkowitz. *The Power and Passion of M. Carey Thomas.* New York: Alfred A. Knopf, 1994.

Huston, James L. *The Panic of 1857 and the Coming of the Civil War.* Baton Rouge: Louisiana State University Press, 1987.

Jacoby, Sanford M. *Employing Bureaucracy: Managers, Unions, and the Transformation of Work in American Industry, 1900–1945.* New York: Columbia University Press, 1985.

Janvier, Meredith. *Baltimore in the Eighties and Nineties.* Baltimore: H. G. Roebuck & Son, 1933.

Kauffman, Christopher J. *Faith and Fraternalism: The History of the Knights of Columbus, 1882–1982.* New York: Harper and Row, 1982.

Kaus, Mickey. *The End of Equality.* New York: Basic Books, 1992.

Kemp, Janet E. *Housing Conditions in Baltimore: Report of a Special Committee.* Baltimore: Association for the Improvement of the Condition of the Poor and the Charity Organization Society, 1907.

Kett, Joseph. *The Pursuit of Knowledge under Difficulties: From Self-Improvement to Adult Education in America, 1750–1990.* Stanford: Stanford University Press, 1994.

——. *Rites of Passage: Adolescence in America, 1790 to the Present.* New York, 1977.

Kwolek-Folland, Angel. *Engendering Business: Men and Women in the Corporate Office, 1870–1930.* Baltimore: Johns Hopkins University Press, 1994.

Lasch, Christopher. *The Revolt of the Elites and the Betrayal of Democracy.* New York: Norton, 1995.

Lawrence, Margaret Woods. *Reminiscences of the Life and Work of Edward A. Lawrence, Jr.* New York: Fleming H. Revell Co., 1900.

Luckett, Margie H. *Maryland Women.* Baltimore: King Bros. Press, 1937.

Macleod, David I. *Building Character in the American Boy: The Boy Scouts,*

YMCA, and Their Forerunners, 1870–1920. Madison: University of Wisconsin Press, 1983.

Mangan, M. A., and James Walvin, eds. *Manliness and Morality: Middle-Class Masculinity in Britain and America, 1800–1940.* New York: St. Martin's Press, 1987.

Marston, Everett C. *Origin and Development of Northeastern University, 1898–1960.* Boston: Northeastern University, 1961.

May, Henry. *Protestant Churches and Industrial America.* New York: Octagon Books, 1963.

Mencken, H. L. *Heathen Days, 1890–1936.* New York: Alfred A. Knopf, 1943.

Meyerowitz, Joanne J. *Women Adrift: Independent Wage Earners in Chicago, 1880–1930.* Chicago: University of Chicago Press, 1988.

Mills, C. Wright. *White Collar.* New York: Oxford University Press, 1951.

Mitchell, Martha. *Encyclopedia Brunoniana.* Providence, R.I.: Brown University Library, 1993.

Mjagkij, Nina. *Light in the Darkness: African Americans and the YMCA, 1852–1946.* Lexington: University Press of Kentucky, 1994.

Modell, John. *Into One's Own: From Youth to Adulthood in the United States, 1920–1975.* Berkeley: University of California Press, 1989.

Monkkonen, Eric H. *Walking to Work: Tramps in America, 1790–1935.* Lincoln: University of Nebraska Press, 1984.

Moore, John F. *The Story of the Railroad "Y."* New York: Association Press, 1930.

Morse, Richard C. *History of the North American Young Men's Christian Association.* New York: Association Press, 1913.

Nelson, Daniel. *Managers and Workers: Origins of the New Factory System in the United States, 1880–1920.* Madison: University of Wisconsin Press, 1975.

Noll, Mark A. *A History of Christianity in the United States and Canada.* Grand Rapids, Mich.: William B. Eerdmans, 1992.

Olasky, Marvin. *The Tragedy of American Compassion.* Washington, D.C.: Regnery Gateway, 1992.

Olson, Sherry H. *Baltimore: The Building of an American City.* Baltimore: Johns Hopkins University Press, 1980.

Osofsky, Gilbert. *Harlem: The Making of a Ghetto: Negro New York, 1890–1930.* New York: Harper Collins, 1963.

Phillips, Christopher. *Freedom's Port: The African American Community of Baltimore, 1790–1860.* Urbana: University of Illinois Press, 1997.

Pivar, David. *Purity Crusade, Sexual Morality, and Social Control, 1868–1900.* Westport, Conn.: Greenwood Press, 1973.

Rabinowitz, Benjamin. *The Young Men's Hebrew Associations (1854–1913).* New York: National Jewish Welfare Board, 1948.

Report of a Conference on Charities. Baltimore: Charity Organization Society, 1887.

Riebenack, M. *Railway Provident Institutions in English-Speaking Countries.* Philadelphia: Pennsylvania Railroad Company, 1905.

Rosenzweig, Roy. *Eight Hours for What We Will: Workers and Leisure in an Industrial City, 1870–1920.* Cambridge: Cambridge University Press, 1983.

Ross, Dorothy. *The Origins of American Social Science.* Cambridge: Cambridge University Press, 1991.

Rotundo, E. Anthony. *American Manhood: Transformations in Masculinity from the Revolution to the Modern Era.* New York: Basic Books, 1993.

Roydhouse, Marion W. "Bridging Chasms: Community and the Southern YWCA." In *Visible Women: New Essays on American Activism,* ed. Nancy A. Hewitt and Suzanne Lebsock, 270–95. Urbana: University of Illinois Press, 1993.

Ryan, Mary. *Cradle of the Middle Class: The Family in Oneida County, New York, 1790–1865.* Cambridge: Cambridge University Press, 1981.

Salamon, Lester M. *Partners in Public Service: Government-Nonprofit Relations in the Modern Welfare State.* Baltimore: Johns Hopkins University Press, 1995.

Scott, Donald M. *From Office to Profession: The New England Ministry, 1750–1850.* Philadelphia: University of Pennsylvania Press, 1978.

Scully, Robert. *A Scarlet Pansy.* Nesor Publishing, 1937.

Sealander, Judith. *Private Wealth and Public Life: Foundation Philanthropy and the Reshaping of American Social Policy from the Progressive Era to the New Deal.* Baltimore: Johns Hopkins University Press, 1997.

Sheldon, Charles Monroe. *In His Steps: "What Would Jesus Do?"* Philadelphia: American Baptist Publication Society, 1898.

Shillinglaw, David Lee. *An American in the Army and YMCA, 1917–1920.* Chicago: University of Chicago Press, 1971.

Sizer, Sandra S. *Gospel Hymns and Social Religion: The Rhetoric of Nineteenth-Century Revivalism.* Philadelphia: Temple University Press, 1978.

Smith-Rosenberg, Carroll. "The Cross and the Pedestal." In *Disorderly Conduct,* 129–64, q.v.

———. *Disorderly Conduct: Visions of Gender in Victorian America.* New York: Oxford University Press, 1985.

Steiner, Bernard H. *Men of Mark in Maryland.* Washington, D.C.: Johnson Winne Co., 1907.

Strayer, George Drayton. *Report of the Survey of the Public School System of Baltimore, Maryland.* 3 vols. Baltimore: 1921.

Syms, Mary S. *The Natural History of a Social Institution: The YWCA.* New York: Woman's Press, 1936.

———. *The YWCA: An Unfolding Purpose.* New York: Woman's Press, 1950.

Teaford, Jon C. *City and Suburb: The Political Fragmentation of Metropolitan America, 1850–1970.* Baltimore: Johns Hopkins University Press, 1979.

———. *The Rough Road to Renaissance: Urban Revitalization in America, 1940–1985.* Baltimore: Johns Hopkins University Press, 1990.

———. *The Unheralded Triumph: City Government in America, 1870–1900.* Baltimore: Johns Hopkins University Press, 1984.

Tocqueville, Alexis de. *Democracy in America.* Ed. Richard D. Heffner. New York: Penguin, 1956.

Trachtenberg, Alan. *The Incorporation of America: Culture and Society in the Gilded Age.* New York: Hill and Wang, 1982.

Trattner, Walter I. *From Poor Law to Welfare State: A History of Social Welfare in America.* New York: Free Press, 1994.

Tucker, Augusta. *It Happened at Hopkins: A Teaching Hospital.* Baltimore: The Women's Board of the Johns Hopkins Hospital, 1960.

———. *Miss Susie Slagle's.* New York: Harper, 1939.

U.S. Bureau of Labor Statistics. Bulletin 250. *Welfare Work for Employees in Industrial Establishments in the United States.* 1919.

U.S. Census. *Thirteenth Census of the United States.* Washington: 1910.

———. *Fourteenth Census of the United States.* Washington: 1920.

Van Vleck, George Washington. *The Panic of 1857: An Analytical Study.* New York: Columbia University Press, 1943.

Watson, Frank Dekkar. *The Charity Organization Movement in the United States: A Study in American Philanthropy.* New York: Macmillan, 1922.

Welter, Barbara. "The Feminization of Religion in Nineteenth-Century America." In *Clio's Consciousness Raised*, ed. Mary Hartman and Lois Banner, 305–32. New York: Harper Torch Books, 1973.

Wheatley, Steven C. *The Politics of Philanthropy: Abraham Flexner and Medical Education.* Madison: University of Wisconsin Press, 1988.

White, Ronald C., Jr., and C. Howard Hopkins. *The Social Gospel: Religion and Reform in Changing America.* Philadelphia: Temple University Press, 1976.

Whiteside, William B. *The Boston YMCA and Community Need: A Century's Evolution, 1851–1951.* New York: Association Press, 1951.

Wiebe, Robert. *The Search for Order, 1877–1920.* New York: Hill and Wang, 1967.

Williams, J.W.M. *Reminiscences of a Pastorate of Thirty-Three Years in the First Baptist Church of Baltimore, Maryland.* Baltimore: J. F. Weishampel, 1884.

Williams, Marilyn Thornton. *Washing "The Great Unwashed": Public Baths in Urban America.* Columbus: Ohio State University Press, 1991.

Williams, Paul Edgar. *The YMCA College.* St. Louis: Educational Council of the YMCA, 1938.

Wilson, Elizabeth. *Fifty Years of Association Work among Young Women, 1866–1916.* New York: National Board of the Young Women's Christian Association of the U.S.A., 1916.

Wilson, Franklin. *The Life Story of Franklin Wilson As Told by Himself in His Journals.* Baltimore, 1897.

Wilson, Grace H. *The Religious and Educational Philosophy of the Young Women's Christian Association.* New York: Teachers College, Columbia University, 1933.

Wilson, William Bender. *History of the Pennsylvania Railroad Department of the Young Men's Christian Association of Philadelphia*. Philadelphia: Stephen Greene Company, 1911.

Wolfe, Albert Benedict. *The Lodging House Problem in Boston*. Boston: Houghton, Mifflin, 1906.

Wrathall, John. *Take the Young Stranger by the Hand: Same Sex Relations and the YMCA*. Chicago: University of Chicago Press, 1998.

Wroth, Lawrence W. "Churches and Religious Organizations in Baltimore." In *Baltimore: Its History and Its People*. New York: Lewis Historical Publishing Co., 1912.

Zahavi, Gerald. *Workers, Managers, and Welfare Capitalism: The Shoeworkers and Tanners of Endicott Johnson, 1890–1950*. Urbana: University of Illinois Press, 1988.

Zald, Mayer N. *Organizational Change: The Political Economy of the YMCA*. Chicago: University of Chicago Press, 1970.

Zunz, Olivier. *Making America Corporate. 1870–1920*. Chicago: University of Chicago Press, 1990.

Dissertations and Theses

Applin, Albert Gammon, II. "From Muscular Christianity to the Market Place: The History of Men's and Boy's Basketball in the United States, 1891–1957." Dissertation. University of Massachusetts, 1982.

Arnold, Adam Bruce. "Growing with Houston: A Centennial History of the YMCA of Greater Houston, 1886–1986." Master's thesis. Rice University, 1986.

Coates, James Roland, Jr. "Recreation and Sport in the African-American Community of Baltimore, 1890–1920." Dissertation. University of Maryland, 1991.

Durr, W. T. "The Conscience of a City: A History of the Citizens' Planning and Housing Association and Efforts to Improve Housing for the Poor in Baltimore, 1937–1954." Dissertation. Johns Hopkins University, 1972.

Gibson, William. "A History of Family and Child Welfare Agencies in Baltimore, 1849–1943." Dissertation. Ohio State University, 1969.

Gilson, James Edward. "Changing Student Lifestyle at the University of Iowa, 1880–1900." Dissertation. University of Iowa, 1980.

Hunt, Alfred Ian. "Mutual Enlightenment in Early Vancouver, 1886–1916." Dissertation. University of British Columbia, 1987.

Lederman, Sarah Henry. "From Poverty to Philanthropy: The Life and Work of Mary E. Richmond." Dissertation. Teachers College, Columbia University. 1994.

Mittleman, Karen Sue. "'A Spirit That Touches the Problems of Today': Women and Social Reform in the Philadelphia Young Women's Christian Association, 1920–1945." Dissertation. University of Pennsylvania, 1987.

Mjagkij, Nina. "History of the Black YMCA in America, 1853–1946." Dissertation. University of Cincinnati, 1990.

Paul, William George. "The Shadow of Equality: The Negro in Baltimore, 1864–1911." Dissertation. University of Wisconsin, 1972.

Stambler, Leah G. "An Historical Investigation of the Transition from Junior to Senior College Status of Four Independent Connecticut Colleges between 1893 and 1970." Dissertation. University of Connecticut, 1986.

Wallach, Stephanie. "Luther Halsey Gulick and the Salvation of the American Adolescent." Dissertation. Columbia University, 1989.

Winter, Thomas. "'A Wise Investment in Growing Manhood': The YMCA and Workingmen, 1872–1929." Dissertation. University of Cincinnati, 1994.

Wrathall, John. "American Manhood and the YMCA, 1868–1920." Dissertation. University of Minnesota, 1994.

Articles

Adams, Herbert B. "Work among Workingwomen in Baltimore: A Social Study." Baltimore: Johns Hopkins University Studies in Historical and Political Science, 1889. 7, number 6.

Antone, George P. "The YMCA Graduate School, Nashville 1919–1936." *Tennessee Historical Quarterly* 32 (1973): 67–82.

Beadenkopf, Anne. "The Baltimore Public Baths and Their Founder, the Rev. Thomas M. Beadenkopf." *Maryland Historical Magazine* 45, 3 (September 1950): 201–14.

Bederman, Gail. "'The Women Have Had Charge of the Church Work Long Enough': The Men and Religion Forward Movement of 1911–1912 and the Masculinization of Middle-Class Protestantism." *American Quarterly* 41 (September 1989): 432–65.

Bender, Thomas. "Wholes and Parts: The Need for Synthesis in American History." *Journal of American History* 73 (June 1986): 120–36.

Blaikie, William. "Personal Purity." *White Cross Documents*. 1888.

Cannon, M. Hamlin. "The United States Christian Commission." *Mississippi Valley Historical Review* 38 (1951–52): 61–80.

Chauncey, George, Jr. "Christian Brotherhood or Sexual Perversion? Homosexual Identities and the Construction of Sexual Boundaries in the World War One Era." *Journal of Social History* 19 (Winter 1985): 189–212.

Clawson, Mary Ann. "Fraternal Orders and Class Formation in the Nineteenth-Century United States." *Journal of Interdisciplinary History* (1985): 672–95.

———. "Nineteenth Century Women's Auxiliaries and Fraternal Orders." *Signs* 12 (1986): 40–61.

Deutsch, Sarah. "Learning to Talk More Like a Man: Boston Women's Class-Bridging Organizations, 1870–1940." *American Historical Review* 97 (April 1992): 379–404.

Findlay, James F. "Religion and Politics in the Sixties: The Churches and the Civil Rights Act of 1964." *Journal of American History* 77 (June 1990): 66–92.

Fine, Lisa M. "Between Two Worlds: Business Women in a Chicago Boarding House, 1900–1930." *Journal of Social History* 19 (Spring 1986): 511–19.

———. "'Our Big Factory Family': Masculinity and Paternalism at the Reo Motor Car Company of Lansing, Michigan." *Labor History* 34 (Spring/Summer 1993).

Fox, Richard Wightman. "The Culture of Liberal Protestant Progressivism, 1875–1925." *Journal of Interdisciplinary History* 23 (Winter 1993): 639–60.

Garrett, John W. "Address by John W. Garrett Delivered on the 30th of January, 1883, before the YMCA on the Occasion of Their 30th Anniversary." Baltimore, 1883.

Gittleman, H. M. "Welfare Capitalism Reconsidered." *Labor History* 33 (Fall/Winter 1992): 1–31.

Gould, E.R.L. "How Baltimore Banished Tramps and Helped the Idle." *Forum* (June 1894): 497–505.

———. "Transients and Tramps in July." *The Charities Record* 2, no. 2 (October 1895).

Harris, Richard. "The End Justified the Means: Boarding and Rooming in a City of Homes, 1850–1951." *Journal of Social History* 26 (Winter 1992): 331–58.

Howard, George Elliott. "Biographical Sketch of Amos Griswold Warner." Baltimore: Johns Hopkins University Studies in Historical and Political Science, 1904. Vol. 22.

Karl, Barry, and Stanley Katz. "The American Private Philanthropic Foundation and the Public Sphere, 1890–1930." *Minerva* (Summer 1981).

Peel, Mark. "On the Margins: Lodgers and Boarders in Boston, 1860–1900." *Journal of American History* 72:4 (March 1986): 813–34.

Putnam, Robert D. "Bowling Alone: America's Declining Social Capital." *Journal of Democracy* 6 (January 1995): 63–77.

Rotundo, E. Anthony. "Body and Soul: Changing Ideals of American Middle-Class Manhood, 1770–1920." *Journal of Social History* 16 (Summer 1983): 23–38.

———. "Romantic Friendship: Male Intimacy and Middle-Class Youth in the Northern United States, 1800–1900." *Journal of Social History* 23 (Fall 1989): 1–25.

Singleton, Gregory H. "Protestant Voluntary Organizations and the Shaping of Victorian America." *American Quarterly* 27 (1975): 549–60.

Skocpol, Theda. "Unravelling from Above: Civic Associations in American Democracy." *American Prospect* (January 1996).

Stapleton, Doris Hopkins. "Margaret Shove Morriss, '48H." *Brown Alumni Monthly* 76 (June 1975).

Steiner, Bernard C. "Maryland's Religious History." *Maryland Historical Magazine* 21 (March 1926).

Vandenberg-Daves, Jodi. "The Manly Pursuit of a Partnership between the Sexes: The Debate over YMCA Programs for Women and Girls, 1914–1933." *Journal of American History* 78 (March 1992): 1324–46.

Wilson, Dreck Spurlock. "Druid Hill Branch, Young Men's Christian Association: The First Hundred Years, 1885–1985." *Maryland Historical Magazine* 84 (Summer 1989): 135–46.

Wrathall, John D. "Provenance as Text: Reading the Silences around Sexuality in Manuscript Collections." *Journal of American History* 79 (June 1992): 165–78.

Index

Jessica I. Elfenbein is assistant professor of history and director of the Center for Baltimore Studies at the University of Baltimore. She is interested in the intersection of religion, philanthropy, and voluntarism in American cities and is the author of *Civics, Commerce, and Community: The History of the Washington, D.C., Board of Trade, 1889–1989*. Her current work is on the role of faith-based organizations and urban revitalization.